STATE-OWNED ENTERPRISE
IN THE WESTERN ECONOMIES

State-Owned Enterprise
in the Western Economies

Edited by
RAYMOND VERNON AND YAIR AHARONI

ST. MARTIN'S PRESS NEW YORK

Library of Congress Cataloging in Publication Data

Main entry under title:
State-owned enterprise in the Western economies.
    1. Government business enterprises. I. Vernon,
Raymond, 1913–   II. Aharoni, Yair.
HD3850.S79   1981   338.7'4   80-19385

ISBN 0–312–75623–2

CONTENTS

PREFACE

This volume of essays grew out of a three-day conference at the Harvard Business School in the spring of 1979, a conference in which 50 participants from the United States and a dozen other countries focused on one central question: what do we know about the state-owned enterprises that are now operating in the market economies of the rich industrialized countries — their objectives, their methods of operation, their consequences at home and abroad?

The participants who came together at Harvard to contribute to that ambitious task had a variety of motives and perspectives. Some participants were interested in the question because they hoped to be able to contribute to improving the management of such enterprises; others were interested in the appropriate public policies relative to such enterprises. Both interests converged in a common desire to pool the available facts and enlarge the existing understanding of the operations of the enterprises.

The costs of the conference were borne principally by the Associates of the Harvard Business School. A grant by the US Department of State to the Center for International Affairs at Harvard was indispensable for the completion of the project.

The conference is one of a number of projects that have grown out of discussions among the members of the Boston Area Public Enterprise Group, BAPEG, an informal organization of scholars who are devoted to expanding the area of knowledge and understanding regarding the operations of state-owned enterprises.

The essays in this volume were written from the vantage-point of a number of different disciplines and by authors of various nationalities and language backgrounds. That fact laid an especially heavy burden on Tobie Atlas, who edited the text with courage, imagination and sensitivity. Eve Berry saw endless drafts through the production processes with unflagging good humour and efficiency.

Yair Aharoni
Raymond Vernon
Cambridge, Mass.

1 INTRODUCTION

Raymond Vernon

If the sheer quantity of publications were any guide, the operations of state-owned enterprises in the advanced industrialized countries could be regarded as a well-researched and well-understood subject.[1] But with a few notable exceptions, most studies of state-owned enterprises share a curious quality: they view such enterprises from a considerable distance. Much of the literature, for instance, analyzes the position of the enterprises in terms of law or public administration, or weighs their contribution to the macroeconomic objectives of the state, or assesses their effects on the political or ideological battles of the nation, or criticizes their shortcomings in large and general terms, or develops concepts of ideal performance as a basis for future policy.

In studies such as these, certain critical facts about such enterprises tend to be slighted: that they are managed by a bureaucracy with values and objectives that can be distinguished from those of the public sector at large; that they are the target of a complex set of pressures emanating from government offices and interest groups; and that they operate in highly imperfect markets, and are frequently in a position to make choices in those markets. Now that many of these enterprises have come to occupy key positions in the national economies of the advanced industrialized countries, it has become evident that these slighted facts need badly to be taken into account in analyzing the behaviour of state-owned enterprises. In short, the state-owned enterprise requires a depth of analysis and understanding comparable to that which scholarship has achieved for the large private enterprise.

The participants who came together at Harvard to contribute to that ambitious task had a variety of motives and perspectives. Some participants were interested in improving the management of state-owned enterprises; others were interested in developing appropriate public policies toward such enterprises. Both interests converged in a common desire to pool the available facts and enlarge the existing understanding of their operations.

As expected, the conference participants found themselves identifying numerous areas in which understanding was murky and facts were contradictory. But some generalizations did emerge, providing a platform for future work on the subject.

7

An Emerging Institution

State-owned enterprises are nothing new in the market economies of
the world. The historians of the Roman Empire and the chroniclers of
the Old Testament offer ample evidence of their ancient origins.

Although systematic data are hard to come by, it is widely assumed
that the state-owned enterprises which existed in the industrialized
countries of North America and Western Europe forty years ago were
mainly of the sort that would be classified as natural monopolies:
railroads, public utilities and the like. The enterprises which fell outside
that category were a motley group. Some governments had long ago
acquired the business establishments of deposed princes, as illustrated
by France's takeover of the Sèvres and Gobelin establishments. Long
ago, too, various countries in Europe had created state-owned enterprises to act as their fiscal agents — to collect taxes on tobacco, liquor,
matches and other products with inelastic demand. Early in the
twentieth century, Britain and France, in response to a compelling
national need, had seen to the creation of their respective state-owned
oil companies, the Anglo-Iranian Oil Company and Compagnie Française
des Pétroles. As Martinelli points out in his essay in this volume, a considerable number of half-bankrupt industrial enterprises in Italy had
been salvaged from the pre-war Fascist regime. But, by and large, these
were the exceptional cases; state-owned enterprises of the public utility
variety remained the dominant category.[2]

World War II gave a strong impetus to the growth of state-owned
enterprises in the rich industrialized countries. Some enterprises were
created to carry on wartime tasks that entailed high risk and little
prospective profit, such as the manufacture of synthetic rubber or the
insurance of plants against war damage in the United States; some were
taken over by governments as the property of the enemy or of native
collaborators, as was the case with Renault in France and with much
of Austria's industrial establishment. Although the United States
government set about systematically liquidating its holdings after the
war had ended, other governments generally retained most of what they
had acquired.

Since World War II, in fact, state-owned enterprise sectors in the
market economies of North America, Europe and Japan have grown in
size, increased in relative importance and diversified in activity.

Perhaps the most general reason for the growth has been a shift in
public opinion regarding the appropriate role of the state in economic
affairs. The exact circumstances and extent of the shift have varied

from one country to the next. The governments of Britain and Sweden, for instance, have from time to time been under the control of political parties that were socialist in ideology; and these occasionally have felt the need for acts of nationalization that represented a symbolic affirmation of their ideologies. For the most part, the governments of the rich industrialized countries have retained their formal allegiance to a market economy; but they have moved a considerable distance from the traditional liberal view that the operation of the system was principally the responsibility of the private sector.

In the past few decades, therefore, government intervention has been increasing. The purposes of such intervention have been various: sometimes to change the distribution of power between the public and the private sector; sometimes to improve the country's bargaining power with foreign enterprises; sometimes to help create industries that seemed necessary for future growth, or necessary to insulate the country from the military and political pressures of other governments; and sometimes to contribute to stability and employment. Some of the intervention has been achieved by rewarding or restraining the private sector, and some by taking over the ownership of industry.

Contributions of Economic Theory

In order to understand why a shift toward the public ownership of enterprises has occurred in the third quarter of the twentieth century, political theory offers a richer set of ideas for the scholar than does economic theory. The objective of our conference, however, was not so ambitious as to require us to explore the contributions of political theory. Our main purpose was to gain a better understanding of the performance of state-owned enterprises and of the forces that lay behind that performance. For this purpose, the theories of the economists seemed more germane.

It goes without saying that economic theorists of a socialist persuasion have always had a considerable interest in the potentialities of the state-owned enterprise as an instrument of the state. But very few have looked at those potentialities in microeconomic terms; and when they have, as in the case of Oscar Lange, they typically have drawn on the common classical economic tradition that they share with their non-socialist colleagues. From that tradition, economists have tended to concentrate upon the monopolistic character of public enterprises, especially those in the public utility field, and have tended to use the analytical tools that were developed from models of the competitive market. For them, the principal focus has been on the following issue: When a monopolist is seeking to maximize social benefit rather than private gain, what are the monopolist's appropriate investment and pricing policies?[3]

Lintner's work in this volume takes off from that established platform of economic theorists, but he broadens the question measurably. He views the state-owned enterprise as an entity the operations of which are financed out of a stream of funds from the rest of the economy, not only through the prices it charges for its services, but also through the terms on which it receives its capital. Exploring those links, he draws conclusions that offer both promise and disappointment for persons who hope to gain from economic theory some added understanding of the state-owned enterprise. The promise lies in the fact that a number of different branches of theory are shown to be germane to the study of state-owned enterprises, including the theory of optimal taxation. The disappointment lies in the formidable limitations that circumscribe the relevant theory's application, a point that Arrow's comments tend to support. Lintner points out, for instance, that the determination of an appropriate social discount rate for the typical products of state-owned enterprises is swathed in theoretical difficulties; and further that the practical application of the theory of optimal pricing and optimal investment commonly demands projections of cost and benefit that are inherently subject to large margins of error — margins so large as to swamp in importance the refinements introduced by typical theoretical embellishments.

Raiffa's paper pushes the theoretical discussions a major step further. Assume that state-owned enterprises set out to serve several different objectives simultaneously, such as economic efficiency, improved income distribution, improved environment and so on. Where multiple objectives exist, Raiffa asks, is there some way of responding to the values and weights of all the parties that are in a position to determine the firm's behaviour, or do all such efforts founder on the problem of interpersonal differences? Raiffa points in the direction of conjoint measurement theory, an approach directed at identifying areas of agreement and disagreement and reducing the points of existing conflict. But he is not sanguine of any easy applications of the theory.

Another branch of theory on which Raiffa draws is the burgeoning literature on the principal–agent problem. How does the principal ensure that the agent acting for him responds to the same information

and the same congeries of objectives as the principal would do if acting
on his own behalf? This is a question that confronts every chief
executive officer operating through the departmental chiefs of an
enterprise. Although it is a universal problem in all organizations,
including large private enterprises, it takes on special difficulties in an
organization the objectives of which are complex and multiple. Arrow
thinks of the problem as a shade more tractable than does Raiffa,
arguing that the agent can be assigned a set of goals that lead him to
respond in optimal fashion.

All told, these papers raise strong doubts as to whether theorists in
years past have been addressing the questions that are central for an
understanding of state-owned enterprises. They raise added doubts
as to whether many of the responses so far provided by theory are
applicable to state-owned enterprises as we find them.

A Confusion of Goals

Different state-owned enterprises, as noted earlier, have been created
to serve quite different objectives — objectives that run the gamut from
the collection of taxes to the stabilization of employment. These
differences, in themselves, are no cause for confusion; as long as policy
makers and scholars can keep the differences in mind, the enterprises
can be operated, controlled, evaluated and appreciated according to
their respective purposes.

Where the confusion begins is in the fact that state-owned enterprises are usually created with many different purposes in mind, with
some parts of the body politic harbouring one main purpose while
other parts harbour another. In the several nationalizations of British
steel, for instance, numerous motivations were evident. Those in the
Labour Party who were committed to a socialist ideology, for instance,
saw it in part as a transfer of economic power from the private to the
public sector with broad ideological overtones. Those tied more closely
to the rank and file of Britain's labour movement, however, tended to
see it as a way of improving labour's bargaining power for more pay and
better working conditions. Those in the Board of Trade hoped that
nationalization could be used to improve the productivity of the steel
industry and increase its exports. And so on. It is in this multiplicity of
goals that confusion lies.

Aharoni's paper in this volume makes a critical point with respect to
that confusion, elaborating a point that also troubles Raiffa. Raiffa asks

speculatively — but not without reservations — whether some process of interaction or trade-off may be possible among the various interests that are concerned with the operations of a given state-owned enterprise, a process that would eventually yield an outcome which could be identified as the position of the government. Aharoni's paper suggests, however, that, as long as Britain and other advanced industrialized countries retain the characteristics of an open, participative democracy, it will be hard to picture a governmental process that leads to the creation of a reasonably unambiguous objective function for the firm.[4] Each ministry and each interest group can be expected to use its power to influence the firm's behaviour, and to reward or punish the firm in measure as the firm responds to its needs. In Aharoni's paper, therefore, the principal disappears and becomes instead a babel of voices and of unrelated pressures.

Even if the original social objective in creating a state-owned enterprise is reasonably clear and simple, Noreng's paper illustrates that the goals of the enterprise often begin to multiply. The enterprise that is created to support a branch of high technology may soon find itself diverted to maintaining jobs. The enterprise that comes into being to support farm incomes may soon discover that its principal role is to hold down urban food prices.

The papers of Aharoni, Cassese and Grassini in this volume all offer a certain amount of evidence on the confusion of goals with which the state-owned enterprise must cope. Grassini's paper graphically describes the wide variety of sources from which demands are made on Italian state-owned enterprises, including the parliament, the parties and the individual politicians; and there are broad hints in various papers in the conference that similar experiences are encountered in other countries. Finally, there is the disconcerting fact that, where conflicting and mutually inconsistent goals seem to exist, politicians may find it undesirable — even dangerous — to try to clarify the ambiguity.

Besides confronting a welter of goals that may be unreconciled and irreconcilable, state-owned enterprises in the advanced industrialized countries also must reckon with the fact that these goals sometimes change with changes in government, including new ministers and new administrations. Accordingly, any manager who can find a way of responding to the commands of all his political masters is still not safely home. He may yet be undone by the fact that a change in the government's leadership will bring with it a change in goals.

These conditions produce some characteristic patterns of interaction between managers of state-owned enterprises and their political masters. One part of the pattern consists of a series of exchanges in which the special tasks of the state-owned enterprise are shaped and their special privileges are determined. A second part of the pattern consists of persistent efforts on the part of most managers of state-owned enterprises to increase their autonomy or discretion or elbow room in their dealings with their political masters.

The interactions between state-owned enterprises and the political structure to which they are responsible are touched on by Anastassopoulos, Grassini and Normanton, supplementing an extensive literature that already exists on the subject.[5]

As a result of the process, state-owned enterprises have been known to take on high-risk projects such as Concorde and the Airbus 300; to hold down prices and forgo profits in periods of inflation, as the British National Coal Board has done from time to time; to favour domestic suppliers, as Air France has occasionally felt obliged to do in its purchase of aircraft; to place plants in backward areas that were in need of development; to hold on to a workforce in periods of slump; and to subsidize selected classes of customers.

The interactive process between state-owned enterprises and the political apparatus, of course, generates not only obligations but also rewards. Among other things, the rewards include access to subsidized capital, guarantees against bankruptcy, exemption from import duties and other import restrictions, preference in governmental purchases, relief from onerous government regulations, and so on.[6]

The second element in the typical pattern of relationships between managers and politicians consists of the managers' efforts to increase their room for manoeuvre. As Anastassopoulos and Aharoni indicate, the search for elbow room has been a persistent characteristic in the behaviour of state-owned enterprises. Perhaps by increasing its independence from government, the firm hopes to increase its strength in the bargaining process. Perhaps the managers want to insulate themselves from the signals and pressures they expect to receive from their political masters. Perhaps some want the opportunity to run their own operations without intervention, simply because they feel they know what the nation needs or else for the pure joy of being in charge. Whatever the reasons for pursuing such a strategy, managers who take the course of attempting to increase their autonomy are not placing the future of the enterprise itself in any great jeopardy. For, whenever the going is rough, as several conference participants pointed out, state-owned enterprises generally have the option of returning to the support and protection of the state. Although the liquidation or sale of state-owned enterprises sometimes occurs, it is a rare event.

In order to increase their room for manoeuvre with government, the managers of state-owned enterprises are said to follow a number of different strategies. Aharoni's paper refers to the managers' efforts to maintain a positive cash flow in order to avoid having to ask for new capital infusions; also mentioned is the eagerness of some enterprises to penetrate foreign markets and acquire foreign partners in order to increase their sources of external support. State-owned enterprises that master complex technologies have also seen themselves as adding to their independence.

In all probability, however, the propensity of managers to look for independence depends partly on the personal circumstances of the manager. Career civil servants who manage state-owned enterprises, for instance, can be expected to respond differently from politicians who assume a management role; temperament may also play some role. Apart from the manager's characteristics, there is also the condition of the enterprise itself. Firms near the brink of insolvency, for example, constitute a less attractive vehicle in which to make a dash for independence than do those with a solid financial base. All told, therefore, the struggle for independence was seen as a complex phenomenon, demanding more analysis and greater understanding.

The Performance of State-owned Enterprises

Each state-owned enterprise ought to be gauged in the light of the unique purposes that led to its creation. But it is also important to try to generalize about the effects of such enterprises without regard to the purposes for which they were created. In various contexts, the conference participants struggled with such questions, producing a number of very tentative judgements.

Various papers in the conference cast some oblique light on what, to some, was the most important question of all: has the growth of state-owned enterprises in the industrialized countries been instrumental in shifting economic power from the leaders of big business in the private sector to leaders elsewhere, such as leaders of government or leaders of labour?

Without much question, there have been some fairly pronounced shifts in the distribution of economic power in the advanced industrialized countries over the past decade or two, during a period in which state-owned enterprises have been on the rise. But defining the nature of that shift is exceedingly difficult. The explicitly socialist parties of the advanced industrialized countries appear no stronger today than they appeared a quarter of a century ago. The labour union movements of those countries are no stronger – perhaps they are even a little weaker – than they were in the early 1950s. Social welfare programmes are more extensive and more firmly entrenched, but most governments have little control over how fast they grow and in what direction; that decision often rests more with the special constituency that benefits from the programme. Therefore, in terms of governmental power – better still, governmental discretionary power – the existence of these programmes is often seen as a source of weakness, a maw to be fed, rather than a source of strength. By the same token, *Mitbestimmungsrecht* – the right of labour to be represented on the boards of enterprises – has been extended, but so far with no obvious increase in the power of the labour unions, let alone the public sector.

In any case, the papers of Normanton, Martinelli, Beesley and Evans, Anastassopoulos, Noreng and Grassini, all of which touch on the question of power, suggest that the decline in the power of the private sector may not have produced a commensurate increase in the power of government or of labour. More than a shift in power to government or to labour, one observes a dispersal of power from business leaders in the private sector to various other claimants, including the public enterprise managers themselves and the interest groups that have built up around each such enterprise. The exact nature of the dispersal, as these papers highlight, has been determined by a congeries of forces. Although regime ideology has played some part in the outcome, so have the personal characteristics and aspirations of individual managers and individual politicians, along with the imperatives of given technologies and given markets.

Despite the seemingly special aspects of the relations between state-owned enterprises and their respective governments in the advanced industrialized countries, some participants in the conference remained unconvinced that these relations were in any material sense different from those between governments and large private enterprises. Governments, they observed, commonly try to achieve their purposes through a judicious application of taxes, subsidies and regulations. It could be argued, therefore, that there is no reason to study state-owned enterprises as a separate subject; that a study of the relations of governments to all their respective enterprises, whether public or private, would be more fruitful.

Indeed, as various papers in the conference suggest, state-owned enterprises do seem to share many characteristics with their private counterparts, especially when they serve similar markets and employ similar technologies. Moreover, with increasing frequency, large private enterprises are being exhorted to behave in a 'socially responsible' manner and to include representatives of labour and the general public in their governing structures. A good case can be made, therefore, for the view that large private enterprises are exposed to all the opportunities of privilege, the ambiguities of purpose and problems of multiple oversight that are the lot of state-owned enterprises.

On our reading of the evidence, however, the state-owned enterprises will probably prove to be distinctive in various critical ways. As was observed earlier, the very circumstances of the creation of state-owned enterprises commonly create a sharp difference from their private counterparts. Although systematic evidence on the point has yet to be developed, it also appears that the managers of state-owned enterprises in most countries are drawn from a different background and are recruited through different channels from the managers of large private enterprises. Moreover, there were frequent allusions in the conference to the view that managers of many state-owned enterprises looked on their financial resources differently from managers of private enterprises. Among other things, public managers looked on their equity capital as entailing little or no cost. If this proves to be the case, its ramifications can be fairly extensive, affecting technological choice, scale of operations and various other aspects of the functioning of the firm. On top of that, public enterprises are insulated from some of the pressures to which private enterprises are subjected, such as the demands of stockholders for profits and for capital appreciation; in an era in which large private firms in some countries are commonly exposed to the threat of takeover bids, the relative immunity of public enterprises from such a threat can be a factor of some consequence in creating distinctive patterns of operation.

Nevertheless, the papers in this conference offer no more than a succession of hints on the inherent differences in performance between state-owned enterprises and large private enterprises in the advanced industrialized countries. Perhaps the strongest statement that can be made about those differences is that state-owned enterprises are not notably profitable undertakings. But that is hardly surprising, in the light of the purposes for which some of them were created. Accordingly, one can easily be misled by making simple comparisons between the profitability of state-owned enterprises and that of private enterprises.

If the performance of state-owned enterprises cannot be directly compared with that of private enterprises, it is still possible to evaluate their performance in appropriate terms. All enterprises ought to be able to meet the test of making a net contribution to social welfare: that is to say, all enterprises ought to be expected to contribute more to society than they use of the things valuable to society. But that test requires a proper valuation of costs and benefits.

Therein lies the rub, for such social cost-benefit analysis presumes that society provides an anambiguous and coherent set of goals for the firm to pursue; that the firm has these goals in view when defining its strategy; and that success is measured by the ability to attain the prescribed goals.

Reality, as was noted earlier, has been much more ambiguous. Because of the ambiguities, it has been possible for the managers of state-owned enterprises to argue that any disappointing financial performance was the result of costly policies and programmes, mandated by their government masters, which were intended as a contribution to social welfare. In many instances, this was no doubt true. Whether true or not, however, it has often been difficult for ministers and politicians to deny that this was the case.

Various conference papers describe the efforts that certain countries have made to cut through these difficulties. Great Britain, Sweden, Italy and France, for example, have experimented at various times with a common approach. They have undertaken to identify the social tasks that they expected the state-owned enterprises to perform; to provide subsidies to such enterprises equal to the cost of these tasks; and thereafter to demand that, with the help of such subsidies, the enterprises should be financially self-sustaining. But at the present reading, according to Beesley and Evans, principles such as these appear to have been applied in a wavering fashion and with uncertain results.

There were considerable differences among the conference parti- cipants on how such difficulties might be surmounted. Some implicitly supported Raiffa's approach of defining carefully the goals and the trade-offs, whatever the difficulties in application might be. Beesley and Evans argue for the use, at least initially, of very simple measures of performance and instruments of control, even if such measures neglect some important social objectives. Others had more complex suggestions to make on how the state-owned enterprise might perform its role more effectively. Few were ready to assume that such enterprises could not be made to serve their governments in socially productive ways.

The International Implications

As nations have reduced their various barriers to the international flow of goods and capital, they have felt an increasing need to find other instrumentalities that might help them to achieve some of their specific domestic goals. One such instrumentaility, of course, is the state-owned enterprise. Such enterprises are likely to affect international trade and investment in numerous ways.

Kostecki's paper, for instance, explores the international implications of the state-trading enterprises, demonstrating that their international trading practices are often equivalent in effect to imposing a tariff or quota or granting a subsidy on imports or exports. Where state-to-state bilateral debts are concerned, of course, the power of the analogy tends to break down; but restriction and discrimination are still implicit.

The conference discussion produced numerous other illustrations of state-owned enterprises with strong international effects: state-owned enterprises granted special support from the state in order to surmount some high barriers to entry into a difficult field, such as aircraft engines; state-owned enterprises granted special support in order to protect a senescent industry, such as textiles or shipbuilding; state-owned enterprises given privileges and exemptions in order to hold foreign-owned firms at bay; and so on.

Conference participants were quick to point out that practically any support to state-owned enterprises which affects the international system can also be made available to private enterprises. Numerous illustrations of such analogous support were introduced, such as the official British support to Rolls Royce before it was nationalized, and the offical United States support to Lockheed Aircraft. The issue turned, therefore, on whether there were inherent reasons why the support extended to state-owned enterprises would prove to be less acceptable than that to private enterprises. Various reasons were expressed for such an expectation, including the possibility that the subsidies would be more extensive and more opaque; but the empirical evidence was sparse.

Another question of importance had to do with the export-pricing policies of state-owned enterprises. Here, the argument was straightforward enough: if state-owned enterprises are subsidized in the use of capital, as various conference papers suggest, they will tend toward capital-intensive techniques with high fixed costs. If they feel obliged to hold onto their labour force in periods of declining demand, as Grassini and others assert, they will look on their labour costs as also being fixed. With high fixed costs and low variable costs, managers who were responding to the usual rules for the firm in a profit-oriented market economy would be especially prone to cut prices in periods of declining demand. That propensity would be increased even further if the enterprises were under pressure to maximize their foreign exchange earnings. There again, however, the speculation rapidly outran the hard data.

Another thread of the argument, however, linked state-owned enterprises to a search for greater stability, not greater instability. Less fearful than private enterprises that they would run out of cash, such enterprises would feel fewer restraints about entering into long-term buy-and-sell commitments. Placing a premium on long-term stability, they may be found promoting long-term state-to-state bilateral agreements with likeminded state-owned enterprises from other countries; and, supported by the patina of their official status, they might be found promoting international cartel arrangements without the onus that attaches to private restrictive agreements.

Finally, there was some speculation that state-owned enterprises might be able to find common ground with multinational enterprises in some circumstances, leading to joint ventures and other arrangements that both sides would see as attractive. In arrangements of this sort, the multinational enterprise might be able to offer its global distribution network and its store of technology, while the state-owned enterprise could contribute access to subsidized capital and preferential access to its national markets. Although illustrations of such arrangements could be found, it was unclear what the future of such ties might be. If co-operative agreements of this sort should flourish, according to the speculation of the conference participants, it could well be that international borrowing at arm's length and international technological agreements would grow in importance while foreign private direct investment was losing some of its relative strength.

Future Work

The scholars and policy makers who have an interest in state-owned enterprises are an exceedingly heterogeneous lot, operating from widely different value systems and with widely different objectives. Some begin with the assumption that state-owned enterprises have a critical political or economic role to play in the national economies in which they operate; they are principally concerned with determining how best to realize the full potential of such enterprises from the viewpoint of each country. Other scholars and policy makers are more qualified, even sceptical, in their views of the desirability of state-owned enterprises; they are more concerned with defining the conditions under which state-owned enterprises represent a superior means for achieving the objectives of society. For them, comparisons with alternative modalities such as the regulated or unregulated private enterprise are of principal interest. Then there are those who are interested in the international aspects of the operations of state-owned enterprises: not only in the effectiveness of state-owned enterprises as the agents of their respective national governments, but also in their role in the international economic system. All groups nevertheless find a great deal of common ground in identifying various areas in which more research is needed.

Some of these needs are so obvious as to require only the most cursory mention. At present, the degree of state participation in the enterprises of the advanced industrialized countries is reasonably well known in terms of general orders of magnitude,[7] but any effort to view this population of firms by useful categories is generally defeated by lack of data. For example, there is no reliable survey at the present time that reflects the relative importance of state-owned enterprises according to the nature of their relationships with government, including such simple questions as the means by which managers and directors are appointed, the nature of the accountability and control systems used, and similar points. Nor do we have much systematic data on the degree of participation of state-owned enterprises in different types of product markets. Even such simple descriptive data as a classification of state-owned enterprises by their asserted objectives have yet to be developed.

Data such as these will no doubt come in time; so too will various studies that fall readily inside the structure of familar economic concepts, such as social cost-benefit analyses of individual firms. What will be much slower in coming and what is much more urgently needed for the intelligent formation of public policy is an intimate understanding of what actually drives the many different varieties of state-owned enterprises: their goals, their restraints, their methods of operations, their consequences. To gain a sufficiently rich understanding of state-owned enterprises in these terms will require many different kinds of studies: for instance, studies by countries, by industries across different countries and by functions across industries and countries. In all these variants, structured comparisons with private enterprises will play a major part in the study design. So will longitudinal studies of individual firms as they move from their early acquisition by the state to a more routine relationship, or as they move from an innovative role to one that is more humdrum, or as they move from a period of losses to a period of profits.

Studies of individual functions offer particularly rich possibilities for increasing an understanding of the state-owned enterprise. Policies with regard to planning, finance, control, pricing, distribution, innovation, technological choice, labour relations and acquisitions are particularly promising.

Perhaps the most subtle and difficult area of inquiry has to do with the decision-making process in state-owned enterprises. The latent hypothesis, of course, is that the public character of the enterprise makes a difference in how decisions are made. The difficulties in testing hypotheses of this sort are well illustrated by similar studies in the field of private enterprise and by studies of governmental decision making; but these will have to be tackled in spite of their formidable character.

This conference, therefore, and the papers that are presented in this volume, should be seen as little more than a prelude, laying the basis for a greatly enlarged effort at understanding in the future.

Notes

1. See, for instance, David Coombes, *State Enterprise: Business or Politics?* (London: George Allen and Unwin, 1971); Charles Dechert, 'Ente Nazionale Idrocarburi: A State Corporation in a Mixed Economy', *Administrative Science Quarterly* (December 1962); André Delion, 'Les entreprises publiques en France', in André Gelinas (ed.), *L'entreprise publique et l'intérêt public* (Toronto: The Institute of Public Administration of Canada, 1978); *The Economist*, Special Report on 'The State in the Market' (30 December 1978), pp. 37–58; Stuart Holland (ed.), *The State as Entrepreneur* (London: Weidenfeld and Nicolson, 1971); Chalmers Johnson, *Japan's Public Policy Companies* (Washington, DC: American Enterprise Institute, 1978); William Keyser and Ralph Windle (eds.), *Public Enterprise in the EEC*, Parts I to VII (Alphen aan den Rijn, The Netherlands: Sijthoff and Noordhoff International Publishers, 1978); Richard Pryke, *Public Enterprise in Practice – The British Experience of Nationalization after Two Decades* (London: MacGibbon and Kee, 1971); William G. Shepherd (ed.), *Public Enterprise: Economic Analysis of Theory and Practice* (Lexington, Mass.: Lexington Books, 1976); *Successo*, Special Report on 'State Enterprises in the Leading European Communities' (February 1972), pp. 87–110; Don

Votaw, *The Six-Legged Dog: Mattei and ENI — A Study in Power* (Berkeley and Los Angeles: University of California Press, 1964); and Annmarie Walsh, *The Public's Business: The Politics and Practices of Government Corporations* (Cambridge, Mass. and London: The MIT Press, 1978).

2. For example, Stuart Holland, 'Europe's New State Enterprises', in Raymond Vernon (ed.), *Big Business and the State* (Cambridge, Mass.: Harvard University Press, 1974), pp. 25–6.

3. For typical works that deal with these issues as the central theoretical questions of state-owned enterprise economics, see P.W. Reed, *The Economics of Public Enterprise* (London: Butterworths, 1973), and Ray Rees, *Public Enterprise Economics* (London: Weidenfeld and Nicolson, 1976).

4. Compare Herbert Simon, 'Rational Decision Making in Business Organizations', *American Economic Review*, vol. 69, no. 4 (September 1979), p. 500: 'To the public works administrator, a playground was a physical facility, serving as a green oasis in a crowded gray city. To the recreation administrator, a playground was a social facility, where children could play together . . . '

5. For example, M.V. Posner and S.J. Woolf, *Italian Public Enterprise* (Cambridge, Mass.: Harvard University Press, 1967), pp. 77–80; Delion, 'Les entreprises publiques en France', p. 129; Anicet Le Pors and Jacques Prunet, 'Les transferts entre l'Etat et l'industrie', *Economie et Statistique*, no. 66, (April 1975), p. 23; *The Economist*, (30 December 1978), p. 48; and Coombes, *State Enterprise: Business or Politics?*

6. For example, Pryke, *Public Enterprise in Practice*, especially pp. 173–283, and the works cited in the preceding footnote.

7. See, for instance, *The Economist* (30 December 1978), pp. 37–58.

2 ECONOMIC THEORY AND FINANCIAL MANAGEMENT

John Lintner

The purpose of this paper is to review some of the principal propositions of economic theory that apply to the financing standards and practices of state-owned enterprises. The analysis will focus on the financial management and policies of public concerns in what may be called the material sectors of the industrialized economies of the non-communist world, mainly the sectors that generate and deliver products and provide public utilities, transportation and communication to the public. In these sectors, one ordinarily finds distinctive enterprises, financially distinguished from the government at large, and operating with some degree of distinction between current and capital accounts and some expectation of a social return that can be directly linked to the enterprise.

The state-owned enterprises with which this paper deals are concentrated in highly capital-intensive industries in the advanced industrialized countries. With a few exceptions such as trucking, they are subject to substantial economies of scale and exhibit strong tendencies toward natural monopoly. Without public ownership or strict regulation, resources would be misallocated and unearned profits (monopoly rents) would distort the distribution of incomes.

Outside the utility sectors, patterns of state ownership in each country reflect particular historical circumstances.* Yet, despite varying circumstances, Pryor (1976) has shown that there are strong, statistically significant industry patterns in the incidence of public ownership. In particular, high nationalization ratios in different countries are found in industries such as steel and transportation equipment. These industries are highly capital intensive, subject to large economies of scale and prone to high concentration ratios; however, they have both the largest industry-wide fixed capital requirements and the highest ratios of fixed to variable costs. Nationalization ratios generally fall through the intermediate ranges of these economic and structural characteristics, with little or no public ownership in industries such as textiles, rubber products and furniture.

* Editors' note: see, for example, Beesley and Evans, Cassese, Grassini, Martinelli and Noreng in this volume.

23

These are precisely the structural characteristics that increase the importance of financial practices and policies in the management of enterprises, whether public or private. Heavy fixed capital requirements necessitate large-scale financing. The long-lived and usually 'lumpy' character of real assets also requires long-term, if not permanent, commitments of capital funds.

The same structural characteristics increase the importance of what are commonly called the 'capital budgeting' decisions of these enterprises. The size and lumpiness of real capital investments create choices between longer-lived and shorter-lived equipment and between technologies with different combinations of fixed and variable operating costs. The longer life of fixed assets involves greater uncertainty regarding cash flows associated with alternative facilities and investment projects. These risks and uncertainties affect the appropriate discount rates when making choices among different assets in capital budgets, and they have a critical impact on the appropriate manner in which the acquisition of assets is financed.

It is universally agreed that state-owned enterprises should operate to serve the public interest and general welfare. Defenders of private ownership accept these objectives for the private sector as well, but argue that the added objective of profit maximization will produce superior results. Since the days of Adam Smith, economists have analyzed the conditions under which 'the greatest good for the greatest number' could be achieved through the invisible hand of free market processes. Their work has produced a substantial body of theory on the optimal operation of state-owned and privately-owned businesses in terms of the ability of these enterprises to maximize social welfare. Although this body of theory is abstract and deals with idealized conditions, it provides an important set of standards against which to examine the central issues in this paper.

Investment and financial decisions depend critically upon the conditional cash flows attributable to the investment; consequently, they require projections of quantities produced, costs and sales prices, together with taxes and subsidies. Differences in the assessment of incremental cash flows attributable to given capital budgeting projects often have a far greater effect on their calculated net present values than differences in the assessment of the appropriate discount rate. Indeed, in numerous instances drawn from personal consulting experiences and the case files of the Harvard Business School (including public firms, private firms and joint ventures), different cash flow assessments discounted at the same cost of capital lead to net present values ranging from more than twice the current investment to substantial negative figures — a range much larger than that produced by any one of the cash flow projections discounted at different reasonable estimates of the relevant discount rate. Obviously, if decisions on prices and production are inappropriate, investment and financing decisions will be distorted even if proper discount rates are used.

Although, for a variety of reasons, results in practice cannot be fully optimal in terms of idealized standards, the goal of 'socially best attainable' decisions must nevertheless be actively pursued by state-owned enterprises. Theoretical analysis provides valuable insights, benchmarks and guides in this effort. Certain complications involved in the application of such theory under less than ideal conditions are explored in this study. As it turns out, theories based on ideal conditions prove inapplicable in some cases — even theories that analyze so-called second-best optimality conditions.

We will examine first the available theory concerning the optimal investment decisions and financial policies of privately-owned businesses where relevant future cash flows are risky and uncertain. This examination will provide a basis for the application of theory to the investment and financing decisions of state-owned enterprises.

Basic Theory: Ignoring Risk and Uncertainty

At any given time, an economy will have a limited supply of resources available to produce the goods and services needed to satisfy its members. The resources will be used in socially optimal ways only if the combination of goods and services being produced is preferred over any other possible combination of alternative outputs. For this to be true, however, the economy must be operating efficiently in several different senses.[1] Given available technology, each firm or business must use its resources to produce at maximum output: it must be impossible to increase the output of any desired product without sacrificing the output of something else. It must also be impossible to reshuffle the use of any resource (or combinations of resources) to provide outputs that consumers would value more highly than the outputs sacrificed by the reshuffling. Finally, after goods and services have been allocated among consumers, it must be impossible to reallocate them in ways that would leave some consumers feeling better off without leaving others feeling worse off.

These are, of course, the standard requirements for the so-called

Pareto optimality of production and distribution. They are usually derived and interpreted in terms of the best allocation of resources in the production and distribution of goods and services to be enjoyed during a given period of time. Any economy having a growing population or seeking a rising standard of living must divert some of its scarce resources from the production of current consumables to investment goods in order to augment its future supply of goods and services. A final efficiency requirement for the optimal allocation of an economy's scarce resources – and one particularly central to the concerns of this paper – is that current consumption must be sacrificed in favour of current real investment outlays to the point (though only to the point) justified by the current valuation of the augmentations of future consumption made available by the current real investment.

Most of the analysis done on welfare maximization has assumed a perfectly competitive factor supply along with product markets in which all participants take the prices generated by the market and in which new producers can enter without restriction. Indeed, considering certain important caveats noted below, it has been shown that any economy in which all markets are perfectly competitive will automatically satisfy all the efficiency conditions given above.

Under perfectly competitive conditions, all prices will be equated to marginal costs and thereby to the marginal value that consumers place on the outputs forgone from alternative uses of the resources. Factor prices equal the value of marginal products and free entry ensures that total costs are minimized. Consumer self-interest ensures that the relative purchase of each good will match its relative marginal utility. Since prices and price ratios are the same for all buyers under perfect competition, the relative marginal utility of any good will be the same for all consumers. Perfect competition ensures that no one can be made better off without hurting someone else. Moreover, ignoring risks, the interest rate will be equal to the marginal time preference of all consumers as well as to the marginal value of the increased future output made possible by investment outlays. The interest rate thus ensures the optimal diversion of resources from current consumption to real investment, and the optimal choices among alternative investment projects.

These ideal results do not necessarily depend upon private owner-ship and management of the business firms in the economy. Indeed, Lange and Taylor (1938) and Lerner (1944) have shown that socialist governments do not need detailed central planning to satisfy the preferences of the members of their economies as fully as possible. At least in principle, they need only compute a set of prices for all primary factors and final products (and a set of 'as if' or shadow prices for all intermediate goods) and require all factory managers to maximize their profits in terms of this set of prices. With all technologies exhibiting constant (or diminishing) returns to scale, marginal cost pricing would be ensured everywhere in the economy and the other optimality conditions listed above would be satisfied.

However, as noted earlier, there are important caveats to be considered. First, the ideal results described above implicitly assume that there are no differences between private and social benefits and no differences between private and social costs. In practice, a number of problems produce major discrepancies between private and social benefits and costs. If the expansion of a certain firm or industry results in lower costs for other firms, some way must be found to credit the expanding firm with the savings enjoyed by the other firms.[2] Second, business units setting their scale of production in terms of their own revenues and costs will produce at more than the socially optimal scale unless some way is found to charge them for the additional costs and losses their activities impose on the rest of the economy. Examples of loss of consumer satisfaction and well-being might be due to the pollution of water, air or land, or the increase in traffic congestion. Finally, the signals of the price system will not ensure optimal scales of outputs and allocations of different goods and services among consumers whenever the satisfaction of individual consumers depends upon the scale and pattern of other consumers' consumption.[3]

The second caveat to consider is that the price system is inherently incapable of signalling the appropriate scales and combinations of the outputs of public goods which are consumed collectively. Public goods cannot be bought and sold in the marketplace like ordinary goods and services. An individual's consumption of public goods is not exclusively his or her own, nor does it reduce the supply available to others. The mix of outputs of this class of goods must be determined by collective decisions; in practice, such goods are provided and financed by public agencies. In the discussion that follows, it will be assumed that all private costs and benefits have been made equal to social costs and benefits by some appropriate set of fees, taxes and subsidies; and that socially optimal decisions have been made regarding the provision of these public goods. Any failure of public policy to satisfy these two conditions will introduce distortions in the rest of the analysis.

The third caveat to consider is that these optimality propositions take the existing distribution of income as given. Each distribution of income produces a different set of outputs, prices and distribution of goods and services among the economy's consumers that satisfies the Pareto-optimal condition. Yet it is evident that changes in the distribution of income through combinations of taxes and subsidies or welfare payments necessarily involve interpersonal comparisons of utility.[4] In the discussions that follow it will be assumed that income tax and welfare policies have been adjusted so that the existing distribution of income can be taken as given and satisfactory, if not ideal.

The fourth caveat to consider is that Pareto-optimality theorems are derived on the implicit assumption that all production functions exhibit constant returns (and costs) to scale. But, as observed earlier, the firms that concern us in this paper are found mainly in industries the technologies of which exhibit markedly increasing returns to scale. Indeed, public ownership increases as industries depart from the competitive norm.

When increasing returns to scale leave a single firm supplying an entire market, unrestricted profit maximization leads the monopolizing firm to charge higher prices and produce smaller outputs than would be socially optimal. If all other firms and industries were operating competitively, the monopolist's marginal costs would reflect the market value of all other outputs in the economy which would be forgone if it increased its output; by assumption, the prices of all other goods and services in the economy are equal to their marginal costs. But consumers value the marginal output of the monopolist at its current price per unit, a price that exceeds the monopolist's marginal revenue inasmuch as the demand for the monopolized product is not necessarily less than perfectly elastic. Consequently, the over-all allocation of resources in the economy is necessarily distorted as the monopolist seeks to maximize profits by producing only to the extent that its marginal costs are covered by its marginal revenue; this is, of course, a lower level of output than one at which the price (the measure of consumer marginal satisfaction) would equal marginal costs.

In principle, a Pareto-optimal allocation of resources can be restored by using either regulation or nationalization to force a monopoly to satisfy all demands forthcoming at prices equal to its marginal costs.[5] However, with strongly increasing returns to scale, marginal costs (and prices) would be substantially below average total unit costs (including normal competitive returns to capital). Therefore, with marginal cost pricing, the firm would suffer a loss. The outcome could be offset by public subsidies. But the payment of public subsidies to offset the loss resulting from marginal cost pricing raises two major problems.

First, payment of such subsidies will have all the adverse effects of 'cost plus fixed fee' contracts. In a monopolized industry, with no possibility of new entrants, there would be no effective pressures to minimize costs and limit the drain on the economy's scarce resources. Unless effective administrative controls could be devised and implemented, serious inefficiencies would probably develop (see discussions below).

Second, public subsidies must be financed; this necessarily involves increasing government tax revenues. If the government were to provide subsidies to industries with increasing returns, it would have to raise new taxes. To be sure, an ideal tax system would not distort any of the marginal choices that may have been made in the economy in the absence of a tax system, and a system of 'lump sum' taxes would meet this ideal condition. But such a system is so impractical as to be ruled out, and all other available forms of taxes (including both income and excise taxes) have been shown to violate this ideal requirement.

The fifth caveat to consider, therefore, is that all feasible tax systems necessarily violate the idealized conditions of an *optimum optimorum*. For this reason, if for no other, the world offers only second-best alternatives. That conclusion holds even if all private and social costs and benefits have been brought into equality, all production is on the 'efficient frontier', and the existing distribution of income (after allowing for income taxes and welfare payments) is accepted.[6]

The situation will be second best (instead of third or umpteenth best) only if the tax structure is optimal under the circumstances. Several economists have derived the optimal structure of commodity (excise) taxes to raise a given amount of required revenue under the three conditions stated above. Their work has shown that, under reasonably realistic assumptions, the best attainable allocation of goods and resources will require a different tax rate on each final product produced in the public and private sectors. (See Technical Note 1.) Producer prices (net of tax) are everywhere assumed to be equal to marginal costs of production and distribution. But consumer prices (inclusive of tax) differ from these marginal costs by proportional amounts that are in principle unique to each product; the amounts for each product are inverse functions of the price elasticities as well as all cross-elasticities of demand for the product.

These results have significance for the appropriate pricing policies, conditional cash flows and financial requirements of state-owned

enterprises. There can be no question that the pioneering work of
Boiteux, Dessus and Massé in France and Turvey and others in England,
which led to the utilities' adoption of marginal cost pricing, has substantially improved these enterprises' social performance. The same can
be said for the later adoption of such pricing in varying degree by
private and public-owned telephone and other communications
companies in the United States and Europe following the work of
Baumol and others. Differences in the marginal costs of providing
different services to different groups of customers at different times
need to be fully reflected in the prices charged. Marginal cost pricing
as such remains optimal for all outputs of intermediate goods;[7] but
the appropriate set of prices for all final goods (such as residential
electricity) must include (optimal) excise taxes.

If state-owned enterprises set their prices equal to marginal costs
on both intermediate and final goods, the government must levy
explicit and appropriate excise taxes on final goods sales; the enterprise
can then be made whole financially with an over-all subsidy. But,
instead of levying excises and remitting subsidies on final goods sales,
governments may have state-owned enterprises vary their prices on
final goods free of excise taxes to reflect the social 'value of service',
so long as the net effects of such price discrimination (relative to
marginal costs) on operating surpluses are fully offset in the amount
of the subsidies provided. (See Technical Note 2.) In such a case,
marginal cost prices on intermediate goods and final goods prices,
inclusive of *pro forma* excises, would determine the appropriate level
of cash remission each state-owned enterprise should make to the state
(or its appropriate net subsidy), rather than the other way around.[8]

In principle, such a set of user prices for each state-owned enterprise is determined independently of any particular level of its
operating cash flow; the appropriate level of the operating cash flow
is derived from appropriate pricing and efficient operations; it is not
a determinant of appropriate pricing and scale of operations. Proper
pricing and scale of operations will probably require substantial subsidies inasmuch as the enterprise could be using technologies with
increasing returns to scale to produce products with elastic demands.
But, on the same grounds, proper pricing by a state-owned enterprise
using technologies with substantially constant returns to scale to
produce products with inelastic demands should provide positive
profits that may exceed the 'cost of capital' rate on its invested capital.

The common practice of imposing separate financial targets for the
operating cash flows of each state-owned enterprise inevitably distorts

socially optimal sets of prices and resulting output levels. The appropriate constraint for determining the levels and structure of excise taxes — and the appropriate margins over marginal costs for all state-owned enterprise sales of consumer goods — is the global over-all revenue requirement of the government. The imposition of an additional or alternative constraint on an individual state-owned enterprise is necessarily suboptimal.

The justification for imposing financial targets is to provide incentives for management to minimize costs and make operations as efficient as possible. These are important goals; but the allocative costs of using arbitrary financial targets not derived from proper pricing standards must be recognized and carefully weighed. Managerial efficiency can better be pursued when divorced from pricing policy. With this understanding, appropriate adaptations of internal budget controls along the lines developed in private business and reviews by efficiency audit commissions as proposed by Robson (1960) can be useful.

As Rees (1968) suggests, further non-distorting incentives for efficiency can be created by offering management bonuses based on the excess of actual operating surpluses over target levels, determined for each state-owned enterprise by calculating the expected surplus that would be implied by its marginal costs, demand conditions and optimal set of prices. But paying bonuses on efficiency gains over target surpluses determined from optimal pricing must not be confused with using financial targets as a basis for setting price levels. As we have seen, any expectation or requirement that state-owned enterprises should produce operating surpluses equal to their cost of capital applied to their investment base is fundamentally misguided and distorting on allocative grounds.

The properly measured cost of capital of a state-owned enterprise, however, enters into its decisions in two important ways: it provides the appropriate discount rate for discounting the conditional incremental cash flows associated with alternative new investment outlays and capital budgets; and, along with proper charges for depreciation, it determines the appropriate economic rent for the use of capital facilities. Determining the appropriate economic rent is an important component of total costs and more specifically of marginal costs, and thereby of allocatively efficient price structures. Under the assumptions of this section (no risk or uncertainty), one would hope that the interest rate would continue to be appropriate for both purposes as it was for the Pareto-optimal world described earlier. However, the requirements for Pareto optimality cannot be simultaneously satisfied in the face of an additional requirement (constraint) that the government raise some given amount of revenue through taxes. According to Lipsey and Lancaster (1956–57), the best attainable set of buyer prices incorporating an ideal tax system can only provide a second-best allocation of resources. These authors proved that if one or more of the Paretian conditions cannot be satisfied, the other Paretian conditions, although still attainable, will no longer be desirable. This raises the question of whether the interest rate is still a sufficient statistic for determining the appropriate scale and composition of real investment outlays in both the greater economy and each of its private and public business units.

Happily, there are grounds for reassurance, provided the capital (bond) market is perfectly competitive, there is no uncertainty and there are no taxes on interest or profits. (See Technical Note 3.) Using interest rates to determine the appropriate scale and composition of investment outlays at any given time involves the optimality of alternative streams of consumption goods and production plans over time rather than cross-sectionally. The existence of a schedule of excise taxes clearly changes the level and mix of the best attainable cross-sectional equilibrium in each time period. Changing incomes, expenditures, producer revenues and costs, and the amounts of conditionally optimal lending and borrowing may change the levels of interest rates. But the marginal conditions for interperiod equilibria are not altered for either producers or consumers; with perfect capital (bond) markets, the interest rate is the same for all members of both groups. The interest rate − or more precisely, the series of single-period rates over time − remains a sufficient statistic for determining the optimal scale and composition of investment outlay for the greater economy and for each firm within the economy, regardless of the nature of ownership.

Indeed, given perfect capital markets with no taxes on interest or profits, the interest rate will induce conditionally optimal amounts and the distribution of saving, borrowing and investing whatever may be the particular price vectors, sets of excise taxes and pricing policies of producers (relative to marginal costs). Apart from the adjustments for risks and taxes not considered in advance, the interest rate will be the proper discount rate for use in evaluating investment outlays even if excise tax structures and pricing policies are not cross-sectionally optimal.

We emphasized at the outset, however, that errors or other differences in the assessment of the levels and time patterns of the relevant cash flows attributed to particular investment projects often have a far greater effect on their calculated net present value (or internal rate of return) than any differences in the choice of the relevant discount rate. As a corollary, the use of improper measurements of social costs and benefits, the reliance on non-optimal price structures across products being sold by the enterprise, and the failure to ensure the efficiency of operations may well distort investment decisions as seriously as the failure to use appropriate costs of capital or discount rates. These policies and procedures may have a greater effect on the social performance of both public and private enterprises than financial policies.

In practice, of course, state-owned enterprises operate in economies in which there is a great deal of managerial slack, inefficiency and oligopolistic independence. Outputs are not everywhere produced at minimum attainable costs. Serious discrepancies exist between private and social costs and benefits. Producer prices net of excise taxes differ from marginal costs in varying (and often substantial) degrees. Because of administrative costs and complexities and the lack of necessary data, the optimal schedule of excises across all privately produced commodities is not in place.[9] As a result, consumer prices are not at appropriate levels elsewhere in the economy. Under such conditions, it is difficult to assess true cross-sectional social opportunity costs as well as just what set of prices in a public sector will produce even a third-best allocation of resources.

Nevertheless, the effort must be made. The managements of state-owned and regulated industries cannot be held responsible for the operating policies of firms in other sectors of the economy, nor for deficiencies in tax structures and other aspects of government policy. All that can be expected of these managements is that they effectively use the best information available concerning demands, costs and technological substitutions and interdependencies to optimize their operations in the context of the existing economy.[10] This will involve making their own operations as cost efficient as possible, making their own decisions in terms of social rather than private costs and benefits, and optimizing the absolute and relative structure of their prices on truly marginal peak load criteria, taking into account minimized marginal costs and all relevant and estimable cross-elasticity and substitution effects.[11]

In the rest of this paper, we will simply assume that maximum efficiency has been achieved in regard to the above-named operations. In the context of the best attainable sets of current policies and *pro forma* projections, the truly incremental cash flows that will be induced by the addition of each possible investment project can be identified and discounted at the appropriate discount rate.

To this point, we have ignored risk and uncertainty. But future outcomes are never precisely known in advance. Managements must allow for the uncertainty involved in their assessments of the cash flows attributable to any investment project in choosing the rate to be used in discounting the expected values of cash flows.

Discount Rates for State-owned Enterprise Investments with Uncertain Cash Flows

We have seen that, in the absence of risk and taxation of private profits, state-owned enterprises and private firms should use the market rate of interest to discount the cash flows of their prospective investments. Apart from tax adjustments, the literature reviewed below suggests that state-owned enterprises should screen risky investment projects with rates closely related or equal to the returns provided in private capital markets on cash flows of comparable risk. Ignoring income taxes for the moment, we begin with the formal theory in a private context. (See Technical Note 4.)

The modern theory of the valuation of risky assets in securities markets is based on the assumption that securities markets are perfectly competitive, frictionless and informationally efficient, and that the large number of investors in the market are all rational, risk-averse maximizers of their expected utility of wealth. Risk-averse investors shift their investment positions whenever they can increase their expected returns without incurring greater risks, and shift their portfolios whenever they can reduce their risk without sacrificing any expected returns. Consequently, they demand compensation in the form of higher expected returns for bearing any added risks. The rate of return on riskless, short-dated government securities determines the opportunity cost of investment in risky securities only if their expected rates of return are sufficiently larger than the forgone riskless return to compensate for the risks incurred. Since each investor's criterion is utility of wealth or consumption, any decision to increase or decrease the scale of investment in a particular security must consider the decision's effect on the rewards and risks involved in the investor's entire risk-asset portfolio. In particular, the risk on any security is its marginal contribution to the total risk of the portfolio, rather than its total variability considered as a single, separate security. By increasing the number of securities in their portfolios, assuming they are imperfectly correlated, investors can average out the risks involved in the unsystematic component of the risk in each security.

The equilibrium prices of all securities in these idealized, perfect and purely competitive security markets will be just low enough to provide expected rates of return that are just large enough to justify investors incurring the risks involved in holding them in well-diversified portfolios. Symbolically,

$$(1) \quad \bar{R}_i = R_f + \beta_i[\bar{R}_m - R_f]$$

where $\bar{R}_i$ is the expected rates of return on an investment in the ith security, $\bar{R}_m$ is the corresponding expected return on the market portfolio of all risky securities, R_f is the riskless rate of return, and β_i is the systematic risk of the ith security relative to that of the market as a whole (automatically normalized to unity).[12] (See Technical Note 5.)

In these informationally efficient markets, the equilibrium prices of each security at each point in time reflect all the relevant information available, including the probability distribution of the aggregate returns on the market as a whole, the regression slope of (or degree of correlation between) the returns on any one stock or other security and the market, and all knowledge available about the company's position prospects (e.g., British Petroleum has just struck oil big on the North Slope). Market prices reflect all this information and fully compensate investors for all systematic market-related risks in each security. But because of the assumed or inferred diversification of individual investors' portfolios, the market in this model provides no additional compensation to the investor for bearing unsystematic firm-specific risks uncorrelated with the aggregate returns on the whole market, regardless of how large they may be in individual cases or for particular companies. (See Technical Note 6.)

One final property of security prices in perfect capital markets is used in establishing criteria for optimal investment decisions by private firms. Let the securities issued by any two companies be selling at market prices justified by their respective systematic risks. Now, if the two companies are merged without any real economies or synergy, the market value of the securities of the firm coming out of the merger will be equal to the sum of the values of the securities of the merging firms in the absence of the merger; this will be true regardless of the degree of correlation between the income streams (or the market returns and values) of the merging firms. The heuristic reason is that the investors in the market will have been holding the outstanding securities of both companies in their well-diversified portfolios and will have already internalized the covariation within these portfolios. Merging the companies will not change the expected returns or the risks of their portfolios.[13]

The prevailing theory of optimal capital budgeting decisions assumes that the proximate criterion for decisions is the maximization of the value of the equity of the firm. As investments increase the value of outstanding shares, they increase the wealth of the shareholders, which is identified as an increase in the shareholders' welfare.

The theory of optimal capital budgeting decisions treats each new investment project as a new, wholly owned subsidiary of the firm considering the investment. Suppose the new investment costs I_j, but the equity claims to its cash flows, using equation (1), have a present value of V_j (based on their systematic risks β_j). If V_j equals or exceeds I_j, the investment should be made, since there will be an immediate increase in wealth which, by the value-additivity principle, will be reflected in the market value of the investing company's shares. Correspondingly, the investment should not be made if V_j is less than I_j. Since V_j is the current present value of the incremental cash flow attributable to the project discounted at the risk-adjusted rate $\bar{R}_j$, the investment rule to make all investments of which V_j equals or exceeds I_j is simply the classical net present value rule; the net present value of any investment should equal or exceed zero after adjusting the discount rates used to allow for the systematic undiversifiable risks involved.[14]

To this point we have assumed that equity capital is used to finance all new investments. In perfect capital markets, risky debt securities will also trade at yields[15] given by equation (1), but these required returns will be lower than those on equity capital because of the prior claims of the debt securities. When a company with a given set of real assets and cash flows finances itself with more debt, the systematic beta risk of its outstanding equity progressively increases; financial risks are added to the basic business risks that would be measured by the beta of the equity shares in the absence of any debt. However, in the absence of profits taxes with interest deductions, the resulting higher required rates of return on the levered equity are balanced by the lower yields on the debt. In these perfect markets, the combined market value of a company's outstanding debt and securities remains constant regardless of the mixture of debt and equity securities used in its capital structure. Its weighted average cost of capital consequently will be the same regardless of its debt/equity ratio;[16] if it has no debt outstanding, this will be equal to the value of $\bar{R}_i$ given by (1) for the equity shares of the company. The appropriate risk premium in the cost of capital of any company as a whole is determined by the systematic risk of its over-all operating cash flows before deducting interest charges on any outstanding debt.

Recalling the value-additivity principle, the same conclusion applies to each individual investment project. When there are no profit taxes, capital budgeting decisions do not depend on the way the particular projects are financed (or the capital structure of the company making the investment). The cash flows of each project should be discounted at the risk-adjusted rate determined by the systematic risk of its unlevered cash flow before deducting interest expense.

Inasmuch as the profit taxes that state-owned enterprises pay represent funds that remain within the public sector, no account need be taken of such payments in fixing the appropriate discount rate. Accordingly, the discount rate that a state-owned enterprise should use to determine the desirability of a new investment outlay depends entirely upon the systematic risks of the cash flow attributable to the project. The appropriate rate will be the same regardless of whether the new project is financed with retained earnings, operating surpluses from the state-owned enterprise's own operations, new equity funds advanced by the government, new borrowing or any other combination of financing. Moreover, regardless of how the project is financed (and regardless of the inherited capital structure of the state-owned enterprise in question), this rate will equal the rate of return the securities market would place on an independent private company the sole asset of which was this investment, financed entirely with equity shares (i.e., by the $\bar{R}_i$ given by (1) if it had used no debt financing).

It should be emphasized that the discount rate required to allow for the risks involved in any investment project will always be higher than the rate on borrowed funds. The return required on debt issues is always less than the equity rate (based on the same underlying uncertain cash flows) because of that shielded position and priorities accorded to bond buyers. The relevant rate is always the unlevered equity rate; only this rate captures and compensates for the entire risks of the underlying cash flows. Moreover, different discount rates are required for projects with different cash flow risks. These conclusions are particularly applicable to state-owned enterprises in view of the common belief among legislators, ministers and managers that the rate on government debt, alone, provides the appropriate standard for all their investments.

If it were not for the fact that private firms are taxed on their profits, the analysis to this point would apply equally as well to their investment decisions as to those of state-owned enterprises. If all private firms and state-owned enterprises made all new investments the net present values of which were positive using the (*pro forma* 'all equity') rates of equation (1), based on the systematic risks of operating cash flows, the economy would have the optimal combination of public and private investments as well as the optimal scale and composition of new investment outlays within each sector and each firm. In particular, no state-owned enterprise investments would displace socially preferred investments by private firms, or *vice versa*.[17]

This conclusion rests on the validity of the position taken by Hirshleifer (1966) and Baumol (1968) who argue that the risks involved in any project are the same regardless of public or private ownership and should command the same rate. Bailey and Jensen (1972) and Rubenstein (1973) have also used the informationally perfect model of equation (1) to urge the efficiency of the private securities markets in spreading risks; and they reach the conclusion that the social rate is likely to be just as high as the private rate for projects with any given degree of systematic risk. Arrow and Lind (1970) agree that, to the extent that the risks of public investments are borne by private individuals (i.e., security holders) rather than by the government *per se*, they should command the same rate; but they conclude that the rate under public ownership should generally be lower since private security markets are incomplete, and risks borne by the government are effectively pooled over far more people than just those who hold risky securities traded in private markets. However, Bailey and Jensen observe that any risks absorbed by the beneficiaries of public projects will be non-marketable risks. They also argue that the discount rate on public projects should probably be higher. Stapleton and Subrahmanyam (1978) argue that second-best Pareto optimality requires tighter investment criteria in the public sector because perfect insurance markets do not exist. Since the (implicit) shares of a public firm's return are untradable, there will be a misallocation of risk bearing if tighter investment criteria are not imposed.[18]

For the balance of this paper, we will adopt the Hirshleifer–Baumol position implemented in equation (1). Readers who believe that the considerations mentioned by Arrow and others cited require an upward or downward adjustment in this benchmark standard are free to make it. Any such adjustment, however, will only add to the adjustments that will be required by the further complications to which we now turn.

All advanced, non-communist countries levy taxes on the profits of private companies, computed after deducting interest paid on outstanding debt. When state-owned enterprises are taxed, however, the taxes are no more than transfers within the public sector. Any given prospective cash flow stream will necessarily provide lower after-tax profits to private companies (and their investors) than the same investment would provide the public sector from the operations of state-owned enterprises.[19] Taxable private companies will require a higher before-tax return on cash flow streams involving a given degree of risk than will state-owned enterprises. To the extent that funds to finance state-owned enterprises' investments are diverted from private investment outlays, the over-all volume of investment outlays by state-owned enterprises will be excessive from a social point of view. To compensate for these private profit–tax effects, the optimal scale of total state-owned enterprise investments and the optimal mix of private and public investments in the economy require that all state-owned enterprise investments be evaluated using discount rates that are higher than the $\bar{R}_i$ given in (1) for cash flows of each level of systematic risks. (See Technical Note 7.) Unfortunately, even after adjusting the criteria in this way, there are problems with this model at a theoretical level, and still other serious problems at a practical level.

Diamond (1967) has shown in a classic paper that a perfectly competitive securities market will yield a Pareto-optimal allocation of risks over any given set of securities being traded. Nevertheless, Stiglitz (1972), Long (1972), Jensen and Long (1972), and Fama (1972) have shown that firms which undertake to determine the optimal scale of their investment in any given project — and, more significantly, the optimum size of their entire capital budget in any one period — by the criterion of maximizing the net present value of their budgeted investment outlays will almost surely select smaller capital budgets and smaller over-all scales of new investment than would maximize the social welfare. (See Technical Note 8.) As a guide to practice, we must conclude that the net present value rule using the risk-adjusted discount rate is an approximation to what is basically desired under all but very idealized conditions. It may be a good working approximation in cases in which all capital budgets are sufficiently small (see Technical Note 9) that they have no significant effect on the aggregate returns and risk of the composite portfolio of all risk-bearing securities. The degree of estimating error will be larger for larger capital budgets than for smaller capital budgets.

When the projects provide cash flows extending over several future periods rather than one, the problems multiply. The risk–asset valuation model in equation (1) will be valid within each future period, but there will usually be no reason to believe that the risk-free rate and the then-contemporary systematic or covariance risks of the project's cash flow with the market return will be unchanging over the life of an extended project. Moreover, as Robichek and Myers (1966) have shown, even if all these elements are assumed to be invariant over time so that all the cash flows of a project are discounted at a constant discount rate, this procedure will still involve an implicit assumption that the relevant risks of a project's cash flows increase at a constant rate as one looks into the future. That assumption is surely not very often satisfied in cases of practical importance.[20]

The most useful and reliable short-cut model has recently been advanced by Myers and Turnbull (1977). We must recognize, however, that it is never possible to demonstrate that any one set of complex assessments involving a stochastic future is uniquely correct. Equally intelligent, well-informed and experienced mortals often differ substantially in the set of assessments of the unknown future they believe are most appropriate in any given case, just as they will differ on the numerical size of the adjustments required in our benchmark models of appropriate discount rates.

But these differences in judgements of appropriate discount rates are probably minor compared with other inescapable problems. If social optimality is properly taken as the objective, the inadvertent distortions in selecting proper prices and scales of operations of state-owned enterprises at a given time are likely to be serious due to inadequate knowledge of all the relevant cross-elasticities in the economy. This is particularly true when it is recognized that a second-best optimal tax system is not in place anywhere, and that the pricing and operations of the private sector dominated by oligopolistic structures, managerial discretion, X-inefficiencies and so on fail to fit the idealized model specifications even of the second- or third-best variety. This is not intended as a conclusion of despair, but of realism. The show must go on; with the co-operative efforts of public and private enterprises, many improvements are possible.

Technical Notes

(1) Optimal Commodity and Excise Taxation

We should explicitly note than in the literature on the optimal structure of commodity and excise taxes, factors of production are treated as negative consumption goods. In effect, consumers are subsidized on their supply of factors (labour) or taxed on their consumption of leisure. The term 'product' will be used throughout in this inclusive sense. With this understanding, the work of Atkinson and Stiglitz (1976), Sandmo (1976), Mirlees (1976), Bradford and Rosen (1976), Baumol and Bradford (1970), Lerner (1970) and Dixit (1970) (and the earlier work of Pigou, Ramsey, Hotelling, Boiteux and Samuelson there cited) may be summarized in three propositions. The first two are included here to rationalize and explain the third which is the conclusion from this work used in the text.

As one special case, if the supplies of all resources (ultimate factor inputs) are strictly invariant to taxes so that all tax shifting only affects other taxable products — and, in particular, if all utility functions are weakly separable between labour and consumption goods and homogeneous in consumption goods (so that all income elasticities will be the same for all goods and all consumers) — all consumer prices (producer prices plus excise taxes) should be strictly proportional to their respective marginal costs of production. The optimal unit excise tax on each final product would also be proportional to its marginal costs of production, and all producer prices (net of excise taxes) would be equal to their respective marginal production costs. Unit subsidies would then be paid back to producers in all industries with increasing return technologies in an amount equal to the difference between their average (minimized) full unit cost and their marginal cost of production (both computed at their optimal scale of output).

But, of course, factor supplies are not in practice invariant to taxes, and some incomes — notably the psychic incomes from leisure, and the incomes from many emoluments and perquisites — are not taxed. Any feasible system of taxes will necessarily involve shifting between the taxed and non-taxed sectors. In particular, the supply of labour is not invariant to the change in real incomes induced by changes in excise taxes, other things being the same, and both the separability and the homogeneity of utility functions are convenient assumptions having little practical relevance.

In another polar case, it has been shown that, if there were no tax shifting among the different items within the taxed sectors so that all relevant tax shifting were between each individual item and untaxed categories, then the optimal structure of tax rates over all taxable items would equalize their respective tax elasticities. The proportional tax rates would vary across items inversely to their respective 'own-elasticities' of demand, rather than being equalized across all items within the taxed sectors as in the preceding special case. However, all producer prices (net of tax) would still be uniformly set equal to their respective marginal costs of production, and subsidies would again be required in order to preserve the financial viability of firms in industries the technologies of which exhibit significantly increasing returns to scale.

When it is recognized that in practice there will be shifting both between taxed and untaxed sectors and between different items within the taxed sector (because all cross-elasticities of demand are not zero), the best structure of tax rates designed to raise any given amount of revenue, in effect, interactively combines the results of these two polar cases while allowing for cross-elasticities of final demands. The formulas are given in Dixit (1970), p. 297 of the text and equation (11), and Baumol and Bradford (1970), p. 275, equation (9). In particular, under these more realistic assumptions, the optimal vectors of tax rates must be simultaneously determined by complex functions of (a) the vector of marginal costs of everything produced or supplied across the entire economy, computed not incidentally at quasi-optimal rather than observed activity levels; and (b) all the elements in the economy-wide matrix of own-price elasticities and all cross-elasticities of output demands and factor supplies; as well as (c) the level of governments' revenue requirements. Clearly, such an ideal tax system involves different tax rates for each final product, service and factor supplier across the economy. Moreover, in principle, any change in consumers' tastes (preference functions), available technologies, supply conditions, or the required level of total government revenues will require recalculation and readjustment of the entire schedule of all excise tax rates. Nevertheless, as in the simpler cases considered previously, all producer prices (net of tax) should be set at marginal costs of production and distribution. Purchasers of intermediate goods would acquire them at marginal costs, while consumers of final goods would pay marginal costs plus the optimal excise tax.

(2) Optimal Subsidies for State-owned Enterprises

We assume that (a) all private and social costs and benefits have been brought into equality, (b) all production is on the 'efficient frontier',

(c) the existing distribution of income (after allowing for income taxes and welfare payments) is accepted, and (d) the optimal set of (differing) excise taxes is being levied on all publicly and privately produced final goods. The derivation of these optimal taxes assumes that all producer prices are set equal to marginal costs ($p_i = MC_i$), which are less than (minimized) average costs AC_i in increasing return industries. Under this pricing regime, applied to sales of final goods (indexed by k) as well as to intermediate goods sales (indexed by j), necessary financial incentives for each state-owned enterprise operating in increasing return industries will require subsidies amounting to the sum of $\Sigma_j q_j (AC_j - MC_j)$ and $\Sigma_k q_k (AC_k - MC_k)$. Note, however, that the net cost to the state will be less than this sum by the amount of the excise tax revenues collected from the state-owned enterprise's sales of final products which will amount to $\Sigma_k q_k (P_k^* - MC_k)$, where p_k^* is price inclusive of the excise tax.

Alternatively, state-owned enterprises can be instructed to price all final goods sales at prices inclusive of *pro forma* excise taxes (while continuing to price all intermediate goods at marginal costs). In this pricing regime, there will be a smaller but still uniquely determined net subsidy for each state-owned enterprise. With normal competitive rates of return included in average costs, the appropriate net subsidy for any given state-owned enterprise (assuming operating efficiency) will be the sum of $\Sigma_j q_j (AC_j - MC_j)$ and $\Sigma_k q_k (AC_k - p_k^*)$ where p_k^* represents the producer price actually charged for the kth final good. The net subsidy to a state-owned enterprise under this pricing regime is clearly the same as the net cost of the gross subsidy required when all prices are set at marginal cost levels. Where this expression is negative, a net profits tax would need to be levied (at a unique rate) on the state-owned enterprise to recapture the excess, which represents the net financial payment of the state-owned enterprise to the state.

(3) Interest Rates as Investment Criteria Under Second-best Conditions

This note establishes that the interest rate remains the proper capital budgeting criterion for capital budgeting decisions even under second- or third-best conditions, so long as the capital (bond) market itself is perfectly competitive, there are no taxes on interest or profits and no uncertainty. The latter conditions are assumed throughout this note.

To avoid confusion, note that the Lipsey–Lancaster general theorem of the second best (1956–57, p. 11) merely states that, if one or more of the Paretian conditions cannot be satisfied, 'the other Paretian conditions, although still attainable, are in general no longer desirable', and formal proofs of this proposition are given on pages 26–7. But in an often quoted sentence immediately following the one quoted above, they write: 'In other words, given that one of the Paretian optimum conditions cannot be fulfilled, then an optimum situation can be achieved only by departing from all the other Paretian conditions.' This, however, is clearly a (misleading) overstatement of their theorem. As two illustrations of the general invalidity of this stronger statement, we note that, even with different (ideal) excise tax rates on all products, all producers throughout the economy should set their prices (net of excise tax) equal to marginal costs of production and distribution. Consequently, $MRT_{ij} = MC_j/MC_i = p_j/p_i$ for all pairs of products and all producers at each point in time, where the p's denote producers' prices net of excise taxes. Correspondingly, consumers still allocate expenditures over goods for current consumption optimally subject to their budget constraint so that we continue to have $MRS_{ij} = p_j^*/p_i^*$ for all pairs of goods and all consumers at each point in time, where the asterisk denotes 'delivered' prices inclusive of excise taxes. Note that both these conditions were requirements of the first-best Pareto optimum in the absence of taxes, and they continue to hold with excise taxes. But differences in excise tax rates across commodities do mean that $p_j^*/p_i^* \neq p_j/p_i$ which makes $MRS_{ij} \neq MRT_{ij}$ at any one point in time. It is the latter inequality which creates a cross-sectionally second-best optimum.

However, using interest rates to determine the appropriate scale and composition of investment outlays at any given time involves the optimality of alternative streams of consumption goods and production plans over time rather than cross-sectionally. Consider the standard multi-period model in which savings earn interest and funds may be borrowed at interest rates (between any two dates) which clear a perfectly competitive 'bond' market. (See Henderson and Quandt (1971), Ch. 8, and Fama and Miller (1972), Chs. 1, 2, 3.) It is well known that any consumer optimizing his consumption plan over time will equate his *MRS* between each pair of commodities in every pair of time periods to the ratio of their discounted prices, and that this is equivalent to his optimizing the combination of goods purchased at each date followed by equating the *MRS* between his optimal expenditures at each pair of dates t and τ to (one plus) the market rate of interest between t and τ. We consequently have $MRS_{t\tau} = 1 + r_{t\tau}$ a common value for all consumers. Clearly, this condition for consumer equilibrium over time remains valid in the presence of excise taxes.

Similarly, when producers have the opportunity to borrow or lend unlimited amounts of funds at market-determined rates, they will reallocate schedules of outputs and inputs across time until all the standard optimizing conditions are satisfied using prices discounted at market interest rates. Between any two dates t and τ, (a) rates of product transformation must equal corresponding ratios of output prices, and (b) rates of technical substitution must equal corresponding ratios of input prices. Also, the discounted value of the marginal product of any dated input with respect to each output in each time period must equal its price (cost). (See Henderson and Quandt (1971), p. 311.) Once again, assuming cross-sectional optimization of production at each point in time, the condition for augmenting any input to increase output(s) at later dates is that all marginal internal rates of return between any two dates must at least equal the market rate of return. All investment outlays with non-negative net present values computed at market rates are desirable.

Note specifically that the marginal conditions for inter-period equilibria are not altered for either producers or consumers and, with perfect capital (bond) markets, this interest rate is the same for all members of both groups. The interest rate — or, more precisely, the series of single-period rates over time — consequently remains a sufficient statistic for determining the optimal scale and composition of investment outlay for the economy and for each firm within it, whether privately or publicly owned.

(4) On CAPM

The observations in the text are systematically used to derive 'The Capital Asset Pricing Model' of equation (1) in most modern textbooks on finance. Mullins (1976) is a good elementary introduction.

Although the early developments of this model in Sharpe (1964), Lintner (1965) and Mossin (1966) dealt with optimization over a single period, Fama (1970) showed that, if each investor is concerned with the utility of his lifetime consumption sequence, risk aversion for consumption in each period validates the use of equation (1) below for each period (though the parameter values will not necessarily be the same in each period, as discussed below).

We should perhaps also note that the theory presented here does not assume that security markets are complete in the Arrow–Debreu sense of there being at least as many distinguishable securities as there are states or possible patterns of cash flows. (See Arrow (1964) and Debreu (1959).) Hirshleifer (1964) and Myers (1968) have developed models of securities prices in such complete markets, but everyone recognizes that the degree of abstraction and idealization in these models is even more extreme and unrealistic than that involved in the models discussed here.

(5) On Betas

It is obvious from equation (1) that the beta of the market return on itself is unity, thereby making each β_i a measure of relative systematic risk. For any portfolio, $\beta_p = \Sigma_i h_i \beta_i$ where the h_i represents the proportion of funds invested in each stock in the particular portfolio. Note also that empirically the β_i represents the regression slope when the returns on any stock are regressed on the market return after adjusting for the risk-free rate. From $R_i = R_f + \beta_i (\tilde{R}_m - R_f) + \tilde{u}_i$ we fit $\tilde{X}_i = \alpha_i + \beta_i \tilde{X}_m + \tilde{u}_i$ where $\tilde{X}_i = \tilde{R}_i - R_f$, $\tilde{X}_m = \tilde{R}_m - R_f$, $\tilde{u}_i$ is the random uncorrelated error term, and the expected values of both $\tilde{u}_i$ and α_i are zero. Observe that the least squares estimate of β_i is $\beta_i = \sigma_{im}/\sigma_m^2$, the ratio of the covariance of the return on the particular stock to the variance of the market return.

Also observe that, since the market compensation for bearing risk on any security is given by (1) which may be written $\beta_i [\bar{R}_m - R_f] = [\bar{R}_m - R_f] \sigma_{im}/\sigma_m^2$, we also have $\beta_i [\bar{R}_m - R_f] = \theta_i \rho_{im} \sigma_i$ where $\theta_i = (\bar{R}_m - R_f)/\sigma_m$, σ_i is the standard deviation of $\tilde{R}_i$ and $\tilde{R}_m$. The risk of premium on any security is thus seen to be proportional to only that part of its total risk (σ_i) which is correlated with the market.

(6) On Systematic and Unsystematic Risks

Some examples of firm-specific risks would be the death of several senior executives of a company in an airplane accident, an explosion shutting down a company's major mine, the unexpected entry of low-cost foreign competition for a company's major product line — all of which may be contrasted with such systematic risks as a sudden embargo on imported oil, or changes in fiscal or monetary policy. As a further illustration, due to Mullins (1976), consider the equity shares of an independent company exploring and drilling for oil. The return will be high if oil in quantity is found, but the entire investment will be lost if it is not. Most of the variability in this return will depend on factors uncorrelated with the returns on other stocks (and the return on the market as a whole). This risk specific to the firm is an unsystematic risk which will add very little to the over-all variability of a well-diversified portfolio, and will not result in larger expected returns for investors in the stock in the marketplace. Only to the extent that the costs of exploration and the price of oil are systematically related to general levels of economic activity and general financial developments will the required expected rate of return on the stock be raised. But these systematic risks are small relative to the unsystematic risk of finding oil in good quantity. Consequently, even though the firm's stock is very risky in terms of total risk, its low level of systematic risk (relative to those of the average stock) would yield a relatively low expected return for new investors, since it is a low-risk security to investors with large, well-diversified portfolios.

(7) Adjustment in Required State-owned Enterprise Returns for (Private) Profits Taxes

Let $\bar{R}_{is}$ as above represent the untaxed required return for a state-owned enterprise given by equation (1) on a given investment. If $\bar{R}_{iau}$ represents the after-tax return on an unlevered private firm, we have $\bar{R}_{is} = \bar{R}_{iau}$. But the deductibility of interest means that the required after-tax return $\bar{R}_{iad}$ for a firm using appropriate amounts of debt financing will be lower than $\bar{R}_{iau}$ or $\bar{R}_{is}$, but the corresponding before-tax private return $\bar{R}_{ibd} = \bar{R}_{iad}/(1 - \tau)$ will be necessarily larger than $\bar{R}_{is}$ (of $\bar{R}_{iau}$). Drawing on the work of Sandmo and Drèze (1971) and Rees (1976), pp. 132–9, under certainty the discount rate for a state-owned enterprise, $\bar{R}_{is}^*$, which will produce socially optimal levels of investment, is the weighted average $\bar{R}_{is}^* = \theta\bar{R}_{is} + (1 - \theta)\bar{R}_{ibd}$, where θ represents the fraction of the investment financed with induced increases in savings (i.e., reductions in current consumption), and $(1 - \theta)$ correspondingly represents the fraction of state-owned enterprises' investments which displace private investments.

(8) Bias in Capital Budgeting Criteria

Essentially, this bias is due to the fact shown earlier by Lintner (1965) and Mossin (1973) that maximizing the increment in the value of a firm's outstanding securities due to its capital outlays involves charging twice the value-covariance risk of the (portfolio of) new projects with that of the firm's own existing assets (or cash flows). Although Leland (1974) has shown that these anomalies disappear in a world in which all product (as well as security) markets are purely competitive – and Merton and Subrahmanyam (1974) have shown they disappear in a world in which all firms regard the economy-wide scale of investment in each product or technology as determined independent of their own investment decisions – these sufficient conditions have little more direct relevance to the real world than the Arrow–Debreu ideal of complete securities markets.

(9) On the Efficient Markets Hypothesis

Even for small, single-period investment decisions, the approximation will be good only to the extent that the private security markets are in fact informationally efficient (as has been assumed throughout the literature being summarized). Extensive sophisticated statistical tests reviewed in Fama (1976, Ch. 5) have generally found that market prices do reflect publicly available information with reassuring efficiency. But several studies have recently developed rather disturbing scientific evidence showing some significant discrepancies even with publicly available information. (See *Journal of Financial Economics* (June/ September 1978), entire issue.) For instance, Rex Thompson shows that investments in discount closed-end funds over the 32 years 1940–72 would have consistently produced risk-adjusted returns 4 per cent greater than the market return! Jaffee (1974) has shown that managers trading on inside information obtain significantly higher-than-average risk-adjusted returns. Further, doubt on at least the 'strong form' of the efficient markets hypothesis comes from the evidence that shareholders of acquired firms in mergers get abnormal returns of over 13 per cent on average, while the acquired firms also on average obtain some smaller abnormal return. The more recent unpublished theses of Bradley and Asquith at the University of Chicago show even larger gains for acquired firms and still some positive average gain for acquirers. While these results do not necessarily show inefficiencies in the security markets, that is surely the most reasonable conclusion. There are also problems even on a theoretical level. Whenever information is not costlessly and instantaneously available to all investors, the capital markets cannot be fully efficient and the market will never fully adjust to new information. (See Grossman (1976) and Grossman and Stiglitz (1976).)

Notes

1. On these matters, see Mansfield (1979), Ch. 15, Baumol (1977), Ch. 16, and Henderson and Quandt (1971), Ch. 17.
2. These so-called 'external economies of production' occur widely. For instance, a firm may train workers as it expands, many of whom later go to work for other firms. The other firms thus avoid training costs. There are also cases where expansions of given industries enable other industries to take advantage of economies of scale that lower their real costs of production.
3. See the discussion of 'external economies and dis-economies of consumption' in Baumol (1977), Little (1951 and 1957), and Henderson and Quandt

(1971). But see also Arrow (1970).

4. Kaldor, Hicks and Scitovsky have suggested criteria for making these comparisons based on whether the gainers (or losers) could compensate the other parties affected and still be better off. But these criteria are suspect unless compensation is actually paid, as Williamson (1970) clearly illustrates; this is generally impractical. Moreover, even if feasible and carried through, reliance on these tests still implicitly assumes that the marginal utility of income is the same for all members of society; this essentially begs most of the basic issues involved. See also Alexander (1970). Although Bergson's conception of a social welfare function (1938) handles these problems constructively at a theoretical level, his conception remains non-operational and subject to further fundamental problems, at least when it is required to be a function of the preferences of all members of society so that everyone's preferences count. See Arrow (1951) and Rothenberg (1961) and later literature, especially Bergson (1976). A more operational but paternalistic approach free of Arrow's paradoxes and intransitivities assumes that the government or some group of individuals determines the collective preferences of society.

5. So-called short-run and long-run marginal costs will, of course, be equal when the combination of technology, plant size, and all other factors are chosen to minimize the costs of producing each given output.

6. Income taxes are not necessarily (and perhaps not even generally) preferable to commodity (excise) taxes on welfare grounds (Little (1951), Friedman (1952), Corlett and Hague (1953–54), and Sandmo (1974)), but probably remain the principal vehicle along with welfare programmes for desired income redistributions. However, Atkinson and Stiglitz (1977) argue that selected commodity taxes (such as housing subsidies or food stamps) may be important components of a tax structure designed to shift income distributions.

7. This is strictly true of all intermediate goods sold to other state-owned enterprises. From the standpoint of the consolidated public enterprise sector, these are the optimal 'transfer prices'. See Hirshleifer (1956) and Arrow (1959). It is also correct for intermediate goods sold to firms in the private sector to the extent that the latter exhibit competitive behaviour; if not, certain adjustments are needed, as shown, for instance, in Rees (1968 and 1976) and references there cited.

8. This analysis also makes it clear that neither price discrimination nor 'cross-subsidization' within any given enterprise are contrary *per se* to the general welfare. This is true under either public or private ownership. As Baumol and Bradford (1970) and others have noted, the optimal pricing problem of a multi-product, private enterprise subject to a regulatory profit constraint is formally identical to the optimal excise tax *cum* marginal cost pricing problem analyzed from a social welfare point of view in the text (when permitted profit under regulation takes the place of the government revenue requirement). See also Meyer *et al* (1959), pp. 172–88, and *passim*.

9. Recall that the optimal schedule of excises is a function of the inverse of the full matrix of all direct and all cross-elasticities across all commodities and products.

10. For a similar position, see Mishan (1962) who vividly advises that it is better to use even rough and ready approximations to the 'attainable best' rather than 'standing by and sadly sucking our thumbs under the sign of second best'.

11. Rees (1976), especially Ch. 6, and literature there cited examines some of the adjustments in state-owned enterprise prices required to allow for non-socially optimal conditions outside the public sector.

12. This is, of course, a holding period rate of return including capital gain or loss as well as cash dividend or coupon payment received.

13. This is just one particularly relevant application of the general

value-additivity principle which Schall (1972) and others have shown to hold in perfect capital markets. The value-additivity principle states that, in perfect markets, the equilibrium value of any claim to several separate income streams will be equal to the sum of the equilibrium value of the separate component streams.

14. The same investment project may be accepted by one firm but not by another because it involves different incremental cash flows in each case; but any project the relevant cash flows of which have the same mathematical expectation and covariance with the market, regardless of which firm undertakes it, will have the same NPV for all firms in this model.

15. The market portfolio will, of course, include all outstanding debt securities as well as equities (and, in principle, all other risky assets).

16. This is the famous Modigliani–Miller (1958) 'Proposition I', which follows as a direct corollary of the value-additivity principle in perfect markets. The original proofs were based on arbitrage considerations ('there is no free lunch'). See also Rubenstein (1973).

17. This conclusion assumes that all cash flow assessments are appropriate and abstracts from all other distortions. The conclusion follows from the optimal allocation of investments among private firms in the absence of profits taxes. See Fama and Miller (1972), Chs 6 and 7. After substituting the risk-adjusted rate of (1) for the riskless rate, the proof exactly parallels Rees (1976), section 8.1, pp. 125–32.

18. Taking a different tack, Feldstein (1964) has argued that there are major externalities of any investment expenditure such as induced increases in productivity and factor earnings in other firms and sectors which should appropriately be credited to public investments even though they are not in the assessment of private returns. Although Feldstein argues that the social opportunity cost rate is less than the private, the public sector's assessment of expected returns should include all induced benefits rather than having the discount rate *per se* lowered for investments of any given degree of relevant risk.

19. This is true even though private companies typically improve their after-tax profits by using prudent amounts of debt financing.

20. For a sizeable investment outlay on a plant, and advertising to launch a major new product, most of the initial uncertainty will be resolved within the first year or so; but the investment must be made beforehand.

References

Alexander, Sidney S., 'Comment on Arrow's Political and Economic Evaluation of Social Effects and Externalities', in Julius Margolis (ed.), *The Analysis of Public Output* (New York: National Bureau of Economic Research, 1970), pp. 24–30.

Arrow, Kenneth J., *Social Choice and Individual Values*, Cowles Commission Monograph No. 12 (New York: John Wiley and Sons, Inc., 1951).

———, 'Optimization, Decentralization and Internal Pricing in Business Firms', in *Contributions to Scientific Research in Management* (Los Angeles: 1959).

———, 'The Role of Securities in the Optimal Allocation of Risk', *Review of Economic Studies* (1964), pp. 91–6.

———, 'Political and Economic Evaluation of Social Effects and Externalities', in Julius Margolis (ed.), *The Analysis of Public Output*, (NBER, 1970), pp. 1–23.

———, and Robert C. Lind, 'Uncertainty and the Evaluation of Public Investment Decisions', *American Economic Review* (June 1970), pp. 364–78.

Asquith, Paul, 'A Two-event Study of Merger Bids, Market Uncertainty, and Stockholder Returns', unpublished PhD thesis in economics, University of Chicago, 1980.

Atkinson, A.B. and J.E. Stiglitz, 'The Design of Tax Structure: Direct vs. Indirect Taxation', *Journal of Public Economics* (July-August 1977), pp. 55-76.

Bailey, Martin J. and Michael E. Jensen, 'Risk and the Discount Rate for Public Investment', in M.C. Jensen (ed.), *Studies in the Theory of Capital Markets* (New York: Praeger, 1972).

Baumol, William S., 'On the Social Rate of Discount', *American Economic Review* (September 1968), pp. 788-802.

———, *Economic Theory and Operations Analysis*, 4th edn (Englewood Cliffs, NJ: Prentice Hall, 1977).

———, and David F. Bradford 'Optimal Departures from Marginal Cost Pricing', *American Economic Review* (June 1970), pp. 265-83.

Bergson, Abram, 'A Reformulation of Certain Aspects of Welfare Economics', *Quarterly Journal of Economics* (1938).

———, 'Social Choice and Welfare Economics Under Representative Government', *Journal of Public Economics* (October 1976), pp. 171-90.

Boiteux, Marcel, 'Sur la question des monopoles publics astreints à l'équilibre budgétaire', *Econometrica*, 24 (1956), pp. 22-40, reprinted in translation by W.J. Baumol and D.F. Bradford, 'On the Management of Public Monopolies Subject to Budgetary Constraints', *Journal of Economic Theory*, 3 (September 1971), pp. 219-40.

Bradford, David F. and Harvey S. Rosen, 'The Optimal Taxation of Commodities and Income', *American Economic Review* (May 1976), pp. 94-101.

Bradley, Michael, 'An Analysis of Interfirm Cash Tender Offers', unpublished PhD thesis in business administration, University of Chicago, 1979.

Corlett, W.J. and D.C. Hague, 'Complementarity and the Excess Burden of Taxation', *Review of Economic Studies* (1953-4), pp. 21-30.

Debreu, Gerard, *The Theory of Value* (New York: Wiley, 1959).

Dessus, Gabriel, 'The General Principles of Rate Fixing in Public Utilities', in James R. Nelson (ed.), *Marginal Cost Pricing in Practice* (Englewood Cliffs, NJ: Prentice Hall, 1964), pp. 31-49.

Diamond, Peter, 'The Role of a Stock Market in a General Equilibrium Model with Technological Uncertainty', *American Economic Review* (September 1967), pp. 759-76.

Dixit, Avinash K., 'On the Optimum Structure of Commodity Taxes', *American Economic Review* (June 1970), pp. 295-301.

Fama, Eugene F., 'Multi-period Consumption-Investment Decisions', *American Economic Review* (March 1970), pp. 163-74.

———, 'Perfect Competition and Optimal Production Decisions Under Uncertainty', *Bell Journal of Economics and Management Science* (Autumn 1972), pp. 509-30.

———, *Foundations of Finance* (New York: Basic Books, 1976).

———, and Merton H. Miller, *The Theory of Finance* (New York: Holt, Rinehart and Winston, 1972).

Feldstein, Martin S., 'Opportunity Cost Calculations in Cost-Benefit Analysis', *Public Finance* (Winter 1964), p. 125.

Friedman, Milton, 'The Welfare Effects of an Income and an Excise Tax', *Journal of Political Economy* (1952), pp. 1-24.

Grossman, Sanford, 'On the Efficiency of Competitive Stock Markets Where Traders Have Diverse Information', *Journal of Finance* (May 1976), pp. 573-85.

———, and Joseph E. Stiglitz, 'Information and Competitive Price Systems', *American Economic Review* (May 1976), pp. 246-53.

Henderson, James M. and Richard E. Quandt, *Microeconomic Theory, A*

Mathematical Approach, 2nd edn (New York: McGraw Hill, 1971).

Hicks, J.R., 'The Foundations of Welfare Economics', *Economic Journal* (December 1939), pp. 696–712.

Hirshleifer, Jack, 'On the Economics of Transfer Pricing', *Journal of Business* (1956), pp. 172–84.

———, 'Efficient Allocation of Capital in an Uncertain World', *American Economic Review* (May 1964), pp. 77–85.

———, 'Investment Decisions Under Uncertainty: Applications of the State-Preference Approach', *Quarterly Journal of Economics* (May 1966), pp. 252–76.

Jaffee, J.F., 'Special Information and Insider Trading', *Journal of Business* (July 1974), pp. 410–28.

Jensen, Michael C. and J.B. Long, Jr, 'Corporate Investment Under Uncertainty and Pareto Optimality in the Capital Markets', *Bell Journal of Economics and Management Science* (Spring 1972), pp. 151–74.

Kaldor, Nicholas, 'Welfare Comparisons of Economics and Interpersonal Comparisons of Utility', *Economic Journal* (1939).

———, 'A Note on Tariffs and the Terms of Trade', *Economica* (November 1940), pp. 377–80.

Lange, Oskar and Fred M. Taylor, *On the Economic Theory of Socialism* (Lippincott, Minneapolis: University of Minnesota Press, 1938).

Leyland, Hayne E., 'Production Theory and the Stock Market', *Bell Journal of Economics and Management Science* (Spring 1974), pp. 125–44.

Lerner, Abba P., *The Economics of Control* (New York: Macmillan, 1944).

———, 'On Optimal Taxes With an Untaxed Sector', *American Economic Review* (June 1970), pp. 284–94.

Lintner, John, 'The Valuation of Risk Assets and the Selection of Risky Investments in Stock Portfolios and Capital Budgets', *The Review of Economics and Statistics* (February 1965), pp. 13–37.

———, 'Security Prices, Risk and Maximal Gains from Diversification', *Journal of Finance* (December 1965), pp. 587–615.

Lipsey, R.G. and Kelvin Lancaster, 'The General Theory of the Second Best', *Review of Economic Studies* (1956–57), pp. 11–32.

Little, I.M.D., 'Direct versus Indirect Taxes', *Economic Journal* (September 1951), pp. 577–84.

———, *A Critique of Welfare Economics* (Oxford: Clarendon Press, 1957).

Long, John B., Jr, 'Wealth, Welfare and the Price of Risk', *Journal of Finance* (May 1972), pp. 419–33.

Mandelpher, Gershon, 'Risk and Return: The Case of Merging Firms', *Journal of Financial Economics* (December 1974), pp. 303–36.

Mansfield, Edwin, *Microeconomics, Theory and Applications*, 3rd edn (New York: Norton and Co., 1979).

Massé, Pierre, *Optimal Investment Decisions* (Englewood Cliffs, NJ: Prentice Hall, 1962).

Merton, Robert C. and Marti G. Subrahmanyam, 'The Optimality of a Competitive Stock Market', *Bell Journal of Economics and Management Science* (Spring 1974), pp. 145–70.

Meyer, John R. *et al.*, *The Economics of Competition in the Transportation Industries* (Cambridge, Mass.: Harvard University Press, 1959).

Mishan, E.J., 'Second Thoughts on Second Best', *Oxford Economic Papers* (October 1962), pp. 205–17.

Modigliani, Franco and Merton H. Miller, 'The Cost of Capital, Corporation Finance, and the Theory of Investment', *American Economic Review* (June 1958), pp. 261–97.

Mossin, Jan, 'Equilibrium in a Capital Asset Market', *Econometrica* (October 1966), pp. 768–83.

—————, *Theory of Financial Markets* (Englewood Cliffs, NJ: Prentice-Hall, 1973).

Mirlees, J.A., 'Optimal Tax Theory: A Synthesis', *Journal of Public Economics* (November 1976), pp. 327–58.

Mullins, David W., 'Diversification, The Capital Asset Pricing Model and the Cost of Equity Capital', (Boston, Mass.: Harvard Business School, Inter-collegiate Clearing House, no. 9-276-183, 1976).

Myers, Stewart C., 'A Time-State Preference Model of Security Valuation', *Journal of Financial and Quantitative Analysis* (March 1968), pp. 1–33.

—————, and Stuart M. Turnbull, 'Capital Budgeting and the Capital Asset Pricing Model: Good News and Bad News', *Journal of Finance* (May 1977), pp. 321–32.

Pryor, Frederick L., 'Public Ownership: Some Quantitative Dimensions', Ch. I in Wm. G. Shepherd (ed.), *Public Enterprise* (1976), pp. 3–22.

Rees, Ray, 'Second Best Rules for Public Enterprise Pricing', *Economica* (August 1968), pp. 260–73.

—————, *Public Enterprise Economics* (London: Weidenfeld and Nicolson, 1976).

Robichek, Alexander A. and Stewart C. Myers, 'Conceptual Problems in the Use of Risk-Adjusted Discount Rates', *Journal of Finance* (December 1966), pp. 727–30.

Robson, W.A., *Nationalized Industry and Public Ownership* (London: Allen and Unwin, 1960).

Rothenberg, Jerome, *The Measurement of Social Welfare* (Englewood Cliffs, NJ: Prentice Hall, 1961).

Rubenstein, Mark E. 'A Mean-Variance Synthesis of Corporate Financial Theory', *Journal of Finance* (March 1973), pp. 167–81.

Sandmo, Agnar, 'A Note on the Structure of Optimal Taxation', *American Economic Review* (September 1974), pp. 701–6.

—————, 'Optimal Taxation: An Introduction to the Literature', *Journal of Public Economics* (July–August 1976), pp. 37–54.

—————, and J. Drèze, 'Discount Rates for Public Investment in Open and Closed Economies', *Economica* (November 1971), pp. 395–412.

Schall, Lawrence D., 'Asset Valuation, Firm Investment and Firm Diversification', *Journal of Business* (January 1972), pp. 11–28.

Scitovsky, Tibor, 'A Note on Welfare Propositions in Economics', *Review of Economic Studies* (November 1941), pp. 77–88.

Sharpe, William F., 'Capital Asset Prices: A Theory of Market Equilibrium Under Conditions of Risk', *Journal of Finance* (September 1964), pp. 425–42.

Shepherd, William G. (ed.), *Public Enterprise: Economic Analysis of Theory and Practice* (Lexington, Mass.: Lexington Books, 1976).

Stapleton, R.C. and M.G. Subrahmanyam, 'Capital Market Equilibrium in a Mixed Economy, Optimal Public Sector Investment Decision Rules, and the Social Rate of Discount', *Quarterly Journal of Economics* (August 1978), pp. 399–412.

Stiglitz, Joe E., 'On the Optimality of the Stock Market Allocation of Investment', *Quarterly Journal of Economics* (February 1972), pp. 25–60.

Thompson, Rex, 'The Information Content of Discounts and Premiums on Closed-end Fund Shares', *Journal of Financial Economics* (June/September 1978), pp. 151–86.

Turvey, Ralph, *Public Enterprise Economics* (Harmondsworth: Penguin, 1968).

—————, *Economic Analysis and Public Enterprises* (London: Allen and Unwin, 1971).

Webb, Michael G., *The Economics of Nationalized Industries* (London: Thomas Nelson and Sons, 1973).

Williamson, Oliver E., 'Administrative Decision Making and Pricing: Externality and Compensation Analysis Applied', in Julius Margolis (ed.), *The Analysis of Public Output* (NBER, 1970), pp. 115–35.

3 DECISION MAKING IN THE STATE-OWNED ENTERPRISE

Howard Raiffa

This paper focuses on two theoretical areas of decision making in large organizations: multiple attribute utility theory and processes of mediation. A hypothetical state-owned enterprise has been introduced to provide a context for discussion. The hypothetical enterprise is not constructed from the experiences of a manager of an existing state-owned enterprise, nor is it a mosaic of the experiences of several managers of several state-owned enterprises. The author, a novice in this field, has imagined what it would be like to manage a state-owned enterprise.*

The Setting

Mr Charles Edgeworth Osgood is the newly appointed chief executive officer of a state-owned enterprise. As chief executive officer, he is responsible for all operational matters, but is guided by the broad strategic policies set by a board of directors. The chief executive officer and the board report to a minister. Several board members serve as directors to protect the interests of other ministries; these directors are in part guardians of special interests. The minister responsible for the state-owned enterprise has been unsuccessful in imposing his preferences upon the board members. The board has power, maintains diverse interests and collaborates with the minister to set broad policy. Although the chief executive officer is not power-less to change the constraints imposed upon him by the board and minister, he has chosen to act in accordance with their directives.

Do the board members have a grasp of the panoply of objectives of this state-owned enterprise? In a formal sense, the answer is yes. Each of the firm's objectives is likely to be mentioned by one member or another at each board meeting. However, different members tend to have different conceptions of the firm's objectives. Certain situations

* Editors' note: Raiffa's imaginings turn out to have much in common with some real situations. See Aharoni, Anastassopoulos, Beesley and Evans, Cassese and Grassini in this volume.

are likely to expose the underlying differences among board members.

Any effort to formalize trade-offs among objectives finds board members disagreeing on which trade-offs are acceptable. The many variables, intangibles and fragile values in the minds of the board members make a consensus on trade-offs very difficult to reach.

If an organic change in the operations of the enterprise is proposed, such as enlarging the product mix, diversifying, or vertically integrating existing operations, basic differences among board members are likely to surface. Despite efforts to reconcile the objections of individual board members, at times, the blocking minority opposes change to protect the special interests of its various ministries; at times, it opposes change for more abstract reasons, such as a pervasive ideology; at times, it simply opposes change.

Although the process of negotiation in board meetings appears restrained and rational, the positions taken by the various members often prove impervious to reason. Each guardian of a right exaggerates his objective and asserts the need for more protection than his interest requires; most are prepared to settle for less than they have demanded, but the minimum requirement is impossible to determine without an actual test.

Marginal changes in the policies of the firm are at times possible, but substantial shifts in the scope and structure of the firm are impossible without a major confrontation. Major decisions are typically made at a political level, beyond the board of the state-owned enterprise, and require various pay-offs to the parties involved.

In this hypothetical state-owned enterprise, the performance of the manager is judged largely by his ability to stay out of trouble; any discernible harm done to an identifiable group creates political difficulties. The secondary and tertiary effects of the state-owned enterprise's policies, good or bad, are disregarded, since they are not visible to the public. The beneficial effects of long-run programmes, in general, are undervalued.

To the extent that decisions entail uncertainty, the manager is judged not by the soundness of his trade-offs between risk and expected return, but by the actual outcome of his decisions. Accordingly, this state-owned enterprise proves more averse to risks than seems justified; this in turn leads to conservative management.

Implications

It is assumed that certain objectives of the state-owned enterprise
cannot be quantified: they are intrinsically qualitative. Given the
panoply of objectives to consider, which objectives can be quantified?
Conjoint measurement theory and multiple attribute utility theory
offer techniques for answering this question.

Suppose there are several potential outcomes – A, B, C, D, – for
one qualitative objective, and that these outcomes are not intrinsically
placed on a physical measurement scale. But suppose, conditional on
the objectives of concern and with other factors unchanged, that a
responsible decision maker can rank these outcomes on a personal
desirability scale. Where rank orders exist, numbers cannot be far
behind.

In conjoint measurement theory, preferences are determined by
playing off one objective against another. By looking at trade-offs
between the qualitative objective (with outcomes A, B, C, D) and other
objectives, one can often quantify and interpret strengths of preferences within one objective, even if there is no underlying objectively
quantifiable measurement scale. The real issue is whether these numbers,
once determined, are helpful for decision purposes.

It is often assumed that, if the board of the state-owned enterprise
were to quantify trade-offs, the end result would be a single net worth
number that would represent the profile of performance measures
reflecting the various objectives of the firm.

Suppose n-objectives are identified $(X_1, X_2, \ldots X_n)$, and a given
policy is evaluated by the n-tuple $(x_1, x_2 \ldots x_n)$ where x_1 is the
performance measure of the proposal for objective X_1. The usual
paradigm is that there is an opportunity set of n-tuples under review;
the decision-making entity must choose an n-tuple from this set. If –
and this is a big 'if' – the decision-making entity has a preference
ordering over n-tuples, represented by a real-valued value function V
that associates a number $V(x_1, \ldots x_n)$ and an n-tuple $(x_1, \ldots x_n)$ the
problem can be reduced to the following: choose an n-tuple $(x_1 \ldots x_n)$
that will maximize $V(x_1, \ldots x_n)$. Embodied in the V-function is a
myriad of delicate trade-off judgements.

I am not sanguine that such an all-encompassing value function can
be derived for the management of a state-owned enterprise, even if
there is dictatorial control over the firm. The essence of the problem
lies in the complex, interpersonal differences of opinion that enter into
any decision-making process. However, conjoint measurement theory

could be used to identify areas of agreement and disagreement, and to exploit areas of relative agreement in order to collapse a large number of objectives into a far smaller number of composite objectives.

If the state-owned enterprise had an over-all, single V-function that associated a single number to each n-tuple $(x_1, \ldots x_n)$, the V could be conceived as generating a single composite objective criterion to maximize. There are vast differences between a world that reduces n-indices into one index and a world that reacts to the full set of n-indices. Conjoint measurement analysis may fulfil an intermediate role by reducing thirty competing indices to perhaps four composite indices. Is this possible? I am not certain, but I believe it is worth trying.

It must be very difficult to manage effectively with a diffuse set of objectives. Private enterprise managers usually have a bottom-line figure that holds them accountable to some extent. In private enterprises, the profit motive is strong and serves as a sieve through which gross incompetents are weeded out and others rewarded. If state-owned enterprises were able to evaluate their performance in terms of a relatively few composite, measurable objectives, their efficiency could be enhanced. A multiplicity of vague objectives serves to protect the inefficient.

Using the limited notation introduced, let me turn to the question of compromise and mediation. The guardian of objective X_i might view current operations as having a performance value of x_i^0; if he is like other guardians, he wants to push x_i to higher heights (assuming the orientation of X_i is 'the more the better'). The set of all objectives other than X_i will be designated as Y_i and the performance measure of the state-owned enterprise on Y_i will be designated as y_i.

Looking objectively at the value of an X_i performance level on the society (holding Y_i at level y_i), a value function as in curve A in Figure 3.1 may be observed. However, the guardian of objective X_i, keeping in mind his mission and role as well as his personal set of rewards and punishments, might have a value function as in curve B. Furthermore, to achieve his personal aspirations, he might exaggerate his value function in the give-and-take of negotiations to that of curve C. What the guardian of objective X_i is doing, so does the guardian of X_j, for $j \neq i$. Hence, the difficulty in reaching an agreement on any innovative programme becomes apparent.

Now, suppose that the chief executive officer contemplates a basic proposal — a proposal that can be shaped in a myriad of ways. The performance index on X_i can range anywhere from point a to b (see

Figure 3.1: Hypothetical Evaluation Functions on Objective X_i

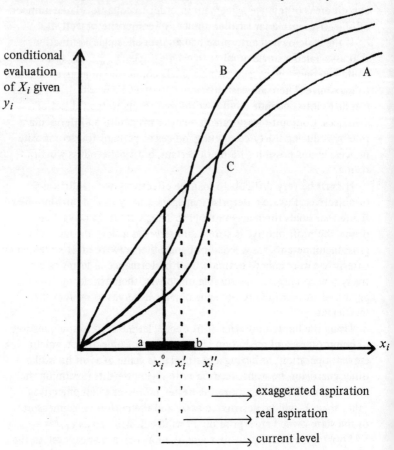

Figure 3.1) depending upon the details of the proposal. If it is shaped in a way favourable to X_i, it might meet the 'real aspiration level', x_i', of the guardian of X_i. But in order to achieve x_i', that guardian tries to hold out for x_i''.

A zone of agreement (or, in the vernacular, a feasible solution) may or may not exist. Consider each possibility in turn.

With honest revelations and hard analysis, the guardian of X_i may be able to shape the basic proposal in order to achieve x_i' (or better); the guardians of other issues may be able to accomplish the same. This can be conceived as a goal-programming problem: choosing a proposal to achieve x_i' or better on a set of critical objectives. However, even if there is a zone of agreement in the abstract, the guardians of the objective might not recognize that it exists, since negotiators strategically exaggerate their demands. In problems such as these, a limited amount of analysis might be crucial in discovering acceptable zones of agreement.

If each guardian holds out for his 'real aspiration level', there will be no acceptable solution. In the absence of a zone of agreement, some negotiators may believe that other board members are acting strategically, exaggerating their demands. Therefore, members of the board may believe that the inability to reach a zone of agreement is more apparent than real.

In either case, whether a zone of agreement exists in principle but is not recognized, or does not exist at all, the chief executive officer and minister still have potential trump cards that they can play to forge a compromise. The chief executive officer and his minister may decide that the excessive personal zeal of the board members is getting in the way of an agreement. They may not agree with the guardians of X_i whose manifest bargaining behaviour reflects an attitude consistent with curve B or C in Figure 3.1. The chief executive officer and minister may believe that trade-offs in the interval from a to b should be smooth (reflecting curve A), and that the sharply inflected curves (B and C) do not capture the public's long-term interests. But the guardian of X_i may be adamant about holding out for x_i', choosing to fight — to go public if necessary — rather than back off. The rub, of course, is that the guardians of other special interests play the same game, making agreement impossible.

The minister is not without power, however. In internal negotiations, he acts as a mediator with clout and muscle. He may be able to convince the guardian of X_i to accept a value to the left of x_i' by cashing in some of his previously gained political chips: demanding the guardian's concession as repayment for past favours. Furthermore, the minister may be able to log-roll by promising concessions on unrelated issues that will enhance the over-all aspirations of the guardians of X_i. The minister also has the option of using force, threatening to replace the adamant guardian on the board. Thus, in the over-all public interest, it may be necessary for the minister to develop artfully a consensus by using the full power of his office. The chief executive officer, acting alone, may be ineffective in shaping compromises within the board. He may need help.

Managing Downwards

The chief executive officer gives orders from his perch at the top of a huge enterprise. He is the principal (decision maker) who delegates authority downwards to diverse agents who act on the principal's behalf. In the principal–agent problem, action is decentralized. Agents, who are closer to the real problems and have information not readily available to their principal, must make choices and convey information through the hierarchy. Instructions and rewards to the agents need to be structured so that agents acting in their own interests are also serving the interests of their principal. The problem of achieving the proper structure is complicated by the fact that there may be constraints on the joint actions of the agents (for example, over-all capital constraints). Furthermore, given an uncertain environment, the principal has to worry about overlapping sets of information patterns, differences in probabilistic perceptions and differences in risk aversions.

The principal–agent problem is further complicated by multiple conflicting objectives. Once again, assume that the principal (the chief executive officer) is concerned about n-objectives; any action is evaluated in terms of n-performance measures $(x_1, \ldots x_n)$. If the principal has a clear-cut V-function that assigns an over-all 'goodness index' $V(x_1, \ldots x_n)$ to $(x_1, \ldots x_n)$, the V-function can be communicated to the agents. Remember that V embodies in its formulation the full set of trade-offs between objectives.

In the state-owned enterprise, a V-function is difficult to elicit. Indeed, it might be divisive to try to get the board to agree on a suitable V. Of course, if the board could agree on how to collapse many objectives into a few composite objectives (say, thirty into four), life could become a bit more manageable. However, as long as the effective number of objectives exceeds $n=1$, the problem remains.

If the chief executive officer is called upon to act, he must either explicitly or implicitly (most likely implicitly) formulate his personal trade-offs among the objectives. As a reasonable chief executive officer, he will balance the interests of the board members, and of his minister, and his perception of the interests of the public. In defending his actions, he will rarely be called upon to articulate his trade-offs; if he is wise, he will refuse to answer even if called upon. But still, in the privacy of his thoughts, the chief executive officer will be forced to make various trade-offs the values of which have not been clearly delegated to him by the board.

Now, enter the agents. How should the principal instruct them? Descriptively, without any empirical evidence to bolster my conjecture, I would guess that the chief executive officer will equivocate. He will want to transmit some of his personal trade-offs to his agents, but not in such a way that his trade-offs will become official policy; to do otherwise will get him into political trouble with the board. After all, it is the board that sets broad policy. What could be broader than fundamental trade-offs?

Now, consider agent Q. In making choices, he knows he should consider an array of objectives $(X_1, \ldots X_n)$; he has some vague guidance about trade-offs from his principal, and has some personal objectives of his own to add to the pot-pourri. In some choice situations, he may be lucky: alternative A may be better than B on all objectives or so much better on most objectives that any reasonable person could not object to A. However, if the situation is not clear, and personal trade-offs are implicitly demanded in the choice of A v B, agent Q can choose one of two strategies: he can defer to his chief executive officer to make the decision, or he can use his own trade-offs to make the choice himself, remembering he is accountable to his principal. If the agent refers the choice to his superior, he has to provide information about the problem; this is not always easily done. Distortions occur, facts are difficult to articulate, and sensitivities have to be protected. If the agent acts himself, he may not be privy to how individual board members feel about various trade-offs. The multiplicity of objectives leads to chaotic control; once again, inefficiency gets protected by complexity.

Controversial trade-offs usually involve highly incommensurable attributes: economic efficiency with safety with health with environmental protection with distributional equity (both spatially and temporally) with desired independence from foreign pressures with attitudes towards the use of market mechanisms. These value trade-offs play a role in major strategic investment choices.

In a few fortunate circumstances, the problem may partially decompose. Agent Q may not be concerned with the full array of objectives $(X_1, \ldots X_n)$ but only with a subset $[X_i, X_j, X_k]$, for example. If preferences over $[X_i, X_j, X_k]$ do not depend upon levels of the other objectives (for example, if the set $[X_i, X_j, X_k]$ is preferentially independent of the complementary set of objectives), the chief executive officer (the principal) need only ascertain that the agent's preferences roughly agree with his own. Thus, it may be relatively easy to make the trade-offs internal to the set $[X_i, X_j, X_k]$.

If the principal has been able to formulate a value function $V(x_1, \ldots x_n)$ over all attributes, he will not need to convey the extent of his formulations to each of his agents. He can convey different information to different agents, and structure incentive schemes so that the agents will act in conformity with the principal's preferences. If a particular agent requires sensitive information about the entire V-function, the principal can reorganize activities so that he assumes some of the responsibility for the actions of the agent.

There are, of course, other ways the chief executive officer can manage his agents without disclosing trade-off information too sensitive to reveal without a full discussion of the board. But the chief executive officer has to be careful not to antagonize the sensibilities of some of the board members in giving his instructions to his agents. Exercising this caution may be burdensome at times, and may force the chief executive officer to manage more conservatively than he might feel desirable.

Thus, the chief executive officer is in an uncomfortable squeeze: he is damned if he formalizes his trade-offs and damned if he does not. The looser the chief executive officer's bonds are to the board, the more he can control his agents. The more explicit the chief executive officer makes his value judgements, the more effectively he can decentralize his organization, and the more accountable his agents become to him. All this is to the good if the chief executive officer (the principal) has the right set of values. But the right set of values should be the collective values of the board and the minister. So it seems we have come full circle in this argument. How nice it would be if the board could articulate a rather comprehensive set of trade-offs that could permeate the organization. Alas, this is easier said than done.

4 ON FINANCE AND DECISION MAKING

Kenneth J. Arrow

The first two chapters of the book have addressed two new theoretical trends, applying them to very real problems in the operation of enterprises in general, and state-owned enterprises in particular. Lintner and Raiffa have summarized the major literature in their areas with extraordinary skill.

The chapters by Lintner and Raiffa are complementary analyses of enterprise behaviour. Lintner's aim is to reduce everything to the right prices and the right interest rates, so that the optimal behaviour of the firm can be determined by optimizing with the right constraints. Raiffa says the world does not work like that. Within an organization, behaviour is determined by a kind of game; personal influences are significant. Instead of having prices as the only signals, Raiffa identifies many power and communication channels. To study these channels, he considers the problems of decision making in collective groups, voting theory, and the strategic misrepresentation of information to achieve specific goals. If everything were reduced to behaviour under competitive prices, it would never pay to misrepresent. Theoretically, a small buyer in a market could buy less than he desired to bring a price down, but his effect would be so small that only he would bear the consequences. On the other hand, if there were a few buyers seeking to change market prices, strategic misrepresentation might become profitable.

Both Lintner and Raiffa are concerned with the role of uncertainty in enterprise decision making. Lintner moves from the world of certainty to the world of uncertainty in his discussions of the discount rates used in evaluating investments. Raiffa considers the principal-agent relationship, an aspect of the problem of eliciting information from others. The principal has to delegate some responsibility to the agent; he cannot know everything the agent knows. The agent has to be induced to act as the principal would act given the same information.

Now, Lintner is right in calling attention to the importance of prices. There is a well-known theory of optimal allocation. To many, the 1938 papers of Harold Hotelling and Abram Bergson made the issues clear. In terms of pure efficiency characteristics, Hotelling and Bergson explained in just what sense parametric prices serve to direct resources efficiently; most of our thinking and practical advice have been dominated by these arguments.[1] We argue that, if the first-best optimum involves some losses to enterprises, the losses should be made up through taxation, but we are not concerned about the details.

Ramsey and Lintner argue that the money has to come from somewhere; there is no such thing as a lump sum tax.[2] Taxes have to be imposed on some economic behaviour. Any tax is essentially an excise tax — that abomination of the welfare economist. Losses in optimal allocation are subsidies, which are simply negative taxes. The classic ideal of a nearly neutral tax is the income tax: in the short run, it is a tax on the labour-leisure choice; in the long run, it is a tax on the consumption-savings choice. The latter can be eliminated by going to a consumption tax, but not the former. In theory, one could even try taxing leisure at the individual's potential wage rate; somehow, however, everyone seems to quail at the suggestion.

The business school professor who could (or believes he could) make much more by working for private industry should really be regarded as earning an additional income. The addition is equal to the difference between his business school salary and what he could earn in private industry, a difference which is equivalent to the pleasure he gets professing. Business school professors enjoy the untaxed benefits of professing while depriving the business world of their valuable services. To avoid distortion, professors should be taxed on that untaxed income.

The Ramsey-Manne-Boiteux optimal taxes recognize inevitable tax distortions and seek to balance them against social gains.[3] Unfortunately, as Lintner has emphasized, calculating optimal taxes requires solving the general equilibrium of the whole economy. The formulas of Boiteux's *Econometrica* paper of 1956 take up half a page. The mathematical complexity of the formulas is really a minor matter; with modern computers, solving 200 simultaneous equations is not difficult. The real problem is where does one get the data for such figures as the cross-elasticities of demand and supply?

The difficulty in securing necessary information is at the heart of the public enterprise question. As Lintner has pointed out, public enterprises are not scattered randomly over the landscape; they are concentrated in certain areas, precisely the ones where the discrepancies between optimal prices and actual prices are the greatest. Typically, public industries operate under increasing returns. Optimal prices are likely to lead to losses. Either the losses will be paid for by a tax on the commodity itself (assuming that public enterprises should break even), or they will be paid for by a tax on something else, such as cigarettes, alcohol, or labour. Unfortunately, the optimal taxes require knowing all possible cross-elasticities which, in turn, requires information from outside the enterprise. Certainly, the firm in question is not the natural focus for collecting information about the general economy, and reliable data are not available for the fully optimal calculation. The logic of decentralization that is used in analyzing the competitive economy implies that outside information is very costly to acquire. Is there some way of operating public enterprises using only information available to them?

In general, public enterprises should not be run to maximize profits narrowly defined since they are usually natural monopolies or high-risk enterprises. However, they should be able to determine their policies by the information available. That does not mean the firm should be run only on information internally generated, such as its own production function and prices. But there is something in between knowing the whole economy in detail and having only local information. The fact that the firm knows more about things that are closer to its operations than those that are unrelated needs to be exploited.

The impact on the state-owned enterprise of optimal prices, optimal taxation and behaviour under certainty can be observed in more practical terms by examining the development of the breeder nuclear reactor. The development of the breeder in the United States and in most other countries has been undertaken by public enterprises and paid for by the government. The commodity being produced in the United States is knowledge about the breeder, rather than the breeder itself. How does the acquisition of knowledge fit into the general picture?

In the United States, knowledge about breeders will be sold free of charge. Perhaps the government will license the use of knowledge. However, the fee will be so low that it will become insignificant when compared to total costs. The first-best argument will be that the price should be zero, since the reproduction cost of knowledge is zero. A zero price may be optimal. The optimal tax theory suggests the possibility of a non-zero price if the research has to be financed. The Nixon administration actually looked into the possibility of a non-zero price, arguing that government-financed development ought to bear licence fees of a type that would at least recoup a significant percentage of research and development. The studies done on this subject yielded mostly negative conclusions.

Perhaps more important than pricing is the need for insight into other questions. How should the United States decide on the scale and timing of the breeder programmes? Should it aim for commercialization in the year 2010 instead of the year 2000? The amounts of money allocated to the breeder programme are large, half a billion dollars a year. What could be learned from Lintner's analysis of risk adjustments based on the securities market?

In principle, the theory of optimal prices will yield a source of revenue; in the case of the breeder, the source of revenue will be mostly subsidies. Assuming the subsidies are correctly calculated, the next question is: what is the discount rate? According to Lintner's analysis, the discount rate is determined by the covariance between the uncertainty of breeder benefits and general economic conditions. The uncertainty is not whether there will be a breeder, but how cheaply it will produce electricity once it is in existence.

Lintner tells us to correlate this uncertainty with a market basket of securities. However, part of the risk will not be compensated in the market. Does this mean that part of the risk should be ignored? Lind and I have argued that the part of the risk not correlated with the market should be spread out, so to speak, over the public at large, and therefore wiped out.[4] To the extent that risk is correlated with the market, the discount rate should be raised.

Whether the correlation of the uncertainties of the breeder with uncertainties of the economy is large or small is difficult to determine. There are two offsetting factors: on the one hand, the bigger the national income, the more electricity needed and, therefore, the greater the value of the savings from the breeder against an alternative; on the other hand, the national income is negatively affected by problems in other forms of energy when the breeder benefits per unit of energy use are greatest. In the first case, variations in GNP that have nothing to do with energy, such as uncertainties about the rate of technological progress, are positively correlated with the value of the breeder. In the second case, a negative correlation exists between GNP and the value of the breeder to the extent that there are fluctuations in other energy sources. The second case offers a stronger insurance argument for the breeder and leads to a lower discount rate. It may be that, on the whole, the correlation will be small; in that case, the discount rate may be only moderately different from the riskless rate.

Now, the problem to consider is that arriving at a negative

correlation, socially desirable as it may be, does not seem satisfactory from the point of view of the enterprise. If the enterprise's performance is to be judged separately from the rest of the economy, the risks become very large for the scale of the firm, small though they may be for the scale of the country. As a result, managers of enterprises will tend to be more conservative than is socially desirable: given a choice, they will take fewer risks than they should. With their decisions partially mandated by different political levels, it may be that political interference may compensate for inadequate risk-taking.

The question, still, is how to make state-owned enterprises accountable, given their limited access to information. Similar problems arise in private enterprises; there, too, managers have some incentive to be more conservative than would be inferred from the pure theory in Lintner's paper. Indeed, there is a new theoretical argument which states that, in a certain sense, every firm is a monopolist in its own stock. By changing the risk characteristics of the firm's behaviour, the firm can create a niche different from that of any other company. Even though it is selling competitively in product markets, the firm's securities may involve different risks from other firms' securities. Thus, there is a declining demand curve for the security — a monopoly position — which leads the firm to keep its scale down.

The considerations discussed above play a significant role in enterprise behaviour. For example, the importance of financing from internal funds and its differential importance in different industries seem to be phenomena that theories of perfect markets have difficulty explaining. As has been pointed out, since state-owned enterprises are typically risky and capital intensive, the financing aspect becomes more important than in the average private firm.

There are two interesting aspects of Raiffa's paper which I would like to discuss briefly. The first point is the repeated emphasis on the *status quo* as a preferred alternative. Raiffa's theory is that, once the organization is going, it is easy for it to stay put, whatever 'stay put' may mean. Raiffa proposes a political model that includes a powerful board of directors; as a member of two boards of directors, I find this hard to believe, but it may be valid. His model of voting in the board is a veto model; changes require extraordinary majorities. I am not clear whether boards of directors of public enterprises necessarily follow such a model or whether more genuinely egalitarian voting is possible. In fact, power in Raiffa's enterprise is distributed in such a way that a cognizant ministry has a predominant role, the other directors serving as conduits for complaints or as information channels. I am unsure whether these conflicting interests lead to paralysis or not. If there are enough different problems and sufficient distribution of opinions, it may be difficult to get a majority of any opinion, even if there is an egalitarian voting process.

Raiffa has discussed arm twisting, the selling of ministerial favours, as a tool of conflict resolution. That constitutes a currency, if you assume that, once power is used, it cannot be used again. With such a currency, the political process may be able to achieve a roughly efficient allocation.

Raiffa has also stressed the principal–agent problem and pointed out some of the great difficulties involved. For the sake of counter-arguments, imagine a complex organization, with any particular agent working in a restricted field. Again, the principle of decentralization is at work, but it is applied internally. It is not necessary to spell out the whole utility function to the agent. All that the agent needs is a restricted optimization problem built on a utility function over a limited set of variables and a set of constraints. This sub-problem can be quite unequivocal and depend only upon information available to the agent.

The constraints, however, are the results of central decisions, most obviously the allocation of capital to individual enterprises or departments. The allocation of capital may be the result of vague and conflicting pay-offs at a higher level, but the agent's performance is not necessarily poorer because of it. Given the allocation of capital, one can determine whether or not the agent is optimizing on his sub-problem — sub-optimizing, to use a popular phrase of a number of years ago. The capital allocation may be poorly solved, but the agent need not concern himself with that problem. The principal–agent problem may not be quite as difficult as Raiffa suggests.

Notes

1. The optimal taxation theory describes one set of prices for consumers and another for producers. In an intertemporal context, apply the same formulas to dated commodities. The natural consequence is that there are producers' and consumers' interest rates. Offhand, I do not see any reason why the real rates have to be the same.

2. F.R. Ramsey, 'A Contribution to the Theory of Taxation', *Economic Journal*, 37 (1927), pp. 47–61.

3. A.S. Manne, 'Multiple-Purpose Enterprise – Criteria for Pricing',

Economica, N. S. (1952), pp. 322–6; M. Boiteux, 'Sur la gestion des monopoles publics astreints à l'équilibre budgétaire', *Econometrica* 24 (1956), pp. 22–40.

4. K.J. Arrow and R.C. Lind, 'Uncertainty and the Evaluation of Public Investment Decisions', *American Economic Review* (June 1970), pp. 364–78.

5 THE ITALIAN ENTERPRISES: THE POLITICAL CONSTRAINTS

Franco A. Grassini

The purpose of this study is to determine how the managers of Italy's public enterprises, controlled by the Ministry of State Shareholdings, are affected by outside political influences and constraints. To observe the political impact on managers, the decision-making processes involved in three major areas will be discussed: management selection; investment; and interactions with trade unions. Instituto per la Ricostruzione Industriale (IRI), Ente Nazionale Idrocarburi (ENI), and Ente Partecipazioni e Finanziamento Industria Manifatturiera (EFIM), the three main Italian state-owned holding companies, are the focus of this research.

IRI, ENI and EFIM control a wide range of operating companies. IRI's holdings span the telephone, electronic, banking, shipping, engineering and metallurgical industries. ENI's holdings extend over the oil and natural gas industry, including the exploration, production, transportation, distribution, refining and marketing of oil and natural gas at home and abroad. EFIM, the youngest of the three enterprises, has operating companies in the field of engineering and agriculture. In this study, IRI, ENI and EFIM have been termed industrial enterprises to distinguish them from the many non-industrial enterprises, such as credit institutions, owned by the Italian government. Much of the resource material comes from confidential interviews with past and present managers of these three enterprises.

Traditional theory has assumed that profit-maximization is the single goal of the firm, the goal towards which all decisions are made. Since the pioneering work of Berle and Means, however, several theorists have argued that decisions, in fact, are made by managers for whom growth, power, salary and personal security are often more important than profit.[1] As Marris has observed, there is always some kind of constraint preventing managers from placing personal goals too highly above profits.[2] Indeed, there are constraints placed on the freedom of decision makers regardless of their goals. It is known that parliament, political parties, ministers, civil servants, directors, trade unions and managers in Italy have a great impact on state-owned enterprises, greater than on private enterprises. It is unclear, however, who the decision makers really are.

The degree of autonomy permitted the managements of state-owned enterprises varies from company to company. In general, according to Pasquale Saraceno, parliament decides a policy, provides funds and sets a limit on the extent to which a state-owned enterprise can try to maximize its profits.[3] At times, the process is reversed: a project or idea is generated by a company and works its way through the government to parliamentary approval. State-owned enterprises are released from the responsibility of earning the full social opportunity cost of the capital used in the approved project. The duty of the Minister of State Shareholdings is to promote the responsive performance of the state-owned enterprise by defining its goals and weighing the social costs entailed in achieving each goal. Thus, from the point of view of the Ministry of State Shareholdings, the public enterprise exists as a resource enabling government to carry out its programme and achieve its goals. How, when, where and to what degree outside influences affect the decisions of management in public enterprises will be discussed in the following sections.

Management Selection

Chairmen for IRI and ENI are chosen by the government. The chairman of EFIM is also chosen by the government but the formal appointment is by decree from the Minister of State Shareholdings. The general manager of IRI, upon recommendation of his chairman, is the only other person appointed by the minister's decree. Managers of controlled companies, though formally appointed by boards of directors, are chosen by the managements of their controlling units.

In the past, boards of directors of public enterprises approved every proposal submitted by their chairmen without question. Recently, however, boards have acquired some power to influence management selection. It is now customary for management to inform the Minister of State Shareholdings of major appointments to be filled. Such advance notice, when carried out, gives the minister a voice in the selection process. Often, however, management reserves the right to select its subordinates, choosing not to inform the minister.

The selection of chairmen and, to a lesser extent, general managers of state-owned enterprises involves political considerations. By examining the kinds of demands politicians have placed on managers of state-owned enterprises, political influences and constraints on managerial decisions can be observed.

Over the last ten years, politicians have asked managers of public enterprises to respond to four main areas of concern: creating new jobs and avoiding firings; responding to labour needs in specific geographic areas; filling positions for political patronage; and financing political campaigns.

Company managers know that, to retain their positions, to be confirmed, or to be promoted, no employee should be dismissed; in fact, whenever and wherever possible, managers should create new factories or expand existing ones. (This will be discussed in more detail in the section on investments.) No large Italian company, private or public, has been able to shut down plants in the last ten years unless it was certain that its workers would be given new jobs. Both private and public enterprise managers operate under the principle that it is sinful to close a plant; however, private managers, not depending upon the government for their positions, are freer to be sinners. In many cases, multinational enterprises have chosen to give away plants and additional cash to avoid the problems a shut-down would cause.

The location of a new factory is extremely important to politicians, for creating new jobs increases the support of their constituencies. The politician who can take credit for bringing new industry to his district will be able to exercise political patronage by placing key people in positions.

Finally, contributions to political parties from private and public enterprises have been an important source of revenue for politicians. Prior to 1974, it was common to find public enterprises making contributions to various parties and campaigns. In 1974, a law was passed prohibiting enterprises holding 20 per cent or more state shares from contributing to political parties; private companies were not restricted from making contributions.

Because top management positions are filled by political appointments, the managers selected tend to be known to the political world. Moreover, those who have held positions within the public enterprise system have a higher probability of appointment than those who have worked within the private enterprise system. Simple political patronage, however, does not dominate the selection.

IRI has had three chairmen and five general managers over the last 25 years. One chairman had been a lawyer and member of parliament, another a university professor and member of the European Economic Community Commission, and the third the chairman of ENI and EFIM. Four of the general managers came from IRI-affiliated

companies and one from another public enterprise. ENI has had six
chairmen over the last 25 years: the first was its founder, the four
following had held the position of deputy chairman within ENI, and
the sixth was a lawyer and former chairman of EFIM. Since its
incorporation in 1962, EFIM has had three chairmen: the first was
a lawyer with a wide range of business experience who later moved
to ENI and IRI, the second was EFIM's previous general manager,
and the third was a university professor. In addition to being known
to the political establishment, most of the chairmen and managers
described above were either members of or closely linked with the
Christian Democratic Party, the majority party in Italy.

Italy is currently ruled by a wide coalition. Recently, the coalition
enacted a law requiring the government to secure the opinion of a
special parliamentary commission before appointing chairmen and
deputy chairmen of public enterprises. The government may still
overrule the commission's majority opinion, but such an act seems
unlikely.

In early 1979, the chairmen of IRI, ENI and EFIM were appointed
under the new ruling. A Christian Democrat was appointed to IRI, a
Socialist to ENI and a Social Democrat to EFIM. The members of the
special parliamentary commission were requested to vote along party
lines. The new chairmen of IRI and ENI were known to support the
platforms of their respective parties, but were not active in politics.
The new chairman of EFIM, however, was a university professor
whose career had been fostered as a result of his active involvement
in party politics. The likelihood that these managers would succeed
in creating new jobs in specific geographic areas appeared to be a
strong criterion in their selection.

Based on the data collected for this study, there is no evidence
to suggest that political patronage in lower-level positions is more
widespread in public than in private enterprises; clearly, it exists in
both business sectors. Political patronage does not appear to be a
major factor in the selection of managers for top managerial
positions in state-owned enterprises. In the 15 major IRI companies
studied, only two of the chairmen had been members of parliament;
both had been chairmen of the Italian Broadcasting Corporation
(RAI), an IRI subsidiary. One president had been a journalist and a
general manager of IBC; his appointment, exceptionally, was subject
to strong political influence.

Among the many interviews conducted with high-ranking managers
of IRI, one manager's rise to power stands out as a clear case of

political patronage. To avoid an imminent firing, a chief executive of an IRI subsidiary joined a particular political party to gain support to remain in office. Other accounts of managerial appointments suggest similar tactics, but there are also many instances where the IRI management refused to promote people supported by the Minister of State Shareholdings or by other government members or politicians.

Thus, in the case of IRI appointments, it appears that political patronage exists, but is not necessarily a key factor. Given the fact that state-owned enterprises and government often have conflicting goals, it is difficult to identify a pattern that guarantees promotion. Certainly, the opinions of fellow managers and one's superiors weigh heavily in the promotion process.

ENI's criteria for selecting managers have changed over the years. Enrico Mattei, ENI's founder, was a powerful man with clear ideas as to how the company was to be managed. His original staff was composed of collaborators from his region and from the rank and file of the resistance movement. In all cases, professional capability was a prerequisite for filling any position, regardless of its level.

Today ENI's hierarchy of management reveals other influences. One of the six major subsidiaries owned by ENI is headed by a political appointee who is clearly the puppet of higher management. Another subisdiary is headed by a man of power and capability who received his appointment through political patronage.

In 1975, a kind of 'middle managers' political revolution' took place in ENI and received wide coverage in the media and significant support from political parties. Since 1975, the political affiliations of management have become increasingly important. Today, those who headed the revolution hold some of the higher internal positions. Since ENI deals predominantly in oil and natural gas, its existence depends to a large extent on political decisions. ENI recognizes its need to be kept abreast of state and world politics, and thus is willing to accept political input.

Since its inception, EFIM has been free to select managers based on professional capabilities rather than political patronage. One of the managers of its four major holding companies is a close political friend of the Minister of State Shareholdings, but is also an expert in his company's line of work. Various interviews at EFIM revealed similar appointments, none of which appeared to involve a compromise of professional expertise.

In the past, those who wished to be selected for top management positions in state-owned enterprises had to be willing to help finance political parties and campaigns. Up until 1974, when the new law was enacted restricting the use of public monies, all Italian political parties depended upon and received contributions from state-owned enterprises. Although managers of these enterprises and government officials believed that financing political parties should not be crucial to effective company management and performance, many justified their actions by arguing that private enterprises had similar means to lobby for their interests. Often, high-level managers willing to grant political contributions were unwilling to allow any political pressures below their administrative levels.

Today, rumours suggest that indirect financing continues despite the 1974 ruling. However, in comparison to what once existed as a crucial factor in management selection, the willingness to contribute to political parties and campaigns no longer appears significant.

The Minister of State Shareholdings, other members of the government, members of parliament and party leaders have all been classified as 'politicians' in this study. To understand the political influences and constraints placed upon managements of state-owned enterprises, it is important to identify who among the many politicians has more power.

The Minister of State Shareholdings has the power to recommend candidates for top-level positions; but, to be appointed, the candidates must be approved by the Prime Minister, cabinet members and party leaders. If the minister's recommendations are not accepted, it is his responsibility to compromise or come up with alternative suggestions. In the last wave of chairmen appointments to IRI, ENI and EFIM, only one of the three new people had the full support of the Minister of State Shareholdings. In late 1978, the incumbent minister requested that IRI's general manager resign; other members of the government, members of parliament and party leaders supported the general manager's position and allowed him to remain in office. A few months later, however, the new chairman of IRI and the same general manager had a quarrel and the general manager resigned.

Governments in Italy are short-lived; since 1957, there have been nine Ministers of State Shareholdings, six in the last ten years. As a result, the minister who makes appointments is seldom the minister who confirms them three years later. With this constant turnover in authority, managers of state-owned enterprises are able to ignore the suggestions of a particular minister as long as they are confident that they have the support of other members of the political establishment.

Members of parliament play a very small part in the selection of higher management in public enterprises. Basically, they are opinion givers and advisors to members of the government and party leaders. As mentioned earlier, the special parliamentary commission on appointments is requested to vote along party lines. Party leaders also consult and advise but have little power in actual management selection.

Investments

In 1957, a law was passed requiring state-owned enterprises to locate 40 per cent of their existing investments and 60 per cent of their new investments in the Mezzogiorno, the area of southern Italy; in 1971, the figures were raised to 60 per cent and 80 per cent, respectively. Such a constraint on public enterprises not only serves to develop southern Italy, but also encourages new investments. To replace plants and machinery, a public enterprise located in northern Italy, as approximately 80 per cent of IRI and ENI subsidiaries were in the late 1950s and all of EFIM was in 1962, needs to increase its investments. To remain within the boundaries of the law, increased investments translate into new investments in southern Italy.

For IRI, new investments are always suggested by its subsidiary companies. The IRI planning manual, printed in 1966, states that the primary responsibility of each company or sectorial holding is to prepare investment plans. High-level IRI management recognizes that its subsidiaries have the most up-to-date knowledge of markets, technologies and competition. IRI must approve each recommendation for investment, taking special care to consider the financing of the project. If a company is able to finance a new investment with internal resources, it can be assured IRI's approval.

High-level investment plans of all state-owned enterprises have to be approved by the Interdepartmental Committee for Economic Planning (CIPE), a government committee of Economic Ministers, and, indirectly, by parliament. So far, there has been only one case where the Minister of State Shareholdings has refused to approve a programme submitted by an enterprise. In 1973, a quarrel began between the chief executive of Alfa Romeo, who wanted to expand his company's northern facilities, and the Minister of State Shareholdings, who wanted all new expansion to be in southern Italy. The quarrel ended with the dismissal of Alfa Romeo's chief executive, and the following reference to the conflict in the *Relazione Programmatica 1974*, the investment programme for state-owned enterprises approved by CIPE:

> It is our duty to question, not only for social reasons, the programme of concentrating all production in Arese [northern Italy], and therefore increasing, by the end of the programme, the number of workers to 35,000 instead of the 28,000 forecast at the beginning. Alfa Romeo, therefore, has been requested to study the opportunity of decentralizing some productions, provided this is not in conflict with the existing productive capacity.

As inferred in the above quotation, it is ultimately the company that plans its production and investment programmes.

IRI has relaxed its screening of expansion proposals submitted by subsidiary companies as a result of incentives to invest in southern Italy. Alfa Sud, an IRI subsidiary, is a case in point.

In the early 1950s, Alfa proposed an expansion of its production and facilities. Its plan was quickly rejected on the grounds that Italy could house only one mass car manufacturer: Fiat dominated the market. In 1958, Alfa opened a new plant near Milan despite some political suggestions to locate the plant in Naples.

Although expanding production is viewed as a positive step, it is the responsibility of higher management to evaluate the risks and benefits of any large-scale expansion plan. In 1968–69, Alfa proposed an ambitious programme with the goal of producing half a million cars (including smaller, popular cars) and constructing a new plant in the Mezzogiorno, southern Italy. The programme was approved and launched the same year.

Between 1973 and 1978, Alfa suffered substantial losses. The oil crisis, a slowdown in the demand for cars, and new labour relations in Italy contributed to Alfa's problems, as well as poor planning at the company level. Had the higher management of IRI conducted a more careful screening of Alfa's original proposal, significant losses might not have been incurred. However, the incentive and pressure for new investments permitted IRI to relax its standards; under heavy pressure from higher authorities, management is induced to take greater risks.

Looking at IRI's investments, one can see that political influence has been used not just to secure new investments but to secure them quickly. IRI's decision to locate Alfa Romeo's southern plant at an industrial site already prepared to begin construction was largely influenced by political pressures to expedite the plant's operation.

Finally, rescuing ailing enterprises is an area in which political pressures are very strong. IRI, however, has successfully resisted such pressures. In 1971, GEPI, a state-owned enterprise, was set up for the express purpose of helping 'lame duck' companies recover. GEPI has kept IRI's involvement to a minimum: from 1970 to 1976 only 11 per cent of IRI's increase in factory employees came from ailing companies it had helped. The government, however, did pressure IRI into acquiring the main private shipyards; today these shipyards account for approximately one-fifth of IRI's employment in the shipping sector.

ENI, being a more specialized enterprise than IRI, has always had a more centralized investment programme. Much of ENI's investments have little relevance for politicians wishing to take advantage of job openings or geographical sites; exploring for oil and natural gas knows no political boundaries and requires a minimum amount of labour. Transporting oil and gas also requires a minimum amount of labour. However, gas distribution for domestic purposes has been used by both ENI management and politicians to earn political favours and connections. Chemicals, textiles and engineering, the three remaining fields in which ENI invests, are much more attractive to politicians for they provide job markets that can be exploited for political patronage.

In the past, there has always been great mobility between the central ENI offices and their subsidiaries. In fact, a few years ago ENI's chairman was also chairman of the main subsidiaries which made the planning of investment proposals an industry-wide project tapping all ENI's resources. Given this structure, it is difficult to determine whether ENI relaxed its screening of investment proposals, as IRI had done, to adhere to the law requiring a percentage of investments to be made in southern Italy. One important case illustrates the impact government had on ENI's investments. In 1971, the Minister of Economic Planning asked ENI's chairman to invest in southern Italy. 'We have bandits in central Sardinia', he said. 'We must create thousands of new jobs to break down the tradition. Government will pay any money you need to cover the bill.' ANIC, a chemical subsidiary of ENI, proposed the construction of a large synthetic fibre plant. The plant was approved with little discussion. Subsequent events proved that excess capacity was created by this new investment and serious losses were incurred for both ENI and the government.

Other examples of political pressures to invest can be seen in ENI's expansion in southern Italy, although, for the most part, these investments have not required compromises on ENI's part. Wherever oil and natural gas have been discovered, ENI has been asked to provide jobs for the people of the area. With few exceptions, locating new plants in these rich areas has proved advantageous to ENI and has coincided with its expansion plans. The government continues to approve ENI's investments with no concern for their economic viability.

Unlike its somewhat passive approach to new productive investments, the Italian government has had a powerful influence on ENI's acquisitions of ailing companies. All the textile and clothing companies ENI has acquired over the last eight years have been 'lame ducks', purchased at the government's request. In terms of labour, 36 per cent of ENI's clothing industry and 22 per cent of ENI's textile industry are made up of workers from politically acquired companies. According to my calculations, these lame duck companies generated a loss in the range of 30 billion lire in 1977. However, losses in the entire chemical industry for ENI in 1977 were 250 billion lire, and in the textile industry, 100 billion; thus, politically acquired companies bear only part of the blame for ENI's poor performance.

To get ENI to rescue ailing companies, the government has used a form of bargaining. In one important case, the government made it clear there would be an increase in the tax on natural gas (amounting to 60 billion lire a year for ENI) unless ENI took over a struggling textile company in the Alps and two clothing plants, one on the Adriatic Sea and the other south of Rome. In another case, the Communist Party promised not to filibuster against an increase in ENI's endowment fund provided ENI rescued a hat-manufacturing concern in a 'red' town in Tuscany.

EFIM's investment proposals, like IRI's, are initiated at the company level and subject to the approval of higher management. However, EFIM differs significantly from IRI in its structure.

EFIM was incorporated in 1962 to manage the remainder of a fund established after World War II to provide financial aid to engineering companies. At the time of its incorporation, EFIM had no subsidiaries in southern Italy. To fulfil its obligation to invest in the south, management created INSUD, a joint venture of EFIM, the special agency for southern Italy (Casa per il Mezzogiorno), and a few banks. INSUD is a financial company designed to create joint ventures among private industrialists. Many of EFIM's investment proposals originate in private companies wishing to merge or expand. As with IRI and ENI,

EFIM's screening process has been weakened by government's pressure to invest.

In 1972, the government asked EFIM to assume responsibility for all the production of aluminium in Italy. In carrying out this request, EFIM rescued two ailing companies belonging to Montedison and Alusuisse. Political acquisitions, however, do not appear to have greatly altered EFIM's performance. In 1976, EFIM lost 50 billion lire in the aluminium industry; only 10 billion lire of that loss can be attributed to lame duck companies.

In summary, managers of state-owned enterprises are able to take higher risks in their investments than managers of private enterprises as a result of state laws and political and financial incentives. The higher managers of enterprises who are appointed or confirmed often receive their appointments through political patronage. As a result, they are freer to take the risks requested by government. The economic performance of the company does not reflect substantially on its capabilities; losses are seen as the consequences of poor political choices or imposed social objectives. The only indicator of successful management is an increase in employment which, inevitably, requires an increase in investments. Furthermore, in the bargaining process described earlier between the manager of a state-owned enterprise and the Minister of State Shareholdings, the manager's position is strengthened through political connections.

The financial incentives for public enterprise investments can be seen in the fact that the Italian government and parliament, to date, have not refused to pay the bills submitted by IRI, ENI and EFIM: endowment funds are increased to cover extra costs. In the late 1960s, government and public enterprises agreed informally to set endowment funds at a percentage of total investments: 10 per cent for IRI, 20 per cent for ENI and 25 per cent for EFIM. As a result, approval of investment programmes means increases in endowment funds.

The theory that endowment funds control investments begins to collapse, however, when one observes that endowment funds are being eaten away by losses. At the end of 1977, for example, IRI's endowment fund was 2,198 billion lire (about 2.7 billion dollars); 1,262 billion lire (57 per cent) had already been lost. In 1978, 1,050 billion was added to the fund, but most of it was needed to cover losses. Furthermore, although the managements of Italian state-owned enterprises are asked to invest and to provide new jobs, endowment funds are not well supplied. There are cases where money promised was never received, such as for EFIM's food programme, and others where money arrived later than expected because the treasury opposed or parliament delayed funding for political reasons. As a result, company balance sheets often reveal deficits that frustrate management.

Finally, as discussed earlier, prior to 1977 it was considered sinful for a state-owned enterprise to close a factory. Today, southern Italy continues to operate under this premise. In that region investing to provide jobs remains a strong incentive despite the many risks involved.

Under a recent law, investment programmes have to be carefully reviewed by a special parliamentary commission — the same commission that advises on management appointments. The problems submitted to the commission, however, neither identify specific projects nor address concerns on expected rates of return on investments. The commission is expected to express its opinions in a broader context.

In early 1979 the commission was debating whether ENI should purchase a private oil-refining and distribution concern. The commission spokesperson presented the proposal with a recommendation that it be rejected. If the majority agrees, it is likely the proposal will be dropped, even if the Minister of State Shareholdings is in favour of the acquisition.

Issues of investments are not voted along party lines and thus leave room for more varied input from commission members. (The exceptions, of course, are the Communist Party members who always vote as a bloc.) In addition to questions of investments and endowment funds, other decisions concerning public enterprises such as highway concessions and financing, telephone rates, subsidies to shipbuilding and airport controls are reviewed by parliament.

Trade Unions

Trade unions constitute another source of political pressure on managements of public enterprises. Italian trade unions are strongly linked with political parties and are widely supported. Apart from making the traditional demands for higher wages and more jobs, trade unions push for new investments in technologically advanced industries and, in southern Italy, strongly support the control and expansion of state-owned enterprises and ardently oppose the conversion of public enterprises into private enterprises.

In 1977, a conflict occurred which illustrates the prowess of trade unions. The Italian government asked a private international firm to rescue Immobiliare, an ailing real estate and construction company. Immobiliare, one of Italy's oldest real estate enterprises, was on the verge of collapse due to management's mistaken speculations. To rescue Immobiliare, the private international firm demanded the right to buy Condotte, a construction company owned by IRI. The national trade unions mounted a strong attack against the possible divestiture of Condotte by IRI, arguing that Condotte was essential to IRI's project development which included providing more housing. The Minister of State Shareholdings deferred to the Prime Minister, claiming that IRI's divestiture of Condotte was a 'political decision'. The Prime Minister decided in favour of the trade unions, refusing to allow IRI to sell.

In general, the anticipation of opposition by trade unions, supported by government, to the divestiture of public enterprises is enough to scare away any prospective buyer. EFIM chose not to sell a motorbike company located in a 'red' area to a private concern rather than confront the opposition of trade unions. In another case, the government intervened and forbade EFIM to sell a food company to a multinational firm.

Trade unions have also opposed joint ventures between private and public enterprises. In 1977, IRI and Fiat proposed a plan jointly to produce special steels. Under severe pressure from trade unions, the government rejected IRI's proposal to collaborate with Fiat.

Trade unions in Italy are more demanding of public enterprises than of private enterprises. One manager of a state-owned company commented on this phenomenon in an interview: 'I do not know whether they are tougher with us because they know we are not going out of business, or because we cannot bribe them.'

At times, the government has used the relationship between public enterprises and trade unions as a political tool. In 1969, during the renewal of labour contracts, C.D. Rumor, head of the minority government in power, sought to form a coalition with the Socialist Party. The Socialist Party was politically left of Rumor's government, closer to the trade unions. To secure socialist approval and to avoid anarchy within the labour movement, the government assumed its traditional role as mediator between employers and trade unions, but also called upon Intersind, the bargaining body of IRI, to ensure an agreement favourable to the trade unions. IRI initially tried to resist the demands of the trade unions but eventually yielded. A long period of strikes and negotiations was terminated by the government's request for IRI to sign a contract within the day. As a result, the unit cost of labour in 1970 rose 22.8 per cent over the previous year. Over the last eight years, the unit cost of labour has continued to rise.

Today, although government plays a role in the discussion of labour contracts, state-owned enterprises are rarely singled out as political tools. Managers of public enterprises are subject to the same kinds of political pressures as are managers of private enterprises: they are asked to avoid long and protracted strikes, they are promised government help to compensate for higher wages and they are persuaded to accept government's many requests as the only alternatives. From the data collected for this study, it appears that the Minister of Labour has replaced the Minister of State Shareholdings as the mediator in most interactions between trade unions and employers.

Management's Reaction to Political Constraints

Recognizing that political connections are necessary to secure top managerial appointments, many managers cultivate good relations with the Minister of State Shareholdings and other prominent politicians. Effective ties are established by performing favours ranging from gathering data for speeches to giving helicopter or aeroplane rides in company planes.

Today, Italy is not as fully developed as its neighbouring countries. The majority of the population and most political representatives believe that public enterprises are needed to achieve the goal of full industrialization. Thus, many managers consider it their duty to invest heavily and take risks; political pressures along these lines are not perceived as constraints. Rescuing lame duck companies, however, is not considered helpful to expansion and development and is therefore not appreciated by management. To minimize political constraints to lend assistance to ailing enterprises, IRI, ENI and EFIM have used their influence to set up companies such as GEPI. As a result, over the last ten years, IRI, ENI and EFIM losses have not been strongly affected by rescue operations: according to my estimates, not more than 5 per cent of total assets can be attributed to these companies.

The reasons why managers of state-owned enterprises are more willing to take risks than are managers of private enterprises have been discussed at length. It should be noted that high-investment and low-risk projects are also possible when a company is investing to exploit a captive market, to achieve a monopoly or to satisfy a government demand. IRI, ENI and EFIM managers have all used these strategies, as have many other public enterprise managers, to achieve desired goals: IRI has invested in the electronics industry to exploit a captive market, ENI has achieved a monopoly on natural gas in northern Italy and EFIM has invested in the helicopter industry with a guarantee that government will buy.

Thus, from the data collected and interpreted for this study, one can see that managers of state-owned enterprises are subject to strong political influences. Although these influences may be constraining, their existence permits higher risks, greater investments and larger budgets than any private enterprise could ever hope to entertain. Managers of public enterprises are able to expand into new areas and new fields without fear of losing profits or their positions. In fact, a state-owned enterprise can go for years losing money without a change in management as long as its losses can be attributed to the cost of responding to social objectives. And in the fact that managers of public enterprises are less threatened by their companies' performance than are managers of private enterprises lies the basis for the difference between public and private enterprises in Italy.

Notes

1. Adolf A. Berle and Gardiner C. Means, *The Modern Corporation and Private Property* (New York: Macmillan and Company, 1932).

2. See, for instance, William Baumol, *Business Behavior, Value and Growth* (New York: Harcourt, Brace and World, 1967).

3. Pasquale Saraceno, *Il Sistema delle Imprese a Partecipazione Statale nell 'esperienza Italiana* (Milano: Giuffrè, 1975).

6 THE ITALIAN EXPERIENCE: A HISTORICAL PERSPECTIVE

Alberto Martinelli

The history of state-owned enterprises in Italy has been subject to
lengthy interpretation and debate. For several decades, the Italian
public sector has been growing at a considerable rate, affecting the
social, economic and political life of the country. Theories on the
development of the public sector have varied, depending upon the period
in question and the approach of the theorists. For example, British
scholars, including Shonfield, Posner and Woolf, and Holland, have
praised the managements of Italian state-owned enterprises for modernizing Italian industries, enabling them to compete in the international
economy, for providing investment in underdeveloped regions of Italy
and for reinforcing competition.[1] In contrast, Italian journalists and
scholars, including Scalfari, Turani, Galli and Tamburrano, have
criticized the managements of public enterprises for their irresponsible
use of power in pursuit of personal and political interests at the expense
of corporate efficiency and national goals.[2] Yet, despite these different
approaches and observations, an incontrovertible fact remains: the
public corporations that once made up the most dynamic component
of the Italian business sector and served as models for other industrialized nations are today riddled with managerial inefficiency and political
corruption. This paper will attempt to explain how and why the
economic performance and public image of Italian state-owned enterprises have deteriorated in recent years.

Structure of the Public Sector

The public sector of the Italian economy forms a complex network of
agencies and organizations producing various goods and services.
Disregarding administrative units, including welfare agencies, schools
and hospitals, the public business sector can be divided into two
categories: public utilities and state-owned enterprises subject to the
authority of the Ministry of State Shareholdings. Within the category
of public utilities, three types of businesses can be identified: public
utilities that have been managed by the central government since their

85

inception; public utilities that were originally private enterprises but were nationalized; and public utilities that are managed at the local government level, the *aziende municipalizzate*. The state-owned enterprises include all joint stock companies for which the government is the controlling shareholder.

A complex system for controlling state-owned enterprises has evolved through various government statutes, acts and corporate laws. The Interdepartmental Committee for Economic Planning (CIPE) oversees all the activities involving state-owned enterprises, including outlining their general strategies, approving long-term plans and authorizing increases in their endowment funds. Directly below CIPE is the Ministry of State Shareholdings which is responsible for enforcing CIPE's directives through the government's financial holdings, creating new firms, purchasing and selling government shares in corporations and informing parliament about the plans and activities of public enterprises. Below the Ministry are the government agencies, known as 'public holdings', that co-ordinate industrial policies, group strategies and finances. These firms are endowed by the state, are free from paying interest on the capital they receive and are able to issue state-guaranteed bonds; 65 per cent of their yearly net profits are transferred to the treasury. The so-called public holdings generally act through sub-holdings in various sectors. The sub-holdings manage the joint stock companies within their sectors. Joint stock companies operate in the market and are subject to the same corporate laws as are private corporations.

The organizational structure described above was first introduced in Italy by the Institute for Industrial Reconstruction (IRI), a state-owned enterprise, to justify the array of enterprises it controlled. IRI's rationale in proposing such a system was to preserve its firms' autonomy by stimulating efficiency through competition in the market. Competition, it was felt, would foster an attitude of independence among managements that would allow them to tolerate nationalization. As a result of IRI's initial efforts, state-owned enterprises in Italy are given considerable autonomy in designing their own strategies.[3]

Since the boom of the early 1960s, the percentage of state-owned enterprises in Italy has steadily increased. In the decade between the boom and the oil crisis, the public sector grew more than any other sector in terms of output, fixed capital and number of employees. With the exception of foreign oil companies, the number of foreign firms in Italy also increased during this decade. The number of Italian private firms, however, drastically decreased, mostly as a result of mergers

with larger corporations.[4] Despite the increase in state-owned enterprises, private corporations continue to dominate the Italian business
market, both in number and in output.

Evolution of the Relationship between State-owned
Enterprises and Government

Italian industries were ready to compete internationally in the early
twentieth century; by that time, however, other countries dominated
the market. To enable growth to continue and to ensure a place in the
world market, the Italian industrial sector requested the protection of
the government through tariffs and contracts for civil and military
supplies. As industrialization developed, the relative scarcity of private
capital helped to spur relationships between banks and corporations.
Commercial banks provided industries with the financial resources
needed to remain in operation.

During World War I, the demand for steel, metal, automobile
equipment and textiles fostered the rapid expansion of the industrial
sector and deepened the involvement of major banks in growing
businesses. After the war, the major banks experienced a liquidity crisis.
To prevent the larger corporations from going bankrupt, the state
intervened. By the early 1930s, the world economic crisis further
aggravated the state of the Italian economy and prompted the government to create IRI. IRI took over the major Italian banks – Banca
Commerciale Italiana, Credito Italiano and Banca di Roma – in order
to provide a unified management for the industrial securities the major
banks had held. Thus, in response to domestic and international
economic crises, the Italian government created a temporary state
agency, IRI, to rescue the country's indebted firms.

Up until the mid-1930s, the Italian experience with state-owned
enterprises was not unlike the experiences of many other nations. In
1936, however, Italy's attitude toward public ownership of business
changed. IRI was granted permanent status as the administrator of
state-owned securities, and a consolidated system of state-owned
enterprises came into being. By the beginning of World War II, IRI's
share of total production included 70 per cent of the shipbuilding
industry, 45 per cent of the steel industry, 39 per cent of the electrical-
mechanical industry and 23 per cent of the mechanical engineering
industry.[5]

Opinions differ as to whether IRI's expansion was the result of a carefully designed strategy to increase the state's control of the industrial sector, or simply a continuation of the rescue operations born of the economic crisis. Shonfield argues that Italy experienced the most casual nationalization ever accomplished by a European country; IRI became a major power in the industrial sector without any political effort to make it the cornerstone of national economic planning.[6] Mussolini referred to IRI as a clinic (*convaliescenziario*) for firms temporarily in trouble.[7] The fact that the enterprises controlled by the state through IRI represented a wide variety of industries rather than a particular area of concentration further supports the idea that the government engaged in nationalization projects to respond to pressures from bankers and businessmen trying to avoid bankruptcy, rather than to carry out a carefully designed strategy.

During the late 1930s, the Italian government continued to place a priority on the growth of private enterprises, permitting state intervention only when a firm's survival was at stake. Yet, despite the priority given to private enterprises, Mussolini's regime had long-range plans that threatened to undermine the development of the private business sector.

The government's autarchic policies implied a determined effort to strengthen basic industries such as steel and shipbuilding through direct state intervention. In addition, in the absence of coherent national planning, a group of public managers argued that state enterprises were needed to overcome economic backwardness and to create a modern industrial sector with up-to-date managerial skills.[8] These managers, enjoying considerable autonomy in their relations with government, succeeded in convincing the state that IRI's rescue operations should be expanded.

In the name of salvaging indebted companies to help develop a strong, modern economy, state intervention in the Italian industrial sector continued throughout the 1930s. The government agencies that were created to oversee the state's involvement in industry existed outside the realm of politics; they were temporary, administrative units charged with specific, limited responsibilities.

The absence of a well-defined political design for state intervention continued after World War II. Various political forces and interest groups disagreed over the extent to which the government should become involved in the industrial sector. Most Italian economists believed that state control of industries was a remnant of Fascism and should be eliminated. Small but influential political parties, including the Liberal Party and the Republican Party, as well as a large component of the Christian Democratic Party, the majority party, agreed with the economists. Other opponents of state intervention included the managements of major industries who feared public competition would destroy their monopolistic positions.

Among the supporters of state control were the Communist Party, the Socialist Party and a component of the Christian Democratic Party — the component that was to become the leading faction of the party in the mid-1950s. Trade unions also supported state control, along with several interest groups which believed that social goals would never be achieved if left in the hands of private, profit-oriented corporations. Supporters of state control agreed that Italy needed to be freed from the Fascist legacy, especially in the public sector. However, they disagreed as to how the freedom was to be won: some wanted to extend the scope of the public sector; others wanted to restrict further growth. Among those who desired to restrict further growth were private business managers who needed low-cost energy and capital to produce intermediate and consumer durable goods.

Neither the opponents nor the supporters of the public sector were totally successful in effecting the changes they sought. The opponents were unable to provide an alternative for the state's ability to generate the resources needed to develop the economy; the supporters were either unwilling or unable to make public enterprises the instruments of anti-monopolistic policies and national planning. Instead, a compromise was reached. At the time it was called a 'mixed economy'; in fact, it is better described as a private economy including a state sector in basic industries.

The industrial bourgeoisie benefited most from the compromise. As the dominant class of the dominant party, the Christian Democrats, the industrial bourgeoisie was able to take advantage of the state's rescue operations as well as the state's ability to help develop necessary but risky businesses. Both private firms and state-owned enterprises were represented by the Confindustria, an employers' association, and, for the most part, were led by the same type of managers. Although there were often conflicts of interest among the managements of private and public enterprises, all shared an interest in opposing the labour movement, an interest that served to unite their business sectors.

In 1953, the government established Ente Nazionale Idrocarburi (ENI), a state-owned enterprise in the oil and gas industry, and for the first time appeared to be actively pursuing a policy of state control of certain industries. ENI was organized as a financial holding and operated under the same guidelines as IRI. Under the aggressive leadership of

Enrico Mattei, ENI's first president, the oil industry in Italy, vital to industrial growth, was developed. Mattei was given considerable autonomy in developing the oil industry, in part because he was an experienced businessman, in part because he shared certain goals with the ruling party. Fanfani, the new secretary of the Christian Democrats, wanted to strengthen the party organization by penetrating the major decision-making centres of civil society; Mattei wanted to achieve national self-sufficiency through ENI by attacking the oil companies' international cartel and the oligopoly of the Italian electric power industry.

ENI was established neither as a rescue operation nor as a response to requests by private businesses to have their losses absorbed by the state; ENI was the result of conscious political strategy. Its close link with the ruling party enabled the enterprise to achieve important results, including dismantling monopolies in the oil and other related industries. IRI also expanded its activities during the 1950s, modernizing the telephone and transportation industries and increasing its production of up-to-date industrial products. The close connections with the government that allowed ENI and IRI to prosper resulted in the systematic exchange of political support for financial aid, a process that eventually contributed to the breakdown of the system of state shareholdings.

The political ramifications of the more active and extended role of state-owned enterprises were far reaching. Conflicts arose between private businesses and the majority group of the government party, a group strongly in support of increasing the power of state-owned enterprises. In 1956, the Ministry of State Shareholdings, a separate government department for state-owned enterprises, was established. The Ministry became a stronghold for the Christian Democratic left. Given their own ministry, state-owned enterprises established their own business association: they withdrew from Confindustria and started Intersind.

As state-owned enterprises began to extend their influence, relations between labour and management began to change. Italian society was developing rapidly; the government wanted the country to enter into an advanced system of industrial relations. In the eyes of the majority party, managing the transition to a modern industrial state demanded strong, centralized control. The Christian Democrats carefully directed the activities of the public sector, minimizing the influence of leftist parties and their related trade unions.

The public sector continued to grow into the early 1960s. While closely controlled by the majority party, state-owned enterprises enjoyed the support of a wide political spectrum ranging from the Christian Democrats to the Communists. Only the conservative Liberal Party and the employers' association, at the time controlled by the less advanced business sectors, opposed the expansion of the public sector. IRI and ENI were extremely successful in the early 1960s; their success served to rally national support for the ideology that state-controlled enterprises would bring modernization and balanced growth to Italy.

As soon as the focus shifted from broad goals to specific strategies, however, relevant differences emerged. By the mid-1960s, overseeing the activities of state-controlled enterprises became an instrument of political control rather than of national industrial development. Managerial efficiency and industrial competition were subordinated to meeting the demands of narrow party interests. Conflicts increased among various party factions and the demands of external pressure groups became more virulent.

The lack of effective parliamentary controls over public enterprises contributed in part to the deterioration of the government's plan for economic development. In some instances, effective controls existed but were not implemented: for example, the Ministry of State Share-holdings was required to submit a report on each state holding but, instead, prepared generalized reports on different industrial sectors. As a result, the different economic performances of specific companies could not be assessed. In other instances, important controls did not exist: for example parliament did not have control over the nomination of company managers nor did it have an effective system for the audit and accountability of state-owned enterprises.

The explosion of labour struggles in the late 1960s and the international economic recession of 1974 revealed the contradictions inherent in the Italian system of state-owned enterprises. As the public sector grew, problems between company managements and government parties increased. In addition, major interest groups became increasingly vocal, vying with the political forces for the priority of social goals. As a result, time-consuming negotiations and costly compromises among the state, political parties and interest groups have become characteristic of the interactions today between the government and the public industrial sector. Furthermore, instead of effective government guidelines and legislative controls geared toward managerial autonomy, there is a confusion over roles and political and economic interests.

As with all government institutions, state-owned enterprises in Italy are expected to perform a variety of functions and are burdened with an overload of demands. With the domestic market, the international market and the ruling party in constant flux, the objectives for state intervention keep changing. Public enterprises are expected to respond to changing goals while maintaining successful operations.

In the absence of a coherent industrial policy, maintaining successful operations becomes a difficult task. Private enterprises in Italy continue to want to retain their profits and have the state absorb their losses. State-owned enterprises are left with less desirable tasks: undertaking risky operations in technologically advanced, low-return activities; making uncertain investments in recession periods; and rescuing failing, inefficient private firms. In addition, the expansion of state-owned operations in certain areas is often constrained by labour unions and leftist political parties fighting to reduce regional and sectorial disequilibria in employment. Furthermore, political parties and major interest groups compete for the financial resources accessible to state-owned enterprises.

Increasingly, the ruling political coalition has attempted to use public enterprises to cope with the social contradictions and tensions stemming from the growth of the public sector and the world economic recessions. Through more effective control of public enterprises, the use of *ad hoc* investment decisions geared toward fulfilling corporate interests, and the enhancement of its role as mediator, the ruling party has tried to implement a stabilization policy without significantly changing class relations or political relations.

The government's use of state-owned enterprises to achieve national objectives, however, has created additional problems in the public sector. The diffusion of targets has made it difficult for managements to implement consistent strategies throughout their industries. The public sector has grown in chaotic spurts, becoming more heterogeneous with new developments and thus more difficult to manage. Poor economic results and increasing indebtedness to the treasury have been a source of growing frustration to managers. In the last few years, business representatives, political leaders and labour unions have become increasingly aware of the costs of state-owned enterprises.

Strengthened by the entrance of leftist parties into the government coalition, the leaders of the business sector have tried to redefine the strategy and structure of state-owned enterprises based on recommendations put forth by a special parliamentary commission, the Commissione Chiarelli, established in June 1975.

The Chiarelli Committee, empowered after the defeat of the Christian

Democrats in the regional elections, was designed to restructure Italy's system of state participation. It began by formulating a set of general recommendations that revealed considerable dissent among its members. Some of the recommendations took important steps toward reforming the public enterprise system: interacting more closely with international economies; establishing a permanent parliamentary commission for the financial control of state-controlled enterprises; allowing parliament to nominate managers for public enterprises within the greater national industrial policy. Some recommendations have been implemented, such as establishing criteria for the nomination of managers of state-owned enterprises; however, given the web of interests and connections between businesses and political groups, reform has been very difficult to achieve. To effect significant changes in the public enterprise system, the pervasive power of the ruling party will have to be reduced.

State-owned Enterprise Relations with Private Business and Labour

Many observers consider the Italian economy to be a mixed economy. However, by examining relations among state-owned enterprises, private enterprises and labour, the Italian economy can be seen as a capitalist system including an internal variant of state-owned enterprises, rather than as a mixed economy including a structural element that approaches or anticipates socialism.

The fact that the Italian economy is, in truth, a capitalist system does not preclude tensions and conflicts between private and state firms. Many of Italy's conflicts are rooted in the fact that, when the state intervenes in a private industry, it brings with it the specific interests of party factions and broader objectives than profit and business growth. In the state-owned sector, a vast array of interests and goals interact to shape policies. The goals include standard economic and social policy goals, such as balanced development, employment, sustained rate of growth, balance-of-payments equilibrium. The interests include industrial and financial bourgeoisie interests that try to use state-owned enterprises to socialize losses, discharging less profitable firms on the state, the interests of the ruling party that aim at tightening control over the decision-making processes of society, and neo-corporate interests of party factions and management cliques that try to bend broader national and class objectives to pursue the maximization of power, wealth and prestige.

The actual performance of public enterprises generally reflects a compromise among the most powerful interests. Sometimes these interests are rearranged into a coherent strategy, as in the boom years; at other times they create a sharp division of areas of influence between the private and public sectors.

As discussed above, the Italian people faced many problems in the late 1950s and early 1960s as they tried to become a mature industrial society. Different sectors of the population had different ideas on what was needed to achieve modernization. The Christian Democratic left saw the need for public enterprises to modernize the country. The traditional power group of employers favoured a reactionary political line, restoring law and order in the factories in the country. Modern private oligopolies wanted to reduce the new strength of the labour unions through a controlled recession. Most small businesses opposed the idea of central planning. The public sector supported the trend toward a more democratic society with elements of planning and selected social reforms.[9]

During this era, a new breed of manager-politician appeared on the scene. These new leaders monopolized key posts in state firms, major banks, financial institutions and state agencies. They had been educated in the same schools (such as the Catholic University of Milan), affiliated with the same political party (the Christian Democrats) and imbued with the same values and attitudes.[10] All were concerned with technocratic efficiency, satisfaction of social needs, political pluralism and collective bargaining, co-operation among capital, labour and government, and the maintenance of the free enterprise system, checked by elements of state planning and anti-monopolistic devices. Although many of these concerns never went beyond rhetoric, they can be seen as attempts to integrate the values and social relations needed by a mature industrialized society with the basic tenets of Catholic social doctrine.

During the 1960s, state-owned enterprises in general were more advanced than private enterprises in work organization and industrial relations. Coexisting with labour unions, particularly the Catholic trade union (CISL), was important to the modernizing strategy of the public sector. Job evaluations were introduced at Italsider, the state steel firm, in the mid-1960s.

During the 1970s, the situation intensified. Intersind, the public employers' association, had introduced 'plant-level collective bargaining' (*contrattazione articolata aziendale*) in agreement with CISL in 1962 'to pave the way to a more modern view of the relationships between business and labour'.[11] The co-ordinated action of Intersind, CISL, the Ministry of State Shareholdings and the Ministry of Labour contributed to the institutional recognition of labour unions.

Intersind's decision to act independently of organized private businesses had strategic significance for the public sector. However, by the late 1960s, Intersind's autonomous role and innovative strategies had all but disappeared; its role had been limited to providing technical assistance to management in labour matters. By the late 1970s, it was impossible to distinguish Intersind from Confindustria.[12] Thus, during the decade from the boom to the oil crisis, public enterprises entertained sympathetic attitudes toward labour, only to return in the 1970s to a more traditional, adversary role to cope with the crisis of modernizing the economy.

In addition to the failure of Intersind to support labour through effective collective bargaining, the interests of labour were further frustrated by the ruling party's attempts to represent all major interests of the country, gaining control of the state and unifying Italian ideology under the Christian Democratic banner. Yet, in their attempts to gain control of the state, the Christian Democrats were constrained by neo-corporatist groups profiting from the lack of adequate parliamentary controls over the state's ability to pursue particularist interests. Special benefits and special privileges were exchanged for political support; broad social goals, such as the industrialization of the Mezzogiorno, were used to allow firms to receive fiscal incentives and financial aid without clear directives and controls. These political strategies contributed to the eventual deterioration of the public enterprise system.

As party management of the economy continued to expand, private businesses were progressively curtailed. Large private groups chose not to oppose the increasing power of state-owned enterprises for two major reasons: they felt at ease in the re-established oligopolistic climate of Italian industry which allowed them to grow while further concentrating their efforts; and the state gave them special attention including access to easy money and tax incentives. In other words, private enterprises chose to expand and restructure their businesses using the state's incentives at the expense of losing their dominant position in the business community. By failing to unite the small and middle-size firms in a coalition against the Christian Democrats, private enterprises relinquished their control of the market to public enterprises.

The labour struggles of the late 1960s and the world economic recession of the 1970s revealed growing tensions between private and public business. Large private firms, capable of introducing changes in the strategy and organization of the employers' association, reasserted their leadership in the business community and tried to limit the power of the ruling party.

In the late 1970s, however, the sharpening of conflicts between Christian Democrats and leftist parties brought about a realignment of organized business with the Christian Democratic Party, paving the way for new compromise. The compromise that has been suggested would give the Christian Democrats control of the industrialized part of the country and the leftist parties control of the Mezzogiorno. Such a plan, in this author's opinion, would perpetuate and actually increase a chronic state budget deficit, making financial resources available only to the most powerful pressure groups.

In general, all groups recognizing the need for basic reform in the Italian economy and society would be victims of the proposed compromise. Public enterprises would act as private enterprises in the industrialized north and as public spending agencies in the south; in both cases, their responsibilities to society would be obscured by either too little political scrutiny or too much political interference.

State-owned Enterprises as Agencies of National Planning

There is a tendency among critics of state-owned enterprises to extend their criticism to the rejection of any type of state intervention in the economy. However, it is important to distinguish between state intervention in the economy in general, which is necessary and useful in advanced industrial societies, and party management of the economy, which is a specific and objectionable form of state intervention. It is not the existence of state intervention that must be questioned, but the quality of state intervention.

The results of comparative research on big business and the state reveal a growing tendency to make use of large national firms to solve specific problems and to consider them as state agencies; they also reveal that the role of the parliamentary process has been reduced while the weight of particular interest groups has increased.[13] These tendencies may in part be responsible for the deterioration of state enterprises in Italy. By strengthening the ability of parliament to set guidelines and control procedures for public enterprises in the framework of national planning, these tendencies could be reversed.

At present, state enterprises are able to waste resources without bearing the costs, as a result of financial guarantees from the state; they pay for this privilege, however, in their subordination to the ruling party and big private businesses. The ruling party uses state-owned enterprises to mediate among major interest groups, to receive special favours and to gain support in times of party struggles. Private businesses use state-owned enterprises to unload their risky operations and to have the state absorb their losses.

Instead of existing as a partial and distorted substitution for a coherent and generalized industrial policy, state-owned enterprises should become key agencies of national planning. Public firms can accept the supremacy of politics only if politics are intended to be a rational strategy for change.

Notes

1. A. Shonfield, *Modern Capitalism: the Changing Balance of Public and Private Power* (London: Oxford University Press, 1965); M.V. Posner and S.J. Woolf, *Italian Public Enterprise* (Cambridge, Mass.: Harvard University Press, 1967); S. Holland (ed.), *The State as Entrepreneur: The IRI State Shareholding Formula* (London: Weidenfeld and Nicolson, 1972).

2. E. Scalfari and G. Turani, *Razza Padrona* (Milano: Feltrinelli, 1974); A. Nannei, *Il capitalismo assistenziale* (Milano: Sugar, 1976); G. Tamburrano, *L'iceberg democristiano* (Milano: Sugar, 1976).

3. M. Colitti, 'Contributo ad una valutazione meno negativa del ruolo delle partecipazioni statali', *Economia e politica industriale,* no. 10 (1975), pp. 83-92.

4. The data apply to a sample of the 150 largest manufacturing firms operating in Italy during the period from 1963 to 1972. See G.L. Alzona, 'Grande industria: sviluppo e strutture di controllo', in A. Graziani (ed.), *Crisi e ristrutturazione nell'economia italiana* (Torino: Einaudi, 1975).

5. F. Guarneri, *Battaglie economiche* (Milano: Gartzanti, 1953).

6. A. Shonfield, *Modern Capitalism.*

7. For Mussolini's views on the rescue function of state intervention, see E. Ludwig, *Colloqui con Mussolini* (Milano: Mondadori, 1932).

8. L. Villari, *Il capitalismo italiano del 900* (Bari: Laterza, 1972), Ch. 4.

9. A. Martinelli, 'Organized Business and Italian Politics: Confindustria and the Christian Democrats in the Postwar Period' in Peter Lange and Sidney Tarrow (eds.), *Italy in Transition* (London: Frank Cass, 1980), pp. 67-87. *European Politics* (forthcoming issue).

10. The distinctive character of managers of state-owned enterprises should not be exaggerated. Our research on the top management of Italy's 563 largest firms showed no striking differences in social background or career patterns among private and public top managers. In fact, there is a considerable amount of mobility between the two sectors of the economy. The different performances are due to the frustrations of public managers as a result of their working environment, rather than to differences in professional competence and cultural attitudes. See A. Martinelli and A. Chiesi, 'Il profilo sociale della classe dirigente economica: primi risultati', *Rassegna Italiana di Sociologia*, no. 3, (September 1978).

11. Intersind, *Dieci anni di attivita contrattuale (1958-1967)* (Roma:

98   *The Italian Experience*

Intersind, 1968), p. 11.

12. A. Collidà, 'L'Intersind', in *La politica del padronato italiano* (Bari: De Donato, 1972).

13. Raymond Vernon (ed.), *Big Business and the State* (Cambridge, Mass.: Harvard University Press, 1974), pp. 25-6.

7 THE FRENCH EXPERIENCE: CONFLICTS WITH GOVERNMENT

Jean-Pierre C. Anastassopoulos

One of the major differences between state-owned enterprises and private enterprises is the relationship of each with the state. Placing a given company under the direct authority of the government allows the public interest to prevail over whatever particular interest the company would serve if it were private. If the company produces and sells goods or services, however, it is bound to find itself caught between two antagonistic logics: the market, which requires straight competitiveness, and public service, which requires a great deal of philanthropy by company standards. Such an antagonism is most evident when each logic is supported by a different entity: one can expect the company to defend its own interests in the name of competition and to fight government instructions based upon a broader conception of public interest. Understanding conflicts between these two entities may reveal how certain contradictions can be overcome and prove enlightening to those who seek to improve the French system.

The questions to be answered in this study are as follows. What are the structural determinants of conflict between government and state-owned enterprises in France? Under what conditions does the public enterprise's interest prevail? What consequences are to be expected if the public enterprise's interest does not prevail?

Conflict has been defined as a situation in which the objective interests and the expressed opinions of the government, on the one hand, and the company, on the other, are clearly antagonistic, i.e., the situation calls for two incompatible solutions. As soon as it can be ascertained that the government would like solution X but the company would like solution Y, provided that X and Y are exclusive of one another, there is conflict.

Conflicts between the state-owned enterprises and government in France have been studied in terms of the definition above. Given the scope of the present paper, the cases shown in Table 7.1 will be presented.

Particular attention has been given to the socioeconomic role played by the company in the country, the organizational structures and patterns of behaviour in the company and in the administration,

Table 7.1: Cases of Conflict between State-owned Enterprises and Government

Companies studied	Sector of activity	Decision area of conflict
Air France	Airlines	Renewing the company's fleet Moving ground operations
Electricité de France	Electricity	Developing nuclear plants Establishing market strategy
Office de Radiodiffusion Télévision Française	Radio – TV	Reporting the news
Renault	Automobile	Locating facilities Setting labour policy

and the personal roles played by the people in command in the company and in the government. Focusing on these three areas will reveal the main factors involved in conflict recognition and resolution.

Case 1: Air France Tries to Replace the French Caravelle

Caravelle was the first short–medium-range jet in the world when it was bought by Air France in 1959. It was, indeed, a very remarkable plane at the time. Its manufacturer, the Société Nationale Industrielle Aéro-spatiale (SNIAS, another French state-owned enterprise), quickly sold approximately 250 units. SNIAS then turned to a new programme, Concorde, and devoted all its resources and technological know-how to building the Franco-Britannic supersonic marvel. Where a whole line of Caravelles could have been developed, only one model was offered, Caravelle III, despite the fact that McDonnell Douglas, after a brief commercial association with SNIAS, was preparing its DC 9. Prestige was more important than doing business, politicians and engineers all agreed; Air France did not agree, but it was ignored.

The DC 9 was an all-time success in plane-manufacturing history, ten times greater than Caravelle. Ironically, the production of the Cara-velle XII, a slightly improved model eventually offered by SNIAS, was limited to twelve units. Boeing proved to be the only manufacturer able to compete with McDonnell Douglas with its B 737. Both American planes have a low-noise, low-consumption engine, the JT 9, which makes them particularly attractive in times of energy shortage and pollution awareness. There has been no 100-seat, medium-range, Franco-European plane to compete with them in the 1970s.

In 1974–75, it became obvious that Air France needed to replace its 28 Caravelles in operation at the time. The plane was obsolete, too slow, expensive in terms of flying and maintenance, and had become unattractive to passengers. The average unit was 15 years old; the other European airlines had more recent planes (mostly DC 9s and B 737s).

After 1974, the year during which almost every airline lost money, all the big companies recovered except Air France. Air France lost $75 million in 1975 and $110 million in 1976. The national company asked the government, as it is legally obliged to do, to authorize the purchase of B 737s. The answer was quickly 'no'. A few weeks later, the Minister of Finance delivered a speech at a press dinner in which he accused certain public managers of acting as if their companies belonged to them and of seeking their particular interests instead of the public interest. 'Should they not consult the government and abide by its instructions', he added, 'we will replace them.' Governmental instructions then came asking Air France to buy Mr Dassault's 'Mercure 100', a 140-seat, short-range jet which Air France had not even considered because it was too big and expensive. Furthermore, only Mercure 100s had been built and sold to Air Inter (the French domestic Airline, also a state-owned enterprise); no other company in the world wanted the plane.

Air France's answer was 'no'. The recently appointed president, Mr Giraudet, was not dismissed, but a long and painful process began in which the company, represented by the Minister of Transportation, and the government, represented by the Minister of Finance, fought each other with every possible argument. A number of alternatives were considered (redesigning the Caravelle motor, improving the Mercure, replacing the 100-seat Caravelles by 260-seat Airbuses), but they were all far more expensive and less adequate for the company's commercial needs than were the B 737s; had this not been the case, the government would not have hesitated to impose its will.

The lack of success – to say the least – of the Concorde, and the unemployment problem in the Toulouse area where aircraft was the major industry and where the political majority was seriously threatened by the opposition, made it impossible for the government to accept a solution to buy foreign equipment. On the other hand, state subsidies to Air France were likely to grow as long as the

Caravelles were not replaced. A decision was blocked for two years.

Eventually, at the beginning of 1978, the government authorized Air France to lease thirteen B 737s while the Airbus programme was being accelerated; Air France promised to buy more A 300 Airbuses and the future version, the B 10, with 200 seats.

Case 2: Air France moves to Charles de Gaulle Airport

In times when air traffic grew at an average rate of 10 to 12 per cent per year, it was necessary for a large city such as Paris to plan the development of its airport facilities far in advance. Orly was built in the 1950s and opened its gates in 1961 to supplement Le Bourget; it immediately became France's largest airport. In the late 1960s, Orly was extended by the construction of the Orly-Ouest terminal, but by that time it had become clear that the site of Orly would not be able to support the future needs of air traffic. An entirely new airport would have to be built. Furthermore, Concorde was being developed, demanding an airport suitable for the supersonic era.

As soon as Orly became operational, the state-owned Aéroport de Paris (AP) began to look for an estate close enough to the city and large enough for the new international airport. Roissy-en-France very quickly emerged as the best location, surprisingly favourable with regard to both criteria. The AP did not lose any time beginning the acquisition process. The new airport was to open in 1972; many airline companies were expected to move from Orly to Roissy, finding Roissy more attractive. The building went on according to schedule, but in 1970-71 air traffic grew at a slower rate than it had in the 1960s. The AP arranged to postpone the inauguration of Roissy to early 1974.

With the decision to postpone the inauguration of Roissy, real trouble began for the AP. The Middle East War and the oil crisis of 1974 made that year the worst in recent civil aviation history. Postponing the opening of Roissy, renamed Charles de Gaulle Airport (CDG) after de Gaulle's death, for eighteen months proved very costly to a company that was already indebted far beyond its normal rate. Ecological concerns were becoming more and more popular and people in developed countries throughout the world were organizing to limit noise pollution around airports. In Tokyo, environmentalists prevented the opening of a new airport. The AP feared that a longer wait would threaten the whole operation.

With government approval, CDG was hastily opened in April 1974. To attract foreign companies with a fully operating terminal, the AP asked Air France to shift a large part of its traffic from Orly to CDG. Air France, however, refused: Orly could match its needs for two more years at least. CDG was already unpopular: people thought it was too far from the centry of Paris (about twice the distance to Orly) and there was no convenient public transportation to Roissy. Moving to CDG was in a way a suicide mission, and Air France was experiencing enough problems with its operating costs. But the AP turned to the government, and the government instructed Air France to move to CDG as requested.

For the national company, moving to CDG meant much higher costs of ground operations: a number of services would have to be duplicated without a corresponding increase in traffic. Certain planes, such as the B 747, would have to fly without passengers from CDG to Orly for maintenance. Air France's facilities for large planes were located in Orly and building new facilities at CDG was, of course, totally out of the question. Space and services were much more expensive at CDG because the AP needed money to repay its debts. Most of all, Air France would be greatly disadvantaged with regard to its competitors, not only because none of them was asked to split its traffic between CDG and Orly (they either stayed in Orly or moved everything to CDG), but because the domestic traffic remained concentrated at Orly-Ouest. Any passenger coming from a local French city and going abroad would prefer to connect flights at Orly rather than take a taxi or bus from Orly to CDG. Air France would thus lose passengers to its foreign competitors, such as Lufthansa or Sabena, located next to Air Inter at Orly.

But Air France lost the battle: the government refused even to discuss it. Had Mr Giraudet been the company's president at the time, the outcome might have been different. As soon as he was appointed, he raised the question — as well as that of the Caravelle and others — and asked the government for proper compensations, which he obtained in a global deal in early 1978, after two years of thorough negotiations. The state agreed to subsidize Air France for most of the increased costs and Air Inter was ordered to shift some of its traffic to CDG. It was not a complete victory for Air France, but certainly a substantial improvement over the former situation.

Case 3: Electricité de France Orders Nuclear Plants

In the technologically advanced sector of nuclear reactors, a French
state-owned enterprise, the Commissariat à l'Énergie Atomique (CEA),
developed an original process called the graphite-gas process. It was
unique of its kind, as the French colour TV SECAM had been. One of
the major difficulties encountered by the CEA was how to make the
process commercially viable. Électricité de France (EDF), the national
power company, was reluctant to use the new technology precisely
because it was new and because its purchasing and maintenance costs
would depend upon its world-wide success. EDF seriously doubted
the likelihood of such a success, but General de Gaulle, then head of
state, was putting every effort into developing French technologies,
French enterprises, French grandeur. Certainly a conflict existed at
the time between the government and EDF, but the personality of
'le général' suppressed its expression.

Shortly after de Gaulle's resignation in 1969, the graphite-gas
process was officially abandoned. EDF believed it was now free to turn
to whichever nuclear process and reactor manufacturer it wished. There
were two processes and two manufacturers competing in France: the
Compagnie Générale d'Électricité (CGE), licensed by General Electric
(USA), and Creusot-Loire (Empain holding), licensed by Westinghouse
(USA). Both companies were French; both proposed an American
technology which assured sales to many clients throughout the world.
EDF looked for the best offer in terms of price and viability. It needed
three 900 megawatt nuclear plants for every year between 1971 and
1975. As CGE's prices were 50 per cent higher than Creusot's, EDF
gave the first order to Creusot and asked both suppliers to make an
offer for the second order. Again, in 1972, CGE's offer was substantially higher than Creusot's. EDF was prepared to give the order to
the same supplier as before. At this point, the government intervened.

The operating strategy among government industrial policymakers
at the time was that, in strategic sectors such as the nuclear industry,
the state should favour a high concentration and help one or two giant
groups emerge and become internationally competitive. EDF, through
its domestic orders, was to be an instrument of that policy. Since
there were already two groups in the industry, EDF was expected to
help both by giving its orders alternately to one or the other. CGE's
president, Ambroise Roux, was an influential man, well known and
supported by the government. CGE did not even try to lower its prices,
for it was convinced it would be given the order this time.

EDF's engineers, however, thought that CGE's process had to be improved. Messrs Delouvrier and Boiteux, chairman and president of EDF, decided to deal with Creusot despite strong pressures from the French government (from the Minister of Industry, in particular). Eventually they had to put their resignations on the line to ensure government neutrality. They won the set, but the match was not over.

A third supplier, Babcock, appeared in 1973 with another American licence. The government first thought that Babcock and CGE should unite and get EDF's next order, but Mr Roux, CGE's president, opposed the idea and insisted that CGE alone should be given the order. Discussions continued between CGE and EDF with CGE offering to lower its price. By 1974 the nuclear programme was accelerated and the government sought a stable solution once and for all: there would be only one French supplier. Creusot-Loire (more precisely its subsidiary, Framatone) was chosen because it was favoured by EDF and had the most experience.

Case 4: Home Electrical Heating and the Energy Crisis

During the 1960s, EDF started to have a grandiose vision of its mission as the main energy supplier of the country by the year 2000. Electricity was to replace any other kind of energy because of its limitless forms of utilization, low price and low pollution. Nuclear electricity would reduce drastically the dependence on foreign energy sources, especially with the new breeder reactors of the end of the century that would produce more fissile material than they would use.

The replacement of traditional energies such as oil and coal by electrical power had to be planned long in advance. Potential customers had to be informed and educated to appreciate the advantages of electricity. In 1970, EDF convinced the government that a strong marketing policy to promote the sales of electricity was a national imperative. Through a 'contrat de programme', a contractual agreement with the Ministries of Industry and Finance, EDF was given relative autonomy to develop its sales.

The ambitious nuclear programme that EDF proposed required the largest possible cash flow, which in turn depended upon a high rate of growth. To be able to cover more than half the energy needs of France in the year 2000, EDF would have to start right away. First, it chose to enter the home-heating market (the technology of electrical heating and insulation is simple and the energy consumed for home heating in France in 1970 was equivalent to the whole production of EDF). Since it was a highly competitive market in which three other forms of energy were already well established (coal, oil and natural gas), EDF started a strong promotional campaign and made every effort to convince promoters, builders, equipment suppliers and finally customers that electricity was the solution of the future. Within a few years, more than one-third of the new homes (houses or apartment buildings) built in France were heated with electricity. It was a massive success, despite an energetic press campaign financed by the oil companies and fought by the ecologists.

Then came the energy crisis of 1974–75. At first, EDF was comforted in its strategy, since it aimed at France's greater independence. Soon, however, it appeared that EDF was inducing French households to consume more energy than they would normally have consumed; this came as a shock to the newly created Agency for Energy Saving (AES).

With this realization, war began between EDF and AES, with the government supporting AES. EDF was asked to stop immediately any publicity favouring the consumption of electricity. AES proposed that a temporary tax be levied on any new housing that would be equipped with electrical heating and demanded that EDF structure its rates so that the more electricity one consumed the more expensive the additional KWh. EDF, of course, opposed all these measures; eventually it was required by the government to oblige.

It is not easy to determine who won this match. Publicity was stopped officially, but EDF continued to promote electricity in indirect ways. The tax was levied, but reimbursed after a few years. Tariffs did not change. EDF oriented its efforts toward industrial uses of electricity and agreed to limit its penetration in the home-heating market to its current level. On the other hand, the head of the AES was replaced. The new Minister of Industry, André Giraud, former president of CEA, strongly supported the nuclear programme.

Case 5: Political Conflict Peaks over the National TV News Reports

The presidential election of 1965 was the first time in French history that a president had to be elected by the direct vote of all citizens. During this campaign, the importance of TV news reports in determining the political life of the country became evident. The opposition (right and left) demanded greater access to television studios precisely at a time when the majority was becoming more convinced that strict control of TV news (if not over all TV programmes) was essential. General de Gaulle was elected not on the first ballot but on the second; everyone agreed that the appearance of opposition leaders such as Mr Mitterand on TV screens had helped to determine the outcome.

Just one year before, French radio and TV had been organized into a state-owned company, the ORTF (Office de Radiodiffusion Télé-vision Française), theoretically autonomous from the state. The TV news reports, one for each of the two channels existing at the time, were placed under the direct authority of a television director, second in command inside the ORTF, in direct contact with the Minister of Information. This system was maintained until de Gaulle resigned in 1969.

ORTF acquired a very poor reputation as far as news reports were concerned. But during the succeeding election campaign, candidate Georges Pompidou promised that things would change. Once elected, he asked his liberal Prime Minister Chaban-Delmas to reorganize the ORTF. Two autonomous divisions were created (among others) to take charge of the news reports, one for the first channel and the other for the second. There was no longer a TV director nor a Minister of Information. Two well-known journalists, Mrs Baudrier and Mr Desgraupes, were appointed to head the two divisions and instructed to compete with one another to give the best possible reports. This resulted in a drastic change in terms of political fairness and increased the quality of both news programmes. The policy of the ORTF management was to give equal authority to both teams and to let them do their jobs with maximum freedom. Even the other TV programmes seemed to enjoy the new wave of liberalism.

Polls indicated that the public was much more satisfied than before, but they also showed that the opposition was growing stronger and that it would be difficult for the neo-Gaullists to win the 1973 congressional elections. Protests came from the congressmen of the majority, won support within the government and reached the President. The news reports, especially those of Channel 1, were increasingly criticized by politicians. It was common for a congressman, or a minister, or sometimes a personal adviser to the President to call the president of the ORTF protesting or asking for programme modifications. The criticism extended to various programmes with a 'political impact'. Although minor changes may have been effected in response to these interventions, the ORTF's top managers resisted and protected the autonomy of their division. In particular, they refused to dismiss Mr Desgraupes, a favourite target of most attacks. They were able to retain him because they had the Prime Minister's support.

Eventually, however, they lost that support. Mr Chaban-Delmas could not afford a conflict with the President; many of his policies were already being questioned by Mr Pompidou and his entourage. Thus, the ORTF lost its battle. Within a reorganization, new programmes were placed under the supervision of a channel director (one for each of the now three channels); the ORTF got a new president-director general (chairman-president), a congressman, Mr Arthur Conte; and one of the most violent critics of the former system was appointed Minister of Information. Needless to say, Mr Desgraupes was dismissed and, in the summer of 1972, Mr Chaban-Delmas was replaced by the more conservative Gaullist Pierre Messmer.

Case 6: Renault Refuses to Invest in Brittany

In the mid-1960s, Renault, the national car manufacturer, was developing at a steady rate and increasing its share of the French market, which already represented one-third of total sales of private cars. It was also engaged in various international activities and was the number one exporter in France. The only real limitation to its expansion came from a structural lack of finances: the only stockholder, the state, was not very generous. While Renault was complaining that its capital stock was 'notoriously insufficient', its major competitor, Peugeot, a private company, was doubling its capital stock (between 1961 and 1966).

With Peugeot on the horizon, Renault had to be especially careful using its scarce resources; any substantial new move required support from the government. The company's good performance, as well as the excellent relationship existing between the chairman-president, Pierre Dreyfus, and General de Gaulle, were guarantees that the state would give support if badly needed.

But some people in the administration thought that they could take advantage of the situation by asking Renault to prove its gratefulness by undertaking certain specific actions. The influential Délégation à l'Aménagement du Territoire et à l'Action Régionale (DATAR), a public agency for regional development created at the beginning of the

1960s, was concerned with areas of high unemployment and was looking for industrial companies that could invest in these areas to create jobs. DATAR had no coercive power with regard to private investors; it could only attract them with various subsidies, low-interest loans to tax allowances. DATAR could also play a co-ordinating role between state and local administration, municipalities, bankers and interested investors to facilitate new construction. It could have done so with Renault, but it was attempting to use more direct means since it was dealing with a state-owned enterprise. DATAR was very close to the Minister of Industry, Renault's tutor. It figured that Renault could be required to make its new investments fit into the agency's regional planning. As a result, Renault was asked several times to take local actions that did not fit with its own plans. Two such cases are particularly interesting.

DATAR wanted Renault to invest in Lorient, Brittany; an old local company was threatened by bankruptcy and had turned to the state for help. When Renault refused to buy the company's completely obsolete facilities, which it did not need, DATAR insisted that it create new jobs in the area. Renault finally had to build a modern electrical foundry in Brittany that it had planned to build near Paris, 300 miles away. One thousand new jobs were created by 1971.

Next, DATAR asked Renault to invest in the harbour of Nantes which was suffering from a recession in its traditional shipbuilding activities. DATAR knew that Renault needed a new assembly plant (such information has to be given to the administration). Such a plant is usually located near plants producing the parts to be assembled (body parts), for parts are costly to transport. Renault's projected location was the already existing complex of Flins, Normandy. DATAR opposed the project categorically and exerted strong pressure through the government to have Nantes chosen as the site. It took a long time and a lot of technical discussions for Renault to demonstrate that Nantes was a bad location and would prove very costly. Finally, it was agreed that Renault would locate the plant in another harbour, but would also build a small plant producing rubber parts in Nantes. Le Havre, also in Normandy, was the harbour chosen for the plant. Twelve hundred new jobs were created by 1971.

Case 7: Renault Workers get Four Weeks of Holiday

Renault has a unique image in France's social life: it has initiated many

social reforms and is usually a good thermometer for measuring the
temperature of labour relations existing at a given time in the country.
In 1950, Renault was the first company to sign a labour agreement
stipulating that wages would follow the rise of the cost of living and
that no strike would be declared without three days' previous notice.
In 1955, a new agreement set the wage increase at a minimum of 4 per
cent a year (much more than the current rate of inflation), and the
duration of paid vacations was extended from two weeks to three
weeks a year.

Under the pressure of unions, three-week vacations were made
compulsory to all French enterprises by a law voted in 1956. In the
agreement of 1955, both parties declared that they considered themselves responsible for the prosperity of the company and would try
every possible means of negotiation before resorting to strike or lock-
out. In 1958, the company created a special fund to compensate the
hours lost by the workers when production was reduced. Many other
social advantages were also given to workers. Renault's labour policy
was carefully planned and played a central role in the company's over-
all strategy.

In 1966, Pierre Dreyfus considered giving his employees a fourth
week of annual holidays for which they had been asking for some
time and which he thought the company could offer. He believed that
such a move would reinforce workers' motivation. Dreyfus's plan,
however, did not fit at all with the government's labour policy. The
country was just recovering from an economic stabilization plan which
had actually caused a recession in 1963–64; the masterword for
industry was productivity. France was increasingly facing international
competition, especially from Germany and the other members of the
European Economic Community, and many smaller firms were in very
difficult situations. To give Renault's workers a fourth week of holidays
would have meant an extension of that privilege to all French enterprises, as had previously happened, within less than a year. Many
businesses would have been threatened; the government could not take
the chance. Besides, it thought that Renault was already 'overdoing it'
and that it should curb its social consciousness. Dreyfus was told not
to consent to the fourth week.

Mr Dreyfus, however, did not listen to the government. Everyone
was stunned when company and union representatives read the
communiqué that outlined the new labour agreement. Among other
points, a fourth week of holidays was immediately granted to all
Renault employees. In political circles it was a scandal, although the

government did not dare to take back what Renault had given. Several
prominent members of the government wanted Mr Dreyfus's head. He
was summoned by General de Gaulle to the Elysée Palace, but he was
not dismissed. The general granted him 'la liberté de réussir', the liberty
to succeed. Mr Dreyfus enjoyed that liberty under close surveillance.
The government carefully watched Renault's labour relations. Of
course, the fourth week was soon extended by law to the whole nation.

Analysis and Synthesis

Drawing from the cases discussed in this paper, a general framework can
be constructed to help determine the important factors involved in
France's recognition and resolution of conflicts.

The first factor to be considered, and quickly rejected, is the nature
of the industry. Conflicts exist in very different sectors; it cannot be
said that the level of technology, the capital or labour intensity, the
degree of maturity of the product or the degree of instability of the
sector determines the situation of conflict. Conflict may happen
anywhere.

Another factor is the degree of market competition or of state
protection. All the state-owned enterprises in this study faced some
kind of market competition; however, some were placed in a highly
competitive market (Renault and Air France), some faced only partial
competition (EDF for electrical heating) and some had no direct
competitors (TV and radio). Thus, competition does not appear an
important factor, even though it may enter into the discussions between
the state-owned enterprise and the state.

The company's performance is another factor to be considered. In
the above case studies, conflict arose whether performances were good
(Renault, EDF), bad (Air France) or difficult to ascertain (TV and
radio). However, the conflicts always concerned decisions that would
have a direct and strong impact on the company's performance or, in
some cases, on its very survival. It seems reasonable to state that state-
owned enterprises rebel when they feel their strength as separate entities
is threatened.

Another factor is the existence of an explicit corporate strategy,
strongly formulated and adopted by the whole organization (any
external pressure to change the strategy being regarded as abusive).
The move towards systematic strategic planning is a recent one in most
French state-owned enterprises. Although it may well increase the

occurrence of conflicts in the future, it does not appear particularly relevant in the present study.

A strong *esprit de corps*, together with the presence of powerful and popular unions, may be a factor to consider. Strong unions distinguish French state-owned enterprises from private enterprises. However, unions did not play a major part in the case studies discussed herein; conflict often concerned exclusively the highest levels in the company. Strong leadership may be a key factor in securing the support of personnel if an appropriate *esprit de corps* exists. Most of the state-owned enterprises observed were headed by strong personalities. It certainly takes great courage to say 'no' to the government, and Messrs Giraudet, Boiteux and Dreyfus had such courage.

Similarly, the presence of strong personalities in the government or close to the government may be a critical factor in conflict resolution. Messrs Fourcade (Minister of Finance), Roux (chairman of CGE) and Guichard (president of DATAR) are such personalities.

Another factor that has to be considered consists of governmental policies. In all cases, it was found that some national objective was at stake, be it the development of an advanced technology (aircraft, nuclear), regional development (airport, job creation), energy saving, labour relations, or political control over TV. Interference with a company's plans was always motivated by the impact of such plans on national policies.

The degree of interaction between the company and the administration — i.e., the extent to which various departments of state administration exert control and intervene in the day-to-day management of a company — is also a key factor. However, in terms of understanding the factors that determine conflict, the form of the conflict may be more violent and overt if the company is traditionally autonomous.

To summarize the observations made to this point, a company's performance, leadership both in state-owned enterprises and in government, and the government's policies are the key factors affecting conflict between state-owned enterprises and government.

By definition, a conflict becomes possible as soon as a company's explicit objective is found to contradict government policy; the possibility is endemic to the existence of two separate entities having two different purposes. The fact that the government has 'higher purposes' than any state-owned enterprise because it is concerned with the nation as a whole, or because it stands as the supervising authority of all state-owned enterprises, does not, as said before, preclude conflicts.

Considering conjointly the recognition of a contradiction (the nature of which may vary in almost infinite ways), the existence of a conflict, and the factors described above, the degree of saliency of an issue from the viewpoint of the company and the degree of saliency of an issue from the viewpoint of the government can be charted. The impact of leadership can then be superimposed on a specific combination of saliency for the company and government to accentuate or moderate the effects of the combination.

If three different degrees of saliency are applied to the chart (high, medium, low), we have the set of situations presented in Table 7.2.

Table 7.2: Company Responses to Situations According to Degrees of Saliency for Company and Government

Issue saliency for Government		Submission	Grievance	Intransigence
	High	Submission	Grievance	Intransigence
	Medium	Lament	Tension	Protest
	Low	Vigilance	Touchiness	Self-confidence
		Low	Medium	High

Issue saliency for firm

A situation of vigilance is one in which there is mild conflict because virtually neither party is interested. However, state-owned enterprises may regard government's tendency to intervene in decisions that have little importance to national policies as dangerous. Therefore, autonomy must be defended with special vigilance, as a sacred principle.

Vigilance turns into touchiness if decisions are more vital to the company than to the government; government intervention should be expected to stop, since no important public policy is really concerned. But in situations where the government is more concerned than the company, the latter can only lament its lack of autonomy.

Submission may be the only alternative if national objectives are at stake. The company may be used by government as an instrument of its policies without substantial consequence to the company's performance. Conversely, the company may have much self-confidence if it can prove that it is vitally concerned with a decision that little affects government.

Special tension begins to appear when both parties are deeply concerned about the outcome. Although it may be assumed that government will impose its will in a forceful way, the personality and influence of the company's top manager and the government's spokesperson may be highly significant.

If government concern is greater than company concern, the only alternative left to the company is to assume an attitude of grievance in order to obtain a just (financial) compensation for whatever damages government has caused. On the other hand, if the balance is in favour of the company (because it can prove that its existence is threatened or because its leader is particularly convincing), protest may be the appropriate attitude to assume. In both cases, conflict is likely to be violent and receive wide coverage in the media (which each party will then use against the other).

Finally, conflict is imminent, leading to intransigence, if both the government and the company are convinced that the decision is essential to their respective goals. It is not certain at all that government's view will prevail; no government would push one of its enterprises to suicide. It would be killing the very instrument it wants to use. Nor is it certain that the company will win; the government may disagree on the reality of the danger the company faces. Personal attitudes and influence, technical arguments, agreement procedures, utilization of the media and public opinion, mobilization of personnel and unions – in short, all means of persuasion and action – may affect the final issue.

Conflicts are not always solved; they may be undeclared, a decision may be made so late that the problem shifts to another area, or a decision to act to resolve the conflict may never be made. Many conflicts could be avoided if certain issues were acknowledged and given attention in due time. One explanation why certain issues remain unattended may be that state-owned enterprises in France have to believe themselves to be in real danger before managements dare to question government policies. Their boldness will largely depend upon whether autonomy or submissiveness has characterized their relationships with the government.

Secondly, the more one waits to put an end to the conflict, the more damaging the consequences to all parties. Indecision or unwillingness to speak out or exert authority will only exacerbate the situation.

It seems reasonable to say that conflict resolution would be better managed if the relationship between state-owned enterprises and government were structured by a set of rules agreed upon and adhered to by both parties. For instance, state-owned enterprises could be obliged to present a strategic plan to the government for approval. Such a plan could be put in the form of a contract between the government and the company to be upheld for three or five years. Thus, both parties could predict potential conflicts, discuss them in advance and incorporate solutions into the plan binding both the government and the company.

EDF, SNCF, ORTF, Air France and CDF (coal mining) have signed contracts with the government at one time or another. However, at present, there is no attempt being made to include contracts as a rule in government and state-owned enterprise negotiations.

It may be necessary to regulate communication and negotiation between state-owned enterprises and government by means of a general law for state-owned enterprises. Such a law should be flexible enough to adapt to particular companies and circumstances, but should also ensure that state-owned enterprises and government are (1) forced to forecast possible conflicts in advance; (2) obligated to find an agreement within a set of rules (e.g., the government has financially to compensate whatever obligation it would impose on the company); (3) bound by the agreement once it is signed. Needless to say, a vote on such a law would be an excellent opportunity for parliament to put some order into the confusion that presently characterizes the regulations and controls concerning state-owned enterprises in France.

Law, however, can only provide a framework to encourage interested parties to negotiate. An agreement can be reached only on specific objectives, which preferably will be quantified. This raises another problem. It is always easier to agree on general statements than on precise figures, and it is often difficult to translate reality into figures. In the case of state-owned enterprises, for instance, is profit a good measure of management performance, or are there better measures, such as the quality of service or the contribution to economic and social objectives? Is the full impact of government intervention on a state-owned enterprise's activity measurable in monetary terms? How can the government be sure that using a state-owned enterprise for a specific purpose is not more costly than using another instrument, or might it be so costly that it questions the very purpose itself?

It seems necessary, therefore, to find better ways to evaluate the costs and benefits to the collectivity as well as to the state-owned enterprise of any given programme of action in which the government would use its enterprise against the enterprise's own interest. Such a problem of evaluation has limitless implications, far beyond the scope of the present study. But, as one could have expected, it is clear that state-owned enterprises are keenly interested in the current research on public policy evaluations.

Conflict between government and state-owned enterprises cannot be avoided in specific circumstances related to company performance, public policies and leadership in management and government. However, there are different ways to manage conflicts and different tools that can be used to solve problems at the lowest possible cost to the national community. Further research into comparative studies of conflict in different countries should focus on processes of communication and negotiation between governments and state-owned enterprises and the measurement of costs and benefits attached to decisions that implicate state-owned enterprises in public policies.

8 THE BRITISH EXPERIENCE: THE CASE OF BRITISH RAIL

Michael Beesley and Tom Evans

In recent years, the formal relationship in the United Kingdom between nationalized industries and their sponsor departments (the ministries responsible for their guidance and control) has been the subject of considerable change and public debate. According to British practice, major statements of policy are published as 'White Papers'; the framework for control of nationalized industries is contained in two White Papers published in 1967 and 1978.[1] A report of the Select Committee on Nationalised Industries (SCNI) in 1974[2] and a full-scale inquiry by the National Economic Development Office (NEDO) in 1976[3] further address the question of control of nationalized industries. These publications have helped to identify and define the underlying perceptions and presumptions that forge the relationship between government and its enterprises. This paper argues that the problems of management in state-owned enterprises are largely ignored or misrepresented in the official policy statements. Analysis of management processes yields quite different strategies for developing the relationship between government and industry.

Historical Background

Attempts to understand and control public enterprises in terms of conventional economics reached a peak in the 1967 White Paper. Allocative efficiency was seen as the major objective and the major principle for organizing public enterprises. The British government sought to give greater discretion to its industries, subject to clear economic rules and performance controls. Social costs were to be dealt with through specific subsidies, and management was to be given discretion to achieve the state's clearly defined goals.

The 1967 White Paper also sought to establish prices based on long-run marginal cost, to appraise investment projects against a test discount rate (TDR), supposedly representing the opportunity cost of capital to the public sector, and to monitor industry's performance against pre-established financial targets. The implied objective was to

117

ensure that returns to resources within and between the industries were equal at the margin. Yet, in the interest of managing the economy as a whole, the treasury imposed short-run budget constraints on the industries.

It is an open question as to whether a system based on the principles described above was ever fairly tested. The trek of the 1970s away from reliance solely on principles of allocative efficiency was largely pragmatic. Most significantly, nationalized industries were used as instruments against inflation. By restraining prices, the government broke the relationship with real costs and stimulated demand. Long-term misallocation of resources was encouraged wherever investments were made to meet the additional demand stimulated by pricing below real costs. When the Select Committee reviewed the resulting confusion, it tried to reinstate something approaching the control offered by the 1967 White Paper, to be exercised 'publicly and according to well-defined ground rules, without interfering with the management functions of the industries themselves'.[4]

The controls of the sponsoring ministries traditionally had focused on appraising individual projects within the constraints of over-all investment budgets. The SCNI supported formal corporate planning and strategy development, arguing that there were in effect shadow prices deriving either from a corporate-wide strategy or from longer-term perspectives that could be considered in individual projects and that should be applied to their appraisal. According to the SCNI, 'corporate planning should give an opportunity for a clearer examination of nationalised industries' objectives and a greater opportunity for the assessment of different methods of achieving them'.[5] It was hoped that the ministers would exercise control by approving explicit corporate objectives and strategic choices rather than by more detailed monitoring and intervention. How this system was to be realized was not specified.

The inquiry by NEDO in 1976 was the largest and most comprehensive study of nationalized industries undertaken in the United Kingdom. It acknowledged the widespread discontent that had grown up between government and the industries, identifying ambiguities in understanding, anomalies in procedures, disparities between formal designations of procedures and practice, and sheer distrust. Three of these findings are of particular relevance to this study. First, in the words of NEDO, 'government has been reluctant to offer, or unsuccessful in providing, adequate indications of its long term intentions for subsidising services'. Second, NEDO observed a gap between the government's intentions to provide corporate planning and its actual practices, the latter often appearing to involve little more than cursory reviews within departments of industry's submitted plans. NEDO emphasized the importance of control through corporate planning and strategy, but did little more than the SCNI had done to specify ways to achieve such control. Third, the NEDO report demonstrated that the framework of rules put forth in the 1967 White Paper had failed. In particular, project appraisal using a TDR was frequently inappropriate, especially for investments with indirect benefits.

The solution proposed by NEDO to this catalogue of discontent was to establish policy councils between sponsor departments and corporation boards. Each council would have an independent chairman and would be comprised of representatives from the departments, the corporations and the treasury.

The 1978 White Paper was the government's response to the NEDO report. It addressed the range of concerns the report had raised in four basic propositions:

1. the concept of policy councils should be rejected, but there should be institutional reforms to enable the major stockholders' interests to be represented in the development of strategy;
2. corporate planning and the examination of strategic options should have a central place in the relationship between nationalized industries and their sponsor departments;
3. inasmuch as allocative efficiency remains an important concern, a revised framework of pricing principles, measures of opportunity cost of capital, and financial targets should be adopted;
4. measures of performance other than financial should be developed and industries should be held accountable to such measures.

In the 1978 White Paper, the commitment to allocative efficiency is much diluted; gone is the appeal to analytical rigour. Marginal cost pricing is advocated only very generally and with caveats. Furthermore, the 1978 White Paper concedes the complexity of much project appraisal by dropping the TDR criterion and by proposing instead a required rate of return based on the whole annual set of investments which each industry must reach. Most importantly, the government's priorities and the government's concerns over the realistic application of those priorities are not examined explicitly anywhere in the report.

Against this historical background, we wish to argue the following points. First, there is no government strategy for the control of state-owned enterprises nor any clear sense of how it might develop. The 1967 White Paper proposed a strategy, but its coherence was bought at the cost of ignoring complexities in its application. Individual sponsor departments in time may develop more successful strategies to deal with their industries; however, in the particular industry in this case study, British Rail, such success is doubtful.

Second, the system that is needed to control nationalized industries should include ways of dealing with the unique concerns and priorities of nationalized industries, including modes of operation and criteria for determining their effectiveness.

Third, managerial perspectives and practices have been either largely ignored or reified; in other words, they have been regarded as if their content and implications were self-evident. Such reification has ignored the problems of designing practices to meet the needs of internal and external controls and, in the face of multiple demands, has made trade-offs in planning and management all the more difficult.

In the light of the arguments presented above, this paper discusses British Rail, one of the most contentious of the UK's nationalized industries.

British Rail and Its Sponsor Department

In early 1976, a study was undertaken for the NEDO inquiry concerning the relationships between British Rail and its sponsor department. This study specifically addressed the management of subsidy—payments by the Transport Ministry to meet British Rail's deficit. Analysis focused on three critical events in the development of the subsidy relationship: the 1968 Transportation Act, the 1974 Railway Act and the 1975 imposition of cash limits.

The 1968 Transportation Act embodied the principle of specific subsidies for rail passenger services. It was perhaps the most explicit adoption in any nationalized industry of arm's-length control and of governmental payment for socially desirable services. The Act intended to work towards a system in which the net social benefits of different levels of individual services could be evaluated, and in which the total level of support could be determined by the individual decisions to expand, control or terminate given rail services.

The 1974 Railway Act took a very different approach. It established an annual public service obligation (PSO) grant to cover the deficit that British Rail incurred by running passenger services. The grant was set at a level comparable to that of the recent past.[6] Fixing a level was widely interpreted as meaning that the government was committed to a base below which passenger services would not be allowed to fall. At the time, the legislation generated markedly little controversy. But, by 1975, strict cash limits were imposed, restricting passenger support to no more than existing real levels and raising the question of how best to cope with the deficit in freight.

At one level, the rapid variations in the governing principles of the subsidy relationship can be explained. In each case, the changes were triggered by a rapid escalation in British Rail's deficit beyond the scale foreseen. Such an escalation could not be accommodated through existing instruments of subsidy or by such devices as capital reconstruction.

Thus, by 1972, it was already apparent that the 1968 assumptions were overly optimistic. A familiar sequence of events that had preceded the 1968 Act, and indeed earlier Acts, ensued. Disagreements between the board and the department increased. Urgent *ad hoc* inquiries and emergency subsidies were called into play. In order to continue the emergency subsidies, legislation had to be passed. In 1974, the Railway Act was enacted to create a long-term settlement. In 1975, cash limits were adopted in response to severe difficulties in macroeconomic policy and public expenditure levels; but, once again, these remedies proved overly optimistic.

The changes that took place during the development of the subsidy relationship have significance for understanding current interactions between government and industry. Each new enactment provided only the outlines and principles of the new subsidy relationship, leaving a great deal to be specified by one or both of the parties involved. The amount of the subsidy to be made available to British Rail was part of an agreement worked out before the 1968 Act; the total subsidy was divided across individual passenger services according to current accounting conventions. Each service was to be reviewed individually. In the 1968 Transportation Act, the precise basis for approving subsidies was left to the department to specify. Thus, if the system were to develop as the Act intended, means had to be found to discriminate between services on the basis of their external conditions, including the potential social benefits to consumers and to the rest of the local community, and the alternative forms and costs of available transport. However, no substantial attempt to develop the system according to the terms of the 1968 Act was made; as expectations were increasingly disappointed, the intended distinctions foundered for want of belief.

The 1974 Act depended upon collaboration of government and industry representatives to implement its programmes. A joint working group was established to co-ordinate the timing of planning and budgeting in order to make the actions of the government departments more responsive to industry's needs. The joint group emphasized the need for government to contribute to corporate planning, especially on such issues as establishing a means of assessing the value of given passenger services and arranging for feedback from the government's monitoring and reviewing of such services.

As discussed above, the 1968 Transportation Act failed to devise effective criteria for determining the scale of rail services. In the negotiations leading to the 1974 Act, the central issue was again the scale of railway activity. At one point there may have been a chance for agreement on a decline in passenger services. However, a premature leak of the department's options, which included drastic pruning, brought an end to negotiations. British Rail, prompted by union pressures, was forced to take an intransigent line against such pruning. As a result, a vague formula referring to a 'comparable scale' of operations was agreed. Both the department and the board were aware that after the 1974 Act there would have to be further decreases in services. Here was an obvious situation in which an explicit combined strategy that developed plans for selective expansion and contraction could have been valuable. But no such plan was ever tried, probably because neither party could test the other's commitment to the proposed decrease in passenger services.

Perhaps the most significant factor affecting the relations of the board and the department during this period was the recurring difference in understanding, interpretation and perspective. In the debate leading up to the 1974 Act, the board and department disagreed over the type of grant preferred. The department favoured an annual grant for public service operations, the PSO option. The board, however, wanted a two-tier grant system: one tier to consist of the costs attributable to unremunerative passenger services; and a separate, short-term grant to cover infrastructure costs. The board's preferred system would involve the department in a commitment to a definite scale of future railway operations. Such a commitment, the board felt, would allow British Rail's management to focus attention on improving its services rather than on ensuring its survival.

The department objected to British Rail's two-tier system, arguing that grants for infrastructure costs would imply special problems of control and accountability: for example, there would be a need to prevent a capital-intensive bias in railway policy. The PSO option, the department argued, would more likely yield the desired output and would have the flexibility to adjust year by year to most contingencies (in effect, adverse, unforeseen shortfalls of revenue). Moreover, the PSO option had the advantage of being compatible with European Economic Community rules on subsidies. Clearly, the board's approach and the department's approach represented very different positions and concerns.

Similar differences surrounded the implementation of the PSO principle after 1974. Disagreement arose about whether grants should be paid according to 'adjustment to actuals' or according to factors defined in advance (e.g., unforeseen inflation, wage agreements, economic recession). The department, which favoured the latter, was obviously mindful of the dangers of being accused by the Public Accounts Committee of lacking foresight. The board was concerned with more conventional corporate budgeting problems such as analyzing and controlling deviations from budget targets. Moreover, the department wanted to give the board management incentives with respect to passenger services; the board apparently wanted such incentives. However, each side meant different things by 'management incentives': the board meant having the freedom, whenever possible, to determine its operations without recourse to the department; the department meant maintaining an inducement to save taxpayers' money.

Thus, the development of the subsidy relationship between British Rail and the UK government can be characterized by the following: a disruption of each arrangement by a mounting financial disorder that could not be managed within existing policy and statutory provisions; an attempt to establish a broad statutory statement of principles to govern the allocation of subsidies, followed by the details for implementing such a plan; the continued presence of major unresolved questions, often unacknowledged by the implementation system; and the ubiquity of divergences of interest and interpretation.

At the time of the NEDO study, discussions ensued over reforming the subsidy relationship. However, of the many participants, no one sought to relate the circumstances leading to the difficulties specifically to ideas for reform. Furthermore, little emphasis was given to predicting the outcomes of specific proposals. Ideas for reform revealed the same differences in understanding and interest that had characterized the history of the relationship and the specific negotiations for the new Acts. Recommended reform also lacked both an explicit analytical framework and effective criteria by which its relative merits could be judged.

Planning in British Rail

Our second source of evidence is current work on corporate planning in British Rail.[7] There are two types of formal planning activities in British Rail: the annual corporate 15-year planning cycle, producing detailed forecasts of the first five years and a snapshot picture of the tenth year; and a study of strategic options over 15 years for the major rail businesses.[8]

The basic corporate planning structure[9] provides forecasts of demand for each of the major British Rail businesses (passenger, freight and parcels) and for the subsidiary businesses (shipping, hotels, etc.), together with physical resource, investment and financial implications. The business as a whole is organized into headquarters and board functions, and geographical regions. The rail businesses are essentially demand oriented; supply is managed by operational and engineering functions. Based on some over-all economic assumptions, each of the three major businesses produces detailed forecasts of service levels and earnings. These forecasts go to the operational planners to be translated into resource requirements and logistical and engineering problems. In principle, these forecasts also determine investment and manpower assessment. The outcomes of the operational, investment and manpower assessments are translated into the financial terms in which the plan is finally presented.

The corporate planning procedure yields a five-year budget. In general, only a simple forecast is produced, though there are means for testing particular assumptions. Some progress has been made in risk analysis, but the principal concern of the plan is to ensure that the expected paths of development of current types of activity are consistent with the over-all constraints to which British Rail is subject – the PSO and the investment ceiling. Should the forecast violate either of these constraints, the plan must be adjusted. In this sense, the planning exercise is a feasibility study of the extension of present commitments into the future.

In the development of a planning framework to guide resource allocation processes, a number of difficulties arise. These problems may be illustrated by considering the process of resource allocation for investment.

British Rail is subject to an anticipated investment constraint over its planning period which is less than it finds sufficient to maintain its current level of service. Two characteristics of investment planning are of particular importance to this discussion.

First, the phasing of replacement is critical. In particular, phasing involves distinguishing between assets the lives of which can be extended by maintenance and those of which the replacement is imperative. The nature of phasing will frequently be determined by the tolerance of professional standards such as safety.

Second, the scale and quality of the replacement are crucial. For example, the impending failure of a section of a signalling system may trigger the replacement of adjacent route sections; modern replacements offer many advantages but also require a larger scale. Consequently the lives of some assets may be shortened in order to pursue a more effective pattern of investment for the system.

Many of the projects, particularly those concerned with infrastructure, are not readily subject to financial appraisal. Rolling stock investment is in some ways an exception, since earnings can be directly attributed to it; but, even here, appraisal is confounded by the need to even out the past bunching of investments in new fleets. Large-scale projects involve a range of professional engineering groups (mechanical, civil, and signalling and communications), as well as the sponsor departments and commercial and marketing groups. Consequently, the designing of investment projects is a complex process that entails considering the needs of several interested parties.

Another element in planning directly related to the development of strategy entails so-called business strategy studies (BSS). These studies are designed to build toward the future, toward the year 1990, in order to identify a 'steady state' for the operation of the railway system. The steady state concept provides for a renewal of the railway system at a level dictated by the demand conditions and technology of the time. This concept is contrasted with what is seen as a currently unsatisfactory state of disequilibrium; the system is not being adequately renewed and there are no clear criteria to judge its operation. It is hoped that the BSS will rectify several disorders, particularly those related to the passenger business.

British Rail has looked to the government to specify corporate objectives derived from public policy and to set the outer limits on its operating deficits. A major concern of the passenger study (PBSS) has been to try to force the government's hand on these issues. One proposal is to correct financial valuations of railway activities by objective economic data that take into account the externalities and consumer surplus generated by British Rail's operations. The corrected values would directly determine the government's allocation of funds. The intention of such a plan is to limit the uncertainty of British Rail's operations by obtaining longer-term commitments from the government. This involves the transfer of uncertainty to government, which, not surprisingly, is unwilling to accept it.

The emphasis in the PBSS and corporate planning has been on preserving British Rail's relations with government. Much of the planning has focused on preparing the British Rail board for the debate that will lead to a new transport policy White Paper and to future commitments from government. The PBSS has also tried to produce a framework for corporate plans within industry and to facilitate the involvement of the board in the two-stage process of choice.

In summary, British Rail's planning system consists of two parts. The first, the annual corporate planning procedure, is essentially an aggregation of intentions for a five-year period. In the future, it may test the legitimacy of operational intentions against aggregate resource constraints; so far, it has been used as a basis for discussions between British Rail and government on emerging operational problems of the rail industry. The second part, business strategic studies, has been handled separately and largely as a means of reducing the uncertainty stemming from British Rail's political environment.

Management Processes and Design

The approach of the government toward British Rail has been one of attempting guidance through strategic choice. By concentrating guidance and control on strategic issues, it was thought that government would be able to reduce its involvement in the day-to-day affairs of its enterprises. But the review of the planning processes and of the fixing of subsidies described above suggests that this approach is far from developed.

Such an approach assumes that strategic guidance is faithfully transferred from the government to lower levels of decision making in the public enterprise, and that budget allocations will correspond to the application of the strategic guidelines. If the government is to have confidence that its guidance has been assimilated by the enterprise, tests have to be developed to verify the fact that such guidance is determining relevant decisions at lower levels and determining budget outcomes. If no such tests exist, *ad hoc* interventions on the part of the government are inevitable. The more managers are required to follow directives that clash with their preferred strategies, the more government will have difficulty imposing its criteria on the corporation. If controlling strategic issues is to be successful, effective criteria for assessing the performance of public enterprises need to be developed.

In present circumstances, there are various reasons why British Rail would be apprehensive about applying strategic guidelines to resource allocation at lower levels. Such application would create many difficulties, particularly in reallocating resources between different activities within British Rail. In any case, the government seems to be concerned primarily with holding actual expenditures as close as possible to target, rather than with effecting shifts between such activities. The emphasis on targets reflects the government's desire to control short-term and medium-term financing. Accordingly, neither British Rail nor the government appears to be pursuing a model of guidance and control through strategic choice. However, because current practices represent a release of certain constraints, such practices came closer to British Rail's point of view than to the government's.

The application of the model of control through strategic choice requires two areas of development: first, it needs the technological and organizational capability to provide relevant and acceptable strategic criteria for resource allocation; second, it needs a co-operative strategy for the development of the model, including a consensus on priorities and a system for dealing with imperfections in order to prevent the rejection of the strategy as complications arise. To satisfy these needs, however, two areas of conceptual ambiguity about planning and strategy development in nationalized industries need to be clarified.

The first area concerns the concept of strategy itself. So far we have identified two strategic needs: limiting the uncertainty that comes from the political environment; and guiding and controlling the resource allocation process. In addition, certain conventional concepts of corporate strategy can also be applied to nationalized industries. Such concepts include the product life-cycle; product mix and diversification, with a heavy emphasis on mobility between product areas; and coping with threats from the market by searching for new opportunities in the market.

Nationalized industries are limited in their ability to apply conventional concepts of corporate strategy. Most importantly, they are unable to diversify on any major scale. As a result, their ability to cope with their problems by changing their markets is limited. In the private sector, diversification enables the company to adapt, to maintain effective use of resources and to ensure organizational growth and momentum. How are these functions to be performed by nationalized industries in the absence of diversification, particularly when existing markets are in decline?

One way a state-owned enterprise can adapt is by changing its structure and practices in order to deal more effectively with problems within the existing sets of constraints. In that case, management's challenging task will be to persuade others to accept the costs of such a limited adaptation. Alternatively, management might attempt to buffer the organization from the cumulative adverse effects of its inability to adapt to the environment. Still another possibility, more complex than those so far suggested, is to develop new internal policies for managing change, maintaining corporate strategy and restoring management's capacity to influence events. So far, none of these approaches is being pursued with respect to British Rail; discussions with the government now seem to focus largely upon public policy issues and market forecasts, with only oblique references to problems of adaptation. The ingredients that are needed to carry out this more complex approach will be discussed in the final section of this paper.

The second area in which clarification is needed concerns the strategy of planning. We have shown how British Rail has adopted a particular strategy of planning, and we have implied that other choices could have been made. British Rail's choice reveals its concern to limit the uncertainty from the political environment and to guide and control the resource allocation process. But there are other ways in which the planning process can be used to achieve certain goals.

Inspection of the literature on corporate planning suggests that the practice of planning is and should be highly situational – that is, should depend more upon the conditions at a particular time and place.[10] Moreover, satisfactory hypotheses relating forms of planning to conditions in which they would be especially effective are hard to find. Many writers have suggested that planning will vary in terms of its purposes and its organizational roles, as well as in response to the specific situations it confronts. For example, rather than being concerned with choosing new strategies through forecasting and analysis, a company may seek to promote change by restructuring its existing mechanisms for coping with problems. Such restructuring may be directed toward increasing the capacity of the company for change by improving its capacity for learning or improving its capacity to interact with different clients or to work toward different goals. The importance of these alternative approaches to planning is emphasized in the work of Ansoff, Declerck and Hayes,[11] who argue that the environment conditions of our time require a shift from strategic planning to strategic management. The critical emphasis of this shift is on coping with the many features of environment change through the development of managerial and organizational capabilities rather than relying wholly on market forces.

Planning, therefore, must be regarded as a discretionary but constrained activity, the nature, form and methods of which are born of the strategy and choices pursued by managers and the expectations and pressures of those who surround the company. Thus, planning appears to be determined both by nature and by choice. We should not expect the corporate planners to concern themselves with how best to foster governmental direction and control. As our evidence suggests, British Rail's managers will view the problem from a corporate standpoint. If the government is to achieve greater effectiveness in guidance and control, therefore, it must be in a position to influence the strategy and setting in which corporate planning is conducted.

A further problem is to create a system of relationships between the board and its sponsor department that is appropriate to the management processes within the firm. To solve that problem, there must be agreement on the criteria by which the relationship between the sponsor department as the subsidizer and British Rail as the subsidized can be judged, and in terms of which proposals for change can be analyzed. Such a system should have the following characteristics.

1. It should be effective in the following senses. For the government, subsidizing should be at least as desirable as any other method available for achieving social goals; this implies some capacity to measure the pay-offs obtained from subsidies. For the company, there should be no reason to value an unsubsidized service more highly, and there should be a willingness to serve both commercial and social goals.

2. The system must be able to justify the social services served by the subsidy.

3. The system should be able to account for the subsidies. Accountability means being able to demonstrate to the subsidizers that social

purposes have been served and that due economy has been achieved.

4. The system should encourage management to have a sense of integrity about its work. In a mixed economy, any industry or firm needs to conduct its affairs in such a way as to maintain its managerial talent. Its managers must have opportunities for self-advancement and job fulfilment that compete with or surpass opportunities in competitive industries. Above all, managerial discretion must be preserved; a company's ability to determine its own scope and development will permit a considerable amount of flexibility. (Of course, an over-all deficit situation threatens managerial discretion.)

5. The system should promote social responsiveness. This is not simply a question of meeting social needs; it also includes promoting a willingness to seek out new opportunities to serve social needs. As a monopolist of supply, and therefore of required technical and other skills, the industry itself must be a principal source of innovation. Moreover, managerial discretion and a capacity for social innovation may be mutually reinforcing.

6. A subsidy system should consider costs in terms of cash outlay and managerial time.

All of the characteristics described above demand mutual trust from government and industry. How to build and maintain that trust remains a question.

A Starting-point

The analysis in this paper suggests that it is unlikely that an acceptable and durable subsidy system could be established immediately. In the absence of such a system, we need to look at ways of developing the subsidy relationship from manageable beginnings.

We suggest that a sensible strategy for developing the relationship between British Rail and its sponsor department would be to formulate the subsidy system in terms of a relatively simple objective for British Rail, but one the sophistication and application of which could be increased as the capacity of both sides to manage complex interactions increases. Such a strategy is already in operation in London Transport's dealings with the Greater London Council: London Transport seeks to maximize passenger miles for a given subsidy level.

Applied to railways, such a strategy would represent a way of relating disjointed decisions about pricing, investment and the scale of particular operations to a single framework. It would be an admittedly crude proxy for social benefit, relying heavily upon a correlation between measured railway passenger output and reduced external congestion. But it would underscore the trade-offs that the department has often seemed to avoid in the past. Furthermore, it could provide a simple but effective basis for management systems. Whatever its initial limitations, the critical quality is the system's potential to provide a fresh starting-point for, and later refinements to, the dialogue between the sponsor department and British Rail. There is nothing particularly novel in proposing the objective to maximize passenger miles under certain constraints. The innovation comes from relating this proposal to a systematic design of learning as a strategy for developing the subsidy relationship.

Agreeing upon the objective to maximize passenger miles under certain constraints can benefit both government and British Rail. For British Rail, it could be a means of linking current budgeting (PSO) exercises to longer-run questions of investment, disinvestment and renewal, and therefore to the over-all scale of passenger output. British Rail management would thus begin the move from more traditional views of its activity as maximizing contributions to a fixed asset base. Moreover, as this corporate objective considers both economic and social aims, it offers a useful way to justify change to those affected.

If the relevant information could be accumulated and interpreted in timely fashion, the department would be in a better position to influence board decisions; agreements could more readily be reached by exchanges between the board and the department, and the department would have less need for subsequent disturbing interventions.

If British Rail's objective is to be specified in passenger miles, it will eventually be necessary to recognize that the social value of a passenger mile may well be different in each of British Rail's many services. When the passenger mile criterion is firmly established, therefore, methods of valuation which reflect that fact should be introduced. When introduced, the subsidies received by British Rail for its various services should be weighed against subsidies provided to alternative recipients, notably buses.

These lines of development have few echoes, either in the preceding history of the relationship between British Rail and its sponsor department, or in the more general debate we summarized in the first section.

Perhaps the greatest problems lie in the initial shift of perspective, but we can see no substitute for systematic experimentation and learning if progress towards an explicit system of guidance and control is to be made.

Notes

1. 'Nationalised Industries: A Review of Economic and Financial Objectives', Cmnd 3437 (London: HMSO, 1967); 'The Nationalised Industries', Cmnd 7131 (London: HMSO, 1978).

2. Select Committee on Nationalised Industries (SCNI), *Capital Investment Procedures*, 1st Report (Session 1973-74) (HC65).

3. National Economic Development Office, *A Study of U.K. Nationalised Industries: Their Role in the Economy and Control in the Future,* Report and Appendices (1976).

4. SCNI, *Capital Investment Procedures,* p.xxxix.

5. *Ibid.,* para. 15.

6. To give some sense of scale, in 1976 the PSO limit was £358 million of which £319 million was actually taken up. Turnover in that year was £1,317 million.

7. The material on which this section is based is part of a study of corporate planning in several nationalized industries, financed by the Social Science Research Council, Contract no. HR 292911, and undertaken by David Chambers, Tom Evans, Max Lehmann and Nick Woodward.

8. The evidence concerns the practice of planning in British Rail as of 1977. Subsequent changes have since taken place in the organization and treatment of strategic analysis.

9. We use the term 'corporate planning' somewhat differently from the way in which it is used in British Rail. There, 'corporate' refers to the aggregation of plans for rail and all the subsidiary businesses, while the 'rail' plan is for the rail business only. We do not make this distinction and, since we are concerned with planning for the rail business, we shall use them interchangeably.

10. See, for example, Peter Lorange and Richard F. Vancil, *Strategic Planning Systems* (New York: Prentice Hall, 1977).

11. H.I. Ansoff, R.P. Declerck and R.L. Hayes, *From Strategic Planning to Strategic Management* (New York: John Wiley and Sons, Inc., 1976).

9 STATE-OWNED OIL COMPANIES: WESTERN EUROPE

Øystein Noreng

Western Europe has been a bastion of state-owned oil companies for over fifty years. The purpose of this article is to examine some aspects of the relationship of control between state-owned oil companies and their supervisory government agencies in four Western European countries: France, Italy, Norway and the United Kingdom.

Origins of the Enterprises

The state-owned oil companies of Western Europe were created to achieve national goals that existing market mechanisms and private enterprises could not achieve alone. The first oil nationalization of Western Europe began in the United Kingdom. In 1914, the British government became part owner of the Anglo-Persian Oil Company, now British Petroleum, to secure foreign oil supplies for military needs.[1] Britain's willingness to enter into a position of ownership in an oil company stemmed from its desire to avoid reliance on foreign oil supplies in times of crisis.

During World War I, the economic and strategic importance of oil was clearly demonstrated. After the war, several West European governments took action to secure foreign oil supplies. France participated in the redistribution of the old Turkish Petroleum Company, securing oil concessions in the Middle East for the first time. In 1924, the French government established a new company, Compagnie Française des Pétroles (CFP), to participate in the oil industry. By 1928, legislation was passed enabling the French government to regulate the domestic oil market to stimulate the development of a French refining industry. In 1929, the French government took a 35 per cent interest in CFP. In 1926, faced with the same concerns as France over depending upon foreign oil suppliers, Italy established Agip, a public company to explore and produce oil abroad.

After World War II, the importance of oil was made even clearer. In 1945, the French government created two public enterprises to explore and produce oil in French overseas territories: the Bureau de

Recherches de Pétrole (BRP) and the Régie Autonome des Pétroles
(RAP). Agip of Italy, however, had lost its foreign concessions during
the war and planned to dissolve the company. Still fearful of dependence
upon foreign oil companies, the Italian government persuaded Enrico
Mattei, the official in charge of Agip, to expand Agip's activities.[2]
Within a few years, sufficient gas supplies were found to make the
company economically viable. In 1953, Agip was placed under
ENI, Ente Nazionale Idrocarburi, and was charged with defending
national oil and gas interests.

The discovery of oil and gas in the North Sea in the 1960s raised the
issue of public control of petroleum production in Norway and the
United Kingdom. Initially, both countries devised means for the state
to participate in the concessions granted to private enterprises. The
British government exercised its rights of ownership through existing
agencies such as the Coal Board. The Norwegian government granted
concessions to private enterprises that explicitly provided for state
participation.

In 1972, the Norwegian government established a wholly state-owned
oil enterprise, Statoil,[3] to care for the government's commercial
interests in Norwegian waters and to secure public control of supplies.
Following Norway's example, the British government in 1975 established
the British National Oil Corporation, BNOC,[4] a wholly state-owned
oil company. Both the British and Norwegian governments argued that
state ownership of oil companies would increase the national revenue
from oil and would promote greater understanding of the world oil
situation.[5]

Thus, two generations of Western European state oil companies can
be distinguished: the first generation of companies, including British
Petroleum, Agip and CFP, was established to secure foreign oil supplies;
the second generation of companies, including BRP, RAP, Statoil and
BNOC, was established to produce oil within national boundaries. The
two generations present different problems of control and thus require
different criteria of judgement.

The state oil companies of the first generation can be judged predominantly by their ability to secure quantities of foreign oil; costs to
the government might enter into their evaluation as a secondary concern.
The state oil companies of the second generation present a much more
complex problem of evaluation. At the microeconomic level, it might
be helpful to determine to what extent the presence of state oil
companies has an impact on issues such as costs, use of domestic goods
and services, concern for labour, safety and environment, raising revenue,

and providing a vantage-point from which government can increase its understanding of the oil industry at large.

The state oil companies of the first generation have been reasonably successful in providing foreign oil supplies. The overseas oil production of British Petroleum has traditionally been much higher than domestic British oil consumption. The overseas oil production of CFP and, in recent years, Elf-ERAP (formerly BRP and RAP) has generally corresponded to French domestic demand. Agip, although initially less successful, secured sufficient oil in the 1950s and 1960s to meet approximately half the domestic Italian demand. Thus, the managements of the state oil companies responded expeditiously to their governments' demands.

With the primary goal of government achieved, state-owned oil companies, for the most part, have been given the freedom to expand without an increase in government controls. The absence of government constraints has allowed state oil companies to co-operate with private oil companies, and has encouraged public enterprises to operate increasingly as private enterprises. The freedom to operate without close government supervision can be seen as a consequence of the successes of state-owned oil companies of the first generation. The question that remains is to what extent this sequence of successes will be repeated by the state-owned oil companies of the second generation.

Patterns of Control

France has two state-owned oil companies: Elf-ERAP and CFP. Elf-ERAP is the younger and the smaller company in terms of production and turnover.

Through its ownership of Elf-ERAP, the French government holds 70 per cent of SNEA, Société Nationale Elf-Aquitaine. The remaining 30 per cent of SNEA belongs to private interests. SNEA is a fully integrated oil company engaged in exploration, production of oil and gas, transportation by tankers and pipelines, refining and marketing of oil products, and other activities such as mining, construction and the production of pharmaceuticals and perfumes. The company is comprised of a number of subsidiaries, many of which are organized in co-operation with other oil companies. SNEA and CFP, for example, have 30 subsidiaries in common.[6] The president of SNEA is appointed by the cabinet. Members of the board represent different ministries and different areas of professional expertise.

CFP, like SNEA, is a fully integrated oil company engaged in exploration, production, transportation, refining, petrochemicals and marketing. It also holds a majority interest in the refining company, CFR, Compagnie Française de Raffinage. CFP has many subsidiaries owned jointly with other oil companies and participates in several industries including nuclear, electrical, mechanical, coal and uranium. The French government owns 35 per cent of CFP's capital and 40 per cent of the votes at the shareholders' meetings. The government also has the right to name the president, but it is not usually represented on the board of directors.[7] In 1979, the board of CFP was comprised of several large French private industrial and financial groups including Elf-Aquitaine.

Each French state-owned enterprise is sanctioned by law and given detailed rules as to how it is to operate. The guiding principle according to law is to have state-owned enterprises operate as commercial managements under public direction.[8] Public enterprises are subject to the same laws and taxes as private firms. The boards of state-owned enterprises are usually comprised of representatives of different ministries, outside experts and employees of the particular companies. The president is usually chosen by the cabinet.

Supervision of French state-owned enterprises is conducted at three levels: government control of investments; government control of expenditures through the Ministry of Finance; and government audit by the Cour des Comptes, the Court of Accounts, France's state auditing agency. The Ministry of Finance oversees the operations of state-owned enterprises through its financial inspectors and controllers. Each public firm is linked with a minister and a technical director; both must be consulted on all important matters. Wage and price decisions have to be referred to the Ministry of Finance for approval.

Elf-ERAP and CFP come under the supervision of the Oil Directorate of the Ministry of Industry. According to the law of 1928, the Oil Directorate is responsible for distributing quotas for oil imports, refining and sales, and for setting prices for oil products. Quotas and prices are set by negotiations between the Oil Directorate and the oil companies. Thus, the Oil Directorate both supervises the state oil companies and controls the domestic oil market.

Italy's state-owned oil company, Agip, was established by law in 1953 and charged with the management and pursuit of national goals in the field of natural gases and hydrocarbons. As a subsidiary company of ENI, Agip is involved in oil and gas exploration, production, transportation, refining and marketing. It also has several subsidiaries engaged in

engineering, construction, contracting and nuclear power. Agip's
activities extend internationally and include joint ventures with private
and foreign industries. Government control of Italian state-owned
enterprises is carried out through the Ministry of State Shareholdings.
According to law, the minister has exclusive control of state-owned
enterprises and is entitled to issue directives, although his actions are
subject to the supervision of an inter-ministerial committee.

The Ministry of State Shareholdings is represented on the boards of
directors of state-owned enterprises. State-owned enterprises are also
subject to control by the Committee for Economic Planning, CIPE,
which co-ordinates investment programmes in private and public
industries on the basis of information provided by the Ministry of
Budget and the Ministry of State Shareholdings. CIPE's plans have
often been unrealistic; as a result, the Ministry of State Shareholdings
has assumed responsibility for the supervision of ENI with only
marginal input from CIPE.[9]

Statoil, the Norwegian state-owned oil company, was established in
1972 by a unanimous vote of parliament. In 1979, Statoil was in the
process of gaining majority or full control of the largest distributor of
oil products in Norway. The aim of the company is to create a vertically
integrated enterprise with total control of the Norwegian oil supply.
The Norwegian government also holds a 53 per cent interest in Norsk
Hydro, a state-owned oil company enjoying the distinction of being
Scandinavia's largest chemical enterprise.

Economic planning in Norway, carried out by the Ministry of
Finance, is essentially macroeconomic in character. State-owned enterprises enjoy a high degree of managerial autonomy. In principle, they
are subordinate to the Ministry of Industry; in practice, they have been
subject to little direct supervision. Furthermore, in order to keep an
arm's-length relationship between government agencies and state-owned
enterprises, Norwegian law prohibits civil servants from serving on the
boards of directors of public companies.

Statoil, created specifically to secure control of the nation's oil
activities, has presented the Norwegian government with new responsibilities of control. Prohibited by law from participating on the
company's board, the bureaucracy has had to devise a special plan to
oversee Statoil's activities. Statoil is now required to submit to its
supervising ministry biannual reports on key aspects of its activities,
including plans for the subsequent year and reports on the status of its
joint ventures. Information of this sort is intended to provide the
ministry with a basis for supervising and participating in the planning of

Statoil. Once a year this information, accompanied by the ministry's observations, is transmitted to parliament.

In 1978, the Norwegian administration was reorganized to include a new Ministry of Oil and Energy. The new ministry assumed responsibility for the supervision of Statoil. Norsk Hydro, as well as the other state-owned enterprises, remained under the supervision of the Ministry of Industry. In addition to the ministries, Norway has a Petroleum Directorate responsible for technical and safety regulations in its industries.

BNOC, the United Kingdom's state-owned oil company, was created in 1975 and reorganized in 1979. It is predominantly active in exploration, production and the marketing of crude oil. As yet, BNOC has not become actively involved in refining and petrochemicals.

BNOC, like most British state-owned enterprises, is organized as a public corporation and is responsible to a sponsor government department, the Department of Energy; its budget is financed through the treasury. The relationship between BNOC and the government can be characterized as arm's length, as can the relationships between most British state-owned enterprises and government.

Problems of Control

Cultural and political differences account, in part, for the different systems of government control of state-owned enterprises in Norway, France, Italy and the United Kingdom. Yet, despite obvious differences in control, the state-owned oil companies discussed in this paper have certain characteristics in common.

French Elf-ERAP and Italian ENI are both wholly state-owned, fully integrated oil companies and perform the principal task of supplying their home markets with foreign oil. However, they greatly differ at the level of government control. The French tradition of centralized administration is visible in its state-owned enterprises; Elf-ERAP is governed by an elaborate control system connected to an even larger economic planning network. The Italian tradition of administration is also evident in its state-owned enterprises: ENI operates relatively independently under a rather simple control system.

Norwegian Statoil and British BNOC also have characteristics in common: both companies are relatively new, and both are subject to considerably more detailed control than are other state-owned enterprises in their countries. In Britain, however, financial control is emphasized; in Norway, open information and participation in corporate planning between the government and its state-owned enterprises are emphasized. Statoil's regular presentation of reports allows the Norwegian government access to the inner workings of the company. Britain's financial control of BNOC allows the government tight control over BNOC's activities.

Despite the differences in control systems, Elf-ERAP, ENI, Statoil and BNOC experience similar problems of control in their interactions with their governments.

In 1974, an inquiry commission of the French parliament prepared a report on the relationship between the French government and its state-owned oil companies.[10] The report was particularly critical of Elf-ERAP and CFP, focusing on three areas of their activities: both companies used the rules of depreciation and reinvestment to avoid paying taxes to France; both companies gave erroneous information on the price of oil acquired abroad; and both companies made illegal arrangements to share the market and fix prices. The commission's report also addressed problems regarding the relationship between the state-owned oil companies and their supervisory government agencies. At best, the companies' accountability was unclear, particularly in the area of decision making. The report questioned whether decisions were made by the Oil Directorate of the Ministry of Industry or by the state-owned oil companies. In fact, it was suggested that the Oil Directorate acted as a representative of the oil industry within the government rather than as its supervisor. Based on its findings, the parliamentary commission recommended that an independent agency be established to control the oil industry, linked to the office of the Prime Minister rather than to any ministry, and that Elf-ERAP and CFP be merged to form one major oil company.

In 1976, the French government reorganized its interests in the oil industry, merging Elf-ERAP with SNPA (Aquitaine) to form SNEA. The state maintains full control of Elf-ERAP; but, to preserve the involvement of private shareholders, the state has restricted its influence over the new company, SNEA, by limiting its votes on the board of directors to 52.2 per cent. (A two-thirds' majority is required to effect any changes in SNEA's statutes.) Thus, as a result of the merger of Elf-ERAP and SNPA and limited representation on the board of SNEA, the French government has apparently loosened its control over the oil industry.

The relationship between ENI and the Italian government has been characterized by a number of political conflicts. ENI, in order to gain access to inexpensive oil, has entered independently into arrangements with foreign countries, creating problems for the Italian Ministry of Foreign Affairs.[11] On the domestic scene, ENI has been at odds with the Ministry of Industry, which periodically has chosen to defend private industrial interests rather than the state's interests.

As with all state-owned enterprises in Italy, the political party in power strongly affects ENI's relations with the state. Prior to 1962, the Christian Democratic Party tended to constrain ENI's activities. With the increase in socialist representation in the Italian government, ENI was able to operate under fewer constraints. In the 1970s, the Communist Party gained influence in parliamentary committees and used that influence to impose more effective controls on state-owned enterprises.

Today, the Italian Ministry of State Shareholdings relies upon ENI to submit relevant information on the corporation's activities to the government. However, because ENI's responsibilities to the government are so poorly defined, the ministry is unable to formulate adequate criteria to evaluate ENI's performance. Furthermore, representatives of the various ministries do not have a significant influence on the boards of directors of state-owned enterprises. Indeed, the spokesperson for the Ministry of State Shareholdings has been accused of being a representative of the large state holding companies in Italy, including ENI, rather than a spokesperson for the government.

In recent years, the Italian parliament has become more actively involved in the affairs of state-owned enterprises; it now approves all company plans and investment programmes. The government has also increased its use of public funds for state-owned company investments. More direct contact between parliamentary committees and state holding companies has strengthened the government's control of ENI and other state-owned enterprises.

Norwegian Statoil and British BNOC are too young to identify clear patterns in their relationships with government. There are, however, certain key factors that affect their control: both Statoil and BNOC want increased independence from their governments; both Britain and Norway are eager to exercise effective controls on their state-owned enterprises.

Statoil is still in the process of consolidating its activities and building experience and competence in the oil industry; but its strategic aims are already discernible. Statoil desires to play a key role in field development and operations, gaining access to domestic goods and services in the oil industry, and engaging actively in downstream operations including transportation, refining and marketing in Norway and abroad. These goals appear to be compatible with the government's goal to make Statoil a fully integrated oil company. However, the achievement of this goal may place Statoil in an extremely powerful position in relation to the Norwegian government and among other Norwegian industries. Cultural and political traditions in Norway have supported a strong central government. Representatives of the private and public sectors have voiced fears that Statoil might become a giant monster, dominating Norwegian economic and political life.

BNOC, on the other hand, has been severely constrained by changing political forces in Britain. British advocates of state-owned enterprises have feared that BNOC's life would be threatened if a Conservative government were in power. In fact, the previous Labour Government allowed BNOC to operate internationally and granted the company a loan of $825 million as a kind of life insurance preventing the possibility of liquidation by a Conservative government. Yet, contrary to liberal speculation, the new Conservative Government of 1979 chose to curb BNOC's activities, not terminate them. Based on past experiences, it can be expected that BNOC's activities will fluctuate depending upon the party in power in the United Kingdom.

Comparisons and Contrasts

The state-owned oil companies of France, Italy, Norway and the United Kingdom share an important characteristic, irrespective of the systems of control under which they operate: all desire expansion into new fields of the oil industry and an increase in market shares. To some extent, the desire to expand may characterize all capital-intensive industries; however, in the case of state-owned oil companies, growth and expansion are particularly crucial. (Research on the differences between public enterprise managers and private enterprise managers may provide insight into why growth and expansion dominate the goals of state-owned enterprises.)

The emphasis on expansion distinguishes public enterprises from private enterprises in the four countries discussed above. Historically, private enterprises in these countries have chosen to remain cautious and conservative rather than involve themselves in risky investments and uncertain business propositions. One explanation for the apparent audacity of state-owned oil companies is that they are not subject to the same set of sanctions as are private enterprises. Dynamic private firms that err in judgement by expanding too fast or misusing funds are punished by the market; they may have to reduce their rate of growth or, in extreme situations, declare bankruptcy. State oil companies, operating under a *raison d'être* that carries them to some extent above market forces, are able to mobilize additional funding in the event of mistaken judgement. As a result, public corporations permit themselves greater risks and higher rates of growth than do private corporations, paying less attention to the most efficient use of resources and capital in deference to other goals.

State-owned oil companies serve multiple interests: they are charged with maximizing profits and achieving national goals. To complicate the matter, governments have conflicting interests: a Ministry of Finance might try to restrict the expenditures of public corporations while a Ministry of Industry might try to encourage investments. Thus, governments have particular difficulty providing clearly defined goals for state-owned enterprises. The absence of clearly defined goals, coupled with the availability of internal funds, permits a considerable amount of managerial autonomy in these public corporations.

In Italy, conflicts between the Ministry of State Shareholdings and the Ministry of Industry reveal a fragmented state: the lack of government consensus on goals for state-owned enterprises allows ENI a high degree of independence. In France, conflicts between the Ministry of Finance and the Ministry of Industry, as well as alleged collusion between the Oil Directorate and state-owned oil companies, have empowered SNEA to act with relative autonomy.

The future of state-owned oil companies will depend in part upon the political culture of the different countries in which they operate. As a class, such companies may experience increased autonomy, given their instincts for expansion and given the evident inability of governments at times either to agree upon goals or to control the complexities of such enterprises.

But state-owned oil companies do not operate in a political and administrative void. With the increasing importance of these companies in many countries, there is also an increasing public and administrative interest in their functioning. This means that in many cases state oil companies will become the subject of increasing pressures to fulfil many different tasks. Their performance, therefore, may well come to be judged by the extent to which they contribute to certain social values, rather than by technical and commercial criteria alone, and hence much more on qualitative than on quantitative criteria.

If there is a shift to social criteria for evaluation, government and political control of state oil companies may well increase. As long as such enterprises are judged on a commercial and technical basis, the companies will tend to have better information than their supervisory agencies. The information that is needed for control by commercial or technical criteria is perforce based upon information provided by the state oil companies themselves. But state oil companies can be selective in their information feedback, and can thus manipulate their supervisory government agencies and reverse the pattern of control. State oil companies have also been known to dominate the control process because numerous government agencies were involved; the situation in France is illustrative of this problem.

A control system that is administered essentially by government and parliament, and that relies upon qualitative standards which rest on political values, can conceivably reduce the power of the state oil companies to dominate the control process. Controls of this sort do not depend on feedback from the companies. Manipulation is made more difficult and political control becomes more feasible. The Italian case seems to some extent to be illustrative of this possibility.

Historically, state oil companies were established because governments did not consider market forces and private enterprise the appropriate instruments for solving certain problems judged to be of prime national importance. Accordingly, it is to some extent inappropriate to judge the performance of state oil companies by the same standards that are usually applied to private oil companies. To a large extent this requires that the initiative for determining the over-all goals of the companies should remain with parliaments and governments, and should not transfer to the companies themselves. But this will not occur until governments and parliaments find an effective means for supervising the performance of state oil companies so that they conform with the objectives of the state.

Notes

1. Christopher Tugendhat and Adrian Hamilton, *Oil – The Biggest Business* (London: Eyre Methuen, 1975), p. 68.
2. Jean Meynaud, 'Rapport sur la classe dirigeante italienne', *Etudes de Science Politique,* vol. 9 (Lausanne: 1964), p. 104f.
3. Kenneth W. Dam, *Oil Resources* (Chicago: The University of Chicago Press, 1976), p. 63.
4. Edward N. Krapels, *Controlling Oil: British Oil Policy and The British National Oil Corporation* (Washington DC: US Senate Committee on Energy and Natural Resources, 1977), p. 26ff.

5. *Ibid.*, p. 32.

6. Patrick Allard, Michel Beaud, Bertrand Bellon, Anne-Marie Levy and Sylvie Lienart, *Dictionnaire des Groupes Industriels et Financiers en France* (Paris: Editions du Seuil, 1978), p. 190.

7. *Ibid.*, p. 45.

8. Bernard Chenot, *Les entreprises nationalisées* (Paris: Presses Universitaires de France, 1972), p. 94f.

9. Romano Prodi, 'Italy', in Raymond Vernon (ed.), *Big Business and the State* (Cambridge, Mass.: Harvard University Press, 1974).

10. Rapport de la commission d'enquête parlementaire, *Sur les sociétés pétrolières opérant en France* (Paris: Union Générale d'Editions, 1975), p. 181.

11. Meynaud, 'la classe dirigeante italienne', p. 90.

10 PUBLIC CONTROL AND CORPORATE EFFICIENCY

Sabino Cassese

Summing up the 1954 Rangoon Seminar on the organization and administration of public industrial enterprises, a United Nations document concluded the following:

> Experience in many countries has demonstrated that it is possible to establish organizational relationships which assure public account-ability without impairing the flexibility necessary for the effective conduct of a public enterprise. The choice is not merely between the equally unsatisfactory alternatives of treating public enterprises as if they were either private commercial companies or traditional government activities. New types of relationships and controls have been developed which reflect the peculiar operating and financial requirements of commercial and industrial undertakings.[1]

A few years later, the French experience disproved the United Nations' optimistic observations. In 1958, speaking at the Fourth World Congress of the International Association of Political Science, Claude Albert Colliard described the inner workings of state-owned enterprises as follows: 'The controls are multiple, confused, crossed, superimposed. They slow down decisions in the enterprises, spread and dilute respons-ibility, limit management's authority without, however, arriving at exemplary sanctions if, eventually, blame or errors are uncovered.'[2] Colliard also concluded that, in many cases, French public enterprises would have had greater success if controls had not existed. A year later, Georges Lescuyer echoed Colliard's conclusions in a book on state control of nationalized industries. Lescuyer observed that 'the lack of precise objectives and means are the essential causes of the failure of state control of the nationalized enterprises'.[3]

Today, not only France but all the advanced industrialized nations have rejected the conclusions of the Rangoon Seminar. It has been observed everywhere that current controls are unsuitable for guiding state-owned enterprises and ineffective for evaluating their activities. On the other hand, it is a growing opinion that, under the weight of controls (as well as the increasing need for the financial intervention

145

of the treasury), state-owned enterprises are becoming increasingly bureaucratic and are losing their peculiar entrepreneurial character. In many countries, the traditional definition of control has drastically changed: we no longer speak only of the obligations of those subject to controls; we also speak of the limits and obligations of those who hold and exercise the power to control.

The search for balance in the control of state-owned enterprises is evidence of the confusion and uncertainty that characterizes current methods of control, an uncertainty reflected in the changes in legislation and control policies of France, Great Britain and Italy.

Historical Background

From 1930 to 1953, controls on state-owned enterprises in France gradually increased. In 1953, a system of *a priori* ministerial approval of enterprise decisions was introduced along with ministerial power to suspend enterprise decisions. But the trend had slowed by 1955. In 1967, the Nora Report, a report produced by a special commission convened by the Prime Minister, proposed a series of measures aimed at 'giving back to the public enterprises a task more in harmony with their entrepreneurial nature, by taking the best possible from the market and [by giving the state-owned enterprises] an autonomy which is indispensable in allowing them to discharge this task'.[4]* The Nora Report proposals were introduced in 1970–71, but shortly thereafter abandoned.

In the 1967 White Paper[5] of the British government on nationalized industries (followed by the report of the Select Committee on Nationalized Industries), the decision was made to treat state-owned enterprises as businesses that had to finance themselves on the market. But this new approach did not last long, partly because of the changing economic situation. Disagreements and uncertainties led the government to step into management operations. In its 1978 White Paper,[6] the government established new guidelines, asserting that public enterprises were to be considered distinct from private enterprises. Decisions regarding their operations were to be left to the management of the enterprises, but the government was to furnish management with both general and specific guidelines. The government also proposed strengthening agency planning (and the controls on it) and introduced

---

* Editors' note: see the essay by E. Leslie Normanton in this volume.

a mechanism for external review.*

Since 1956, the year when the Italian government established its Ministry of State Shareholdings, governmental control of state-owned enterprises has progressively increased, but the effectiveness of these controls has not. In fact, many have regarded the ministry's handling of public enterprises as useless or even counter-productive and have proposed its disbandment.

Thus, the problem of control of state-owned enterprises can be seen from the enterprise's and the state's point of view. For the enterprise, control is viewed as a means of defining the enterprise's objectives; for the state, control ensures the enterprise's conformity with government guidelines. Simplifying matters a great deal, we can say that the changes that have taken place in several countries with respect to the control of state-owned enterprises have addressed problems of both the enterprise and the state. Often controls have proved to be too heavy, diminishing or nullifying entrepreneurial responsibilities. They have also proved unsuitable for the pursuit of public objectives. As a result, confusion has prevailed.[7]

The public enterprises referred to in this study are those at the national level, not the local level, which present different problems. We will treat public enterprises as if they were homogeneous in nature, but we must caution that this is really not the case. Differences in purpose (from bail-out operations to national champions) go side by side with organizational differences (as state agencies, public corporations, joint stock companies with or without private shareholders). Differences in legal capacity (English public corporations must operate within special powers whereas Italian public corporations are not so limited) have an influence; so do differences resulting from the sector in which the enterprise operates. This last element of differentiation is particularly relevant; one need only recall the differences between manufacturing, services (in which monopolistic public enterprises normally operate), banking and the agriculture and food sectors. It is no coincidence that the British White Paper of 1978, cited earlier, underlines at the very start the differences between the two new manufacturing corporations (British Aerospace and British Shipbuilders) and the traditional nationalized sectors (public services).

The situation, therefore, is very complex. When considering the problems of control, one cannot overlook whether a public enterprise is in a position of natural monopoly, part of a group of public corporations or organized as a company with private shareholders. If the

* Editors' note: see the essay by Michael Beesley and Tom Evans in this volume.

public enterprise is a natural monopoly, consumer protection controls must be considered; if it is part of a group of public corporations, the controls of the individual company as well as the group must be considered; as a company with private shareholders, the balance between public and private controls must be considered.

'Control', in the context of this study, refers solely to state controls (by ministries and parliaments, for example), not to other types of controls (by consumers, for example). As a further qualification, only those controls relating to the fact that the enterprise is owned by the state will be considered. For example, controls over the prices of petroleum products or controls exercised in connection with concessions to exploit deposits being directed at both public and private enterprises will be excluded.

Bureaucratic Control

Bureaucratic control is the type of control carried out by the traditional organs of the state using performance criteria designed to measure the state's concerns. This type of control prevails in the older public enterprises, organized originally as autonomous agencies or as organs of the central administration. Because of their autonomous nature, these public enterprises have not developed further since the end of World War II; in almost every country, attempts are being made to replace the few remaining with public agencies.

Bureaucratic control has also been applied to the newer public enterprises, in most cases with rather negative results. The controller in these enterprises has failed effectively to lead; the controlled have refused to be led. As we will see below, the function of controlling state-owned enterprises in France and Italy has frequently been turned around into the activities of advising or defending the interests of the public enterprises subject to control.

Let us consider two cases. In France, state control of public enterprises was introduced in 1935 and subsequently underwent a series of changes. Today, the responsibility for control resides in the Court of Accounts (Cour des Comptes), a court under the Ministry of Economy and Finance. But the Nora Report of 1967 observed that the court's subordination to the ministry was more formal than real. The report stated that the court was staffed by older civil servants and served more as a career outlet for ministry employees than as an agency for control of public enterprises. The controllers, the report found, neither interacted nor received direction from a central source. Each was isolated from the other, and thus controlled as each saw fit. None of the controllers conducted market comparisons (prices, salaries, financing) to judge effectively the enterprise's performance. Over-all, these functionaries (some of whom had been assigned to the same agency for over 15 years) acted more as advocates and defenders of the enterprises than as their controllers.

Italy's Court of Accounts (Corte dei Conti) has experienced many of the same problems as France's Court of Accounts since it began in 1968 to control firms receiving subsidies. Within the Italian court, there is a delegate charged to observe the operations of state-owned enterprises and to report to the court and to parliament. However, the court-appointed delegate does not work together with other members of the court's public agency control department; he serves as a court magistrate, a counsellor of the court, having extensive legal training but little knowledge of budgets and economics. Thus, he 'tries to assert certain rules of conduct for the various actors present in the system of state shareholdings, rather than control concretely the actual results of the financial operations'.[8] Neither the law nor the Court of Accounts dictates the activities of public enterprises. The court contents itself with establishing criteria for the formal regulation of the enterprise's activity. The delegate thus becomes a *de facto* collaborator and adviser to the board of directors of the enterprise and turns to parliament only when he is ignored by the board.

Over-all, bureaucratic controls have not worked. The principal causes of their failure can be found in the inadequacy of bureaucratic control for entrepreneurial organizations. Bureaucratic control, in fact, is best suited to activities carried out according to specific criteria and along lines laid down by the law in advance, where such control serves to evaluate the changes in activities according to predetermined criteria; it does not work if it is applied to an enterprise having many different functions. The fact that bureaucratic controls are ineffective for complex corporations explains why public enterprises have tended to avoid these controls or manipulate them in such a way as to make them work in favour of the enterprise itself.

Control by Direction

In the absence of objective measures to assess the activities of an enterprise, governmental guidelines have provided a means of controlling the performance of the public enterprise. For example, the 1978 British White Paper states that industries expect the government to provide guidelines on industrial policies, economic prospects and if need be, sectoral policies, including any social objectives that affect the allocation of public funds. The government, in turn, expects the industries to provide data on markets, supplies and adequate production. But in actual experience, numerous problems have arisen, and three in particular have direct relevance to our discussion.

The first problem lies in the limits that government has felt in imposing guidelines on public enterprises, a problem that has occurred periodically in Britain. The government has devolved day-to-day management of its enterprises to the respective managements and, according to the 1978 White Paper, has stated that the power to issue general guidelines does not allow a minister to instruct an individual industry on specific matters, regardless of how important the matters may be. Lacking this power, the government has had to resort to informal processes of persuasion. These processes have often provoked conflicts. As a result, the government has concluded that it is necessary to enact a law permitting a minister to intervene on certain matters. This raises important questions. When the guideline power is exercised on specific matters, does it not then lose its special characteristics? Can an organization subject to this type of guideline still be considered an enterprise?

The second problem has had to do with the legitimacy of controlling the management of public enterprises without similarly controlling private enterprises. This issue has been raised in Italy, partly because of the increase in the size of the public economy sector. Several critics have asked whether a government guideline addressed only to part of the economic sector, the public sector, can be a legitimate guideline; others have questioned whether such a guideline creates an excessive differentiation between public and private enterprises. These and similar questions gave rise to the idea of global planning, formulated in 1962 and realized three years later, which called for the establishment of guidelines for all enterprises, both public and private. Naturally, it was assumed that the guidelines of global planning would be more binding on public enterprises. As is commonly known, this strategy failed. Technical difficulties on the part of the government and hostility on the part of the enterprise obstructed the practical application of the first five-year plan and militated against repeating the experience.

The third problem has been that of avoiding the fragmentation of controls over state-owned enterprises — a widely experienced phenomenon. When several government authorities have the power to control a public enterprise, and when each minister is responsible for the public enterprises in his sector, it is extremely difficult both to manage effectively and to guarantee guidance of the public sector. In most countries, public enterprises are controlled by more than one ministry. In several countries, however, the Ministry of Finance predominates. The supremacy of the Ministries of Finance can be explained by recalling the time when public enterprises were merely instruments to guarantee revenue for state treasuries rather than instruments to carry out official economic policies.

France's Commission de Vérification des Comptes des Entreprises Publiques, CVCEP, in its 1967 report, upheld the necessity of having only one organ for co-ordination and guidance of state-owned enterprises. In 1968 the British Select Committee on Nationalized Industries proposed the establishment of a single Ministry of Nationalized Industries. However, the Italian experience with a single controlling ministry, the Ministry of State Shareholdings, established in 1956, does not set a favourable example. Its staff is ill equipped to handle the control of state holdings; in fact the staff appears reluctant to undertake such control of state enterprises. Instead, the ministry acts either as the advocate within the government for state-owned enterprises or as an instrument to enlarge the minister's political following in such enterprises.

Control Through Information

In some cases, governments attempt to maintain control over state-owned enterprises by requiring and publicizing data, particularly financial data, on the operations of such enterprises. An example is Italy's law of 1962 which lays down criteria for drawing up the budgets of the National Board for Electric Power (ENEL). Another example, also in Italy, is the law of 1978 on the parliamentary review of candidates nominated by the government as presidents of public agencies.

Control through information, like other means of control, seems to be experiencing a crisis. An examination of two experiences, one Italian, one French, will illustrate this crisis. Both experiences refer to reports aimed at the public in general and parliament in particular. The parliaments that receive the results of these reports perform more as representatives of the public ('the country's eye') than as decision-making bodies (legislative assemblies).

The law that established the Italian Ministry of State Shareholdings decreed that the ministry should present planning reports in addition to the public enterprises' final accounts to parliament. These planning reports, however, have done nothing to improve public enterprise operations. First, they are usually presented too late. Second, the ministry lacks adequate personnel to prepare the reports; the reports, although ostensibly those of the ministry, are actually drawn up by the personnel of the enterprises under examination. It is obviously in the interest of the enterprise's personnel not to divulge news related to the company's activities and to defend the company's actions. Finally, parliament takes no interest in the reports, neither examining nor debating their findings.

Equally ineffective was France's CVCEP, established in 1948 and abolished in 1976.[9] It lacked authority over certain important categories of enterprises, such as those not in industry and those in which public bodies held a minority interest, and it suffered from insufficient means and personnel to carry out its investigations.[10] After the commission was abolished, the auditing of accounts and management of public enterprises were assigned to the Court of Accounts. It is still too early to assess the performance of the court.

If the traditional control of the formal and bureaucratic type is impossible, and control through guidelines and plans is hard to achieve, hope for the greater visibility of management operations of public enterprises through information control is also unrealistic. As with guideline control, however, the reasons for the failure of information control should be sought chiefly in the inadequacy of the control instruments and in the fact that public enterprises are unwilling to expose their operations to public view.

Market-oriented Control

Market-oriented controls are relatively new attempts at control, developed in response to the partial or total failure of other types of control. Not much is known about these efforts, however, so that evaluation is difficult. Of the many different types of market-oriented controls, the most well known are those introduced through contracts between the state and public enterprises and those set up by introducing competition among different public enterprises.

In Italy, market-oriented control through contracts was applied in the early years after the establishment of the Ministry of State

Shareholdings. These contracts involved the joint determination by the Ministry of State Shareholdings and the managements of enterprises of objectives or policies for enterprises and the subsequent issue of directives by the minister to the enterprises in which the agreement was publicized. A British NEDO study of 1976 also proposed that control be carried out 'by cooperation and agreement'. Only in extreme circumstances were formal guidelines to be issued to the public enterprises. According to the 1978 White Paper, the minister was instructed not to issue specific guidelines without previously consulting the industry concerned. Thus, an agreement became the first form of control; if it failed, specific guidelines were to be called into action.

The Italian experience, however, was brief, and the British experiment is still new. The French experience, on the other hand, has a longer history. The planning contracts in France have their origin in the frequently cited Nora Report. According to the Nora Report, the state's role must be limited to fixing the 'rules of the game'. In 1970 and 1971, agreements were reached with the public electricity, railway and radio enterprises of France. These agreements accorded the enterprises freedom to set tariffs and organize and manage services. Much less freedom existed with respect to new investments. In exchange for a considerable amount of autonomy, the French public enterprises were obliged to meet the objectives set down in their initial agreements with government. In 1974, however, the possibility of abandoning the entire policy of using planning contracts began to be discussed; and after 1977, no further agreements were consummated.[11]

The possibility of controlling public enterprises by having them compete with one another has been much discussed among scholars and politicians. Despite extensive discussions, the approach has been applied sporadically and has yielded few definitive results. Simulating the conditions in the market place and introducing rewards and punishments have long been advocated by Gabriel Ardant and Pierre Mendès-France.[12] The competition between IRI and ENI in Italy over control of the electric enterprises provides the sole example of competition as a means of control.

From Financial Control to Efficiency Control

The persistence and size of the deficit of many public enterprises and their need for financial support from public sources have given financial authorities enormous power over such enterprises. Some may argue that the weaknesses of public enterprises give the financial authorities their strength. Unfortunately, this strength has not been properly used. The power of the purse has always been a source of power *de facto*, unregulated by law. Furthermore, such power has risen or fallen with changes in the economic situation of the sector or enterprise. Finally, as has been observed in France, the power of the purse has not served the interests either of the state or of public enterprises. Government offices have acted independently, causing confusion at the state level and making entrepreneurial management extremely difficult.

The Italian situation is even worse. When state enterprises have no need for financial support from the government, they look on the Minister of State Shareholdings as useless. But when a crisis occurs, the minister becomes the indispensable link between the public enterprises and parliament. Unfortunately, the minister's efforts as mediator have not proved very useful to either the public enterprises or the government. They have proved useful, perhaps, to the minister and the party he represents. As a remedy to some of these problems, when government contributions are made to the enterprises they should be accompanied by legislative indication of how they are to be used. However, such a strategy reduces the public enterprises' discretion in using their allocated capital.

The basis of financial control is the demand by the treasury that funds be used efficiently. Curbing expenses, however, does not necessarily guarantee efficiency. Toward this end, William A. Robson proposed in 1937 the establishment of an 'efficiency audit commission' in England. According to Robson's proposal, the commission should conduct inquiries to achieve three goals: ensuring the efficiency of the public enterprises; ensuring that there is no exploitation of monopolistic positions to the consumer's detriment; and ensuring sound trade union relations. The commission's examination should cover the quality and quantity of the services offered, price policy, bureaucratic efficiency, personnel policy, consumer relations, and costs and financing. No explicit action, however, has been taken on any of these recommendations, though traces of Robson's proposal can be found in the NEDO report of 1976 and in the British government's 1978 White Paper, as well as in France's report on the reform of public establishments prepared by the Conseil d'Etat in 1971.

Conflict in Control

In our overview of the major types of control, we have observed that, in general, existing types of control are ineffective. The exception to this observation is financial control based on the power of the purse. Reactions to the failure of controls have not advocated placing more stringent controls on state-owned enterprises. As discussed earlier, the growing consensus is that limits should be placed on the government's control of public enterprises, and that these limits should be exceeded only if accompanied by proper compensations to the enterprises.

In actual application, such an approach to control encounters numerous difficulties. First, the accounts and operations of the public enterprise should be sufficiently detailed to allow the government as well as the individual enterprise to determine when government-imposed guidelines have been the cause of losses. Second, it is difficult to determine the 'improper charges' imposed by the government on state-owned enterprises. (The extra-agency fees imposed by government were termed 'improper charges' by the Italian State Railway in its budget reports, and by the Italian Institute for the Reconstruction of Industry (IRI) in its 1976 'Closing report of the Technical-Consulting Committee for the areas of loss'.) In France, the Nora Report proposed reversing 'the burden of proof', requiring the government financially to motivate and compensate the public enterprises. However, in France, as in Italy, the compensation mechanism has been purely theoretical.

The countries considered in this study have not succeeded in finding adequate ways to control their public enterprises without destroying the entrepreneurial nature of their industries. Single types of control are clearly ineffective: they are either excessively restrictive or excessively flexible, and they are often transformed into means for public enterprises to exercise their power in government, rather than into means for the government to guide public enterprises.

Notes

1. United Nations, 'Some Problems in the Organization and Administration of Public Enterprises in the Industrial Field' (New York: 1954), p. 31.
2. See the report in *A.A.V.V.*, 'Il controllo dell'impresa publica' (Milano: Vita e Pensiero, 1960), p. 87.
3. Georges Lescuyer, *Le Contrôle de l'Etat sur les Entreprises Nationalisées* (Paris: LGDJ, 1959), p. 316.
4. The Nora Report, 'Rapport sur les entreprises publiques' (Paris: La

Documentation Française, 1967), p. 89.

5. 'Nationalised Industries: A Review of Economic and Financial Objectives', Cmnd 3437 (London: HMSO, 1967).

6. 'The Nationalised Industries', Cmnd 7131 (London: HMSO, 1978).

7. An exemplary illustration of the case is given by P. Bruneau in 'Le contrôle du Parlement sur la question des Entreprises Publiques', in *Revue du Droit Public* (Paris: LGDJ, 1975), p. 1199ff; the general problem of the conflict between autonomy and control was already made clear in W.A. Robson, *Nationalized Industry and Public Ownership* (London: George Allen and Unwin, 1960), p. 138ff.

8. The passage quoted and the evaluations are from D. Serani, 'I controlli esterni sulle partecipazioni statali', in 'Partecipazion Statali: Strategie e Assetto', *Giurisprudenza Constituzionale* (Milano: Giuffrè, 1977), no. 9, p. 107ff.

9. It suffices to read A.G. Delion, *L'Etat et les Entreprises Publiques* (Paris: Sirey, 1959), p. 94ff.

10. For an account of the problem see R. Muzellac, 'Le contrôle de la Cour des Comptes sur les entreprises publiques', in *AJDA* (November 1976), p. 540 *et seq.*

11. See also P.G. Brachet, *L'Etat patron − théories et réalités* (Paris: Syros, no date).

12. See G. Ardant, *Technique de l'Etat − de la productivité du secteur public* (Paris: PVF, 1953); and S. Cassese (ed.), *Note sulle imprese pubbliche in Francia e sulla misura dell'efficienza* (Milano: Ciriec, 1960).

11 ACCOUNTABILITY AND AUDIT

E. Leslie Normanton

This study examines the role of government, or 'state', auditors in the over-all process of accountability and control for state-owned enterprises in three industrialized countries, the United States, the United Kingdom and France. It will show that this role, at least on the European side of the Atlantic, continues to be a highly controversial one; indeed, it is increasingly so. Large-scale expropriation of industry by governments has created new – and often still unsolved – problems for the national auditing bodies, founded many years ago and for very different purposes.

United States

A governmental audit for federal enterprises in the United States was established in 1945, at just the same period when the United Kingdom and France were beginning to nationalize selected industries on a massive scale.

American government corporations, however, were different from their European counterparts. The political creed seeking public owner-ship to eradicate the real or supposed evils of capitalism never became a major force in American political life. There was thus almost no history of 'nationalization' in the sense of taking over existing private enterprise. Instead, by Acts of Congress or by executive order, wholly new corporations were created to respond to specific and often temporary national concerns, such as organizing the home front for two world wars or resurrecting the economy after the great depression.

Between 1933 and 1945, there was a profound increase in the number of government corporations. The New Deal created, among others, the Reconstruction Finance Corporation, the Commodity Credit Corporation and the Tennessee Valley Authority. A great complex of corporations, largely under the financial direction of the Reconstruction Finance Corporation, was charged with reinforcing the national war effort in World War II. The Defense Plant Corporation alone owned over 2,000 factories. By 1945, 58 corporations held combined assets worth $30 billion.

A prolonged controversy raged in the government over the autonomy of public corporations. State-owned enterprises were financially independent of annual appropriations from Congress and were not clearly subordinated to federal departments. Private enterprises feared competition from the government. Congress felt that the public corporations were being used to promote policies without legislative authority or budgetary approval; and its auditing agency, the General Accounting Office (GAO), had almost no powers of scrutiny over their financial affairs.

The Government Corporation Control Act of 1945 gave Congress exclusive power to create government corporations and provided a formula for their financial control, combining a business-type budget with a commercial-type audit to be performed by the GAO. The Act appeared to please all parties. The GAO itself benefited from the creation of a new Corporation Audits Division, the first to employ professional accountants on a large scale and to develop a comprehensive, on-site audit. Eventually the GAO adopted these innovations for all its auditing activities.

For the GAO the audit of state-owned corporations quite soon became almost indistinguishable in terms of procedures from its main task, the auditing of direct federal government services. Such job integration would be impracticable in Europe, where government services and state enterprises are two quite distinct species and have to be treated as such for auditing purposes.

The GAO's audit had a significant impact upon the Reconstruction Finance Corporation, the Panama Canal Company and other important American corporations. But the corporation audit, and probably the corporations themselves, have declined in importance in recent years. Since 1 July, 1974, the statutory requirement for annual corporate audits has been reduced to once every three years.

Today, the GAO nevertheless continues to audit and report on pressing problems facing the public corporations of the United States government. Like most other countries, the United States is now unable to operate rail services profitably. Two large public corporations attempt to keep the trains moving and restore health to the accounts: the National Railroad Passenger Corporation (AMTRAK), and the Consolidated Rail Corporation (CONRAIL). In 1973, the GAO reported that AMTRAK needed to improve its repair and maintenance schedule; during 1972, one-third of its passenger cars had been out of service. By 1978, the GAO reported that, despite new equipment and improved stations and tracks, some AMTRAK routes continued to be highly unprofitable and wasted energy. It was suggested that these routes be abandoned.

The Consolidated Rail Corporation was established in 1976 to acquire six bankrupt railroads, including the once powerful Penn Central. Despite federal funding totalling $3.4 billion, the GAO has expressed doubts that CONRAIL will be able to become profitable in the near future.

The United Kingdom

In the United States the motive for creating government corporations has been expediency: they responded to current needs rather than political ideology. This was also broadly true of state enterprises in Great Britain before 1945; the Port of London Authority (1908), the Central Electricity Board (1926), the British Broadcasting Corporation (1927) and the London Passenger Transport Board (1933) were set up to meet specific needs. They enjoyed as much autonomy and as little public accountability as the early creations of the Roosevelt administration. There was no provision for any sort of audit reporting to government.

In 1945, the Labour Party, which since 1918 had been committed to a policy of 'the progressive elimination from industry of the private capitalist',[1] came to power with a large majority in a country just emerging from a long war. Some industries, especially coal mining and railways, were in a state of serious decrepitude and needed large and immediate transfusions of capital, which were not available from private enterprise.

In the next few years, Acts of Parliament transferred into state ownership – against compensation to the former owners – a whole series of industries and public utilities: coal and civil aviation (1946), railways, electricity, inland waterways and long-distance road haulage (1947), gas (1948) and steel (1949). Many hundreds of thousands of workers became employees of state-owned enterprises.

These great industries were organized as 'public corporations', following basic ideas traceable to the Crawford Committee of 1926 which advised on future arrangements for public radio broadcasting. The committee proposed that the radio services 'should be conducted by a public corporation acting as a trustee for the national interest', and its object would be 'to bring an important industry or service within public control without making it an ordinary government department.[2]

The public corporation is neither part of nor officially subordinate to a government department, nor are its staff civil servants. Although its governing board is appointed by a minister and is subject to the minister's directives when government policy so dictates, it is free from the full and continuous accountability to parliament which applies to a department of state through its minister. The finances of the corporation are separate from those of the government. The public corporation has been called 'a kind of half-way house, attempting to combine public responsibility with freedom for day-to-day operations'.[3]

Moreover — and this concerns us particularly here — although it submits annual reports and professionally audited accounts (the private auditors are appointed by the minister), the corporation, unlike the government corporations in the USA, is exempt from audit by the British state auditing body, the Exchequer and Audit Department (E&AD). In this respect the British nationalized industries are virtually unique; and to some minds, this lack of an audit reporting to parliament and the public represents a very serious defect in the British public enterprise system.

The idea that something resembling a state efficiency audit should accompany nationalization can, nevertheless, be traced in some early writings of British socialist thinkers (Sidney and Beatrice Webb, 1920, and Professor W.A. Robson, 1937[4]).

The test case for the great new post-war corporations was during the preparation and passage of the Coal Industry Nationalization Act, 1946, which led to the first take-over of a major industry. The view of the Conservative Opposition, expressed in an amendment to the Act, was that the minister should transmit the accounts of the new National Coal Board to the chief auditor of the realm, the Comptroller and Auditor General (C&AG), for his examination, certification and report; this would have involved an audit similar to that applied to government departments. But the amendment was defeated by the Labour Government, and the usual statutory requirement adopted in the Nationalization Acts was — and still is — that the responsible minister was required to appoint private auditors and to lay the audited accounts of the corporations before parliament. This procedure in effect follows the audit requirements prescribed for private firms under the Companies Acts; it does not involve any formal examination of the accounts by parliament, nor provide inside information about the corporations' affairs.

It is thus ironic that the party which had favoured nationalization, partly on the ground that it would bring the managements of powerful industries within the scope of public accountability, with all the changes of fundamental motivation which that was expected to imply, was nervous, when the time came for policy decisions, of easy access to information about the industries, which could and would have been exploited by those who opposed nationalization on principle. As one student of the subject put it:

> It is to be expected that Labour members naturally and instinctively set out to prove that the Boards can do no wrong and resent criticism as a form of attack. In the eyes of Conservative members, on the other hand, it is doubtful whether they can do anything right.[5]

This was certainly a factor which militated against the establishment of a state audit able to publish informative and perhaps critical reports about the activities of the SOEs. It is also perhaps true that the Conservatives, who might be happy to obtain reports which could provide political ammunition, paradoxically sympathize with the nationalized boards' desire for secrecy, since that is part of the tradition of management in British private enterprise.

The issue is further obscured by the fact that various alternative devices were provided which tend towards public accountability for the industries. These are sometimes cited as an adequate substitute for a proper public audit.

In parliament, questions addressed to ministers have never been received in the same way as questions about the ministers' own departments; in view of the corporations' considerable independence, the ministers cannot obtain answers directly from their own staffs and they endeavour to avoid all concern with what are called 'matters of day-to-day administration', which may include such momentous concerns as staffing and procurement. Parliament can debate the corporations' own statutory annual reports, although the managements cannot be expected to use these as channels for revelations and self-criticism.

'Nationalization', it has been said 'was not intended primarily to benefit consumers'.[6] However, the major Nationalization Acts provided for consumers' councils, which still exist, although little known by the general public. Nevertheless, despite early allegations of ineffectiveness, they remain part of the official panoply of accountability, and a government White Paper of 1978 expressed a desire to refurbish their image.

The most important channel of accountability, however, is probably the House of Commons' Select Committee on Nationalized Industries, which has been fairly continuously active, at least since 1956, after an experimental start in 1951. At that time the Select Committee recommended that its examination of the nationalized industries be undertaken with the aid of an officer of status roughly equivalent to that of the Comptroller and Auditor General. The C&AG himself was asked whether his department could, or would wish to, undertake the task itself. He replied that he was fully aware of events in the USA in 1945, including the Government Corporation Control Act and the extensive recruitment by the Comptroller General of professional accountants. It was clear that he did not wish to follow suit. The committee did not insist and the matter was dropped. The E&AD did not become professionalized – it was staffed with middle-grade permanent civil servants, recruited in the same way and from the same educational/social group as the equivalent grades in the ministries. Only in the mid-1970s has the department adopted a form of professional-ization: the practice is to enlist young graduates from miscellaneous disciplines and then require them to qualify as associates of a new body, the Chartered Institute of Public Finance and Accountancy (CIPFA).

The Select Committee did not obtain any outside assistance for its inquiries, which have continued on the basis of questions addressed directly to board members, civil servants and other interested parties. In 1968 the committee published a report in which it expressed many arguments for an efficiency audit of the industries and then paradoxically rejected the idea.[7] A retired senior civil servant, Mr Maurice Garner, criticized the Select Committee's attitude:

> The basic mistake . . . was to attach undue weight to the suscept-ibilities of management and insufficient weight to the public interest in the efficiency of management . . . Having opted for managerial autonomy the Committee closed its mind to the necessary corollary; proper accountability.

The National Economic Development Office (NEDO) issued a report in 1976 on the future role and control of nationalized industries, in which it stated the view that the boards were not required to account for their performance in a systematic or objective manner and pointed out that there was no external audit mechanism which might provide reassurance to government and parliament about the effectiveness of management organization and procedures within the industries.

Mr Garner visited France, Sweden and Austria and reported that these
countries were, in their different ways, developing state auditing
institutions which were making substantial progress towards the
objective mentioned by NEDO. He concluded:

> I believe that it will not be possible to judge the quality of the
> industries' strategic direction (including in this the part played by
> Ministers) and also intelligently assess the industries' current
> performance until an institution has been created to undertake
> these tasks and been provided with the necessary independence,
> powers and resources for what would be a regular effectiveness and
> efficiency audit of each board . . .

In the mean time the government had published a White Paper in
answer to NEDO, in which it declined to make any innovation in the
domain of external audit, and maintained that it was 'the responsibility
of each Board to monitor performance and efficiency within its
industry', whilst recording in its annual report information on how it
was measuring up to its objectives. Here we have a curious doctrine
of self-monitoring and self-audit; whoever is to control managers and
administrators, and render them publicly accountable, it can scarcely
be themselves; nor can they satisfactorily fill the broad role of judges
of their own success or failure.

Since July 1977, when the Expenditure Committee of the House of
Commons made a sharp criticism of the whole of the existing state
auditing arrangements in the United Kingdom, which it described as
out of date,[8] the specific problem of audit for state enterprises has
become part of a wider debate about the reform of state audit in general.

The findings of the Expenditure Committee on the need for such
reform were supported by the Commons' Select Committee on
Procedure in July 1978.[9] The veteran Committee of Public Accounts
recommended that the C&AG should be given access to the books and
records of two very important public enterprises of recent creation, the
National Enterprise Board and the British National Oil Corporation.[10]

For the first time in many years, the reform of state audit in Great
Britain is a subject of intense debate, in parliament and the civil service
and in the press. On 18 January 1979, the then Secretary of State for
Industry announced that the government had decided to put in hand a
study of the C&AG's present role, with a view to 'fresh legislation
defining more directly and explicitly' his responsibilities in modern
conditions. The change of government following the General Election

of May 1979 has not halted the process and a further announcement of government policy on state auditing reform has been made.[11]

It is, however, too early to say whether the specific problem of the nationalized industries will, as part of a general change, be solved by the creation at an early date of a strong, learned and tactful efficiency audit body, staffed by persons with administrative experience and high qualifications in a variety of disciplines (those of the private accountancy profession alone will not suffice), and charged to study the endless problems of the nationalized sector. But this paper does maintain that such a creation would provide a greatly improved and constantly available form of public accountability, which would make a major contribution to parliamentary, ministerial, public and even managerial understanding of state-owned enterprises.

France

With some minor exceptions, nationalization in France began during the Popular Front government of 1936–37, which took over the armaments industries and the railway system (SNCF). But, as in Britain, the main series of nationalizations followed closely upon the Second World War: the Banque de France, the four great deposit banks, Renault and Air France (1945), coal, gas, electricity and 34 insurance companies (1946), and the two leading steamship lines (1948).

Control over this great complex of enterprises quickly became a political question. In March 1947, parliament created by law two sub-committees charged 'to follow and evaluate the administration of the public enterprises', and equipped them with very wide powers of investigation. However, 'citing the necessity of administrative autonomy for the enterprises, and even in some cases the imperatives of commercial secrecy and the dangers of a confusion of responsibilities, the government has generally sought to limit the parliamentary prerogatives'.[12]

One possible solution would have been to charge the French national audit body, the Cour des Comptes, with control of the state enterprises, and, indeed, as early as 1927 the Cour had proclaimed in a report that it should have such control.

The Cour des Comptes is a unique body, founded in its present form by Napoleon in 1807 and recruited for many years largely from aristocratic families, or such members of them as had passed through the *grandes écoles* of Paris, institutions of a prestige far above that of the mere university. The members of the Cour are classed as magistrates with irremovable status, rather than simple officials, since the Cour is quite literally a court of law, and is equated with the highest court of appeal. It exercises a jurisdiction of very ancient origin, the judicial audit of the accounts of the receiving and paying officers of the treasury service, the *comptables* of France, who alone are entitled to hold public funds. But this venerable function, from which the Cour derives its judicial dignity and ceremonial, is increasingly difficult to reconcile with the working requirements of a modern audit office.

The solution adopted by a law of 1948 was the creation of a new body, the Commission de Vérification des Comptes des Entreprises Publiques (CVCEP). This was a compromise because, although the commission was autonomous, the Cour des Comptes provided its president and its senior deliberative personnel. It was 'a technical organization sheltered from political influence to the greatest possible extent', and for a generation it was the standard bearer of public accountability for French state enterprise; after November 1958, when the Fifth Republic of General de Gaulle suppressed the sub-committees of parliament, the CVCEP was more or less alone in the field.

The law prescribed that it should regularly address an individual report on the accounts of each enterprise to the ministers concerned, containing comments as appropriate and 'an opinion as to the quality of the commercial and financial management of the enterprise'; this was a confidential document, released only to designated members of parliament under controlled conditions.

The commission was also charged to produce a general report for publication, which was to contain, when required, recommendations for organizational changes in the enterprises and 'an opinion as to their prospects for the future'. The CVCEP published, altogether, 14 such general reports before its functions were terminated in 1976. The commission earned a reputation for impartiality, and its relations with the heads of the enterprises were good. But there were doubts as to its profundity, the main reason for which was constantly stressed by the CVCEP itself. It was never given authority or funds to recruit a permanent auditing staff. It had to make do with a fairly small and changing group of 'rapporteurs', bright but unspecialized young men on loan from the *grands corps* and the technical civil service. This part-time base always exposed the commission to the risk and the charge of superficiality; it admitted that its control was 'relatively light'. The problem of staffing was never solved.

This was probably no accident, since the commission was

administratively subordinate to the Ministry of the Economy and Finance, which denied it an adequate budget. The ministry also limited extensions of its control which were called for by the evolution of the public sector, which became extremely ramified as state enterprises created their own subsidiaries and invested in those of others. The CVCEP was unable to make much penetration here; yet for a long period the government refused all notable improvements in its procedures and resources.

Finally, in November 1975, the Minister of the Economy and Finance admitted the idea of reform; he agreed to consider the transfer of the commission's functions to the Cour des Comptes. Legislation in 1976 extended the competence of the Cour 'to the whole of the industrial and commercial public sector, to the limit of its most extreme ramifications', wherever the total of all public shareholdings exceeded 50 per cent of its capital, or the state had effective authority through majority representation on its board. The intention is to conserve, as far as possible, the familiar methods of the commission, and particularly its so-called 'contradictory procedure', which means that reports are finalized only after frank discussion with top management.

This reform involves a heavy new task for the Cour des Comptes, which received assurances both from parliamentarians and the minister that adequate staff reinforcements would be forthcoming. The number of divisions (*Chambres*) in the Cour was increased from five to seven, but until recently the new posts created were insufficient. In any case, the expansion of such a small elite corps as the magistracy of the Cour must create personnel problems and encounter the fear of 'dilution'. Moreover, the members of the Cour are men of learning but not qualified commercial accountants. They have to cultivate relationships not only with parliament, the committees of which are again active, but with the accounting firms who audit some of the SOEs. And the problem of the borrowed young 'rapporteurs' still exists. Whether the government is fully sincere in wanting a powerful audit of the public sector remains to be seen. The system has much to recommend it, but is short of manpower.

Like the GAO, the Cour has reported (already) upon that very tenacious problem, the profitability of state-owned rail transport. According to the report, there has been, in the 1970s, a rapid rise in deficits, and the state's agreement of 1969, under which the SNCF was to break even in 1974, has failed and been almost forgotten. There has been a steep and general increase of the cost to the public in subsidies. Some were to compensate for reduced fares decided by the state for 'large families, the poor, those entitled to annual holidays, the military, the scholars, students and apprentices, the children on excursions'. These corresponded, said the Cour, 'less to the application of logical criteria than to practices accumulated over half a century'.

The Paris suburban services were heavily in the red, and the local authorities, who were supposed to bear 30 per cent of the deficit, objected on the grounds that they were insufficiently associated with the original decisions.

But, despite subsidized tariffs, traffic had fallen, and the effects of the economic crisis were worse than for other forms of transport, especially in the freight sector. The over-all financial consequences were critical: 'these subsidies, which already represent the equivalent of the product of the SNCF's own operations, and nearly 5 per cent of the State's budget, will reach, unless some new element intervenes, a level difficult to accept.'

The SNCF could not be guaranteed, in all circumstances, against all possible losses and miscalculations.

> If the present tendency is confirmed . . . and appears to have long-term causes arising from changes in transport techniques, its influence on the State budget could lead to a total re-examination of the operating conditions of the railways and their relations with the State.[13]

Conclusion

The problems of public accountability for SOEs appear to have two elements in common, judged by those countries which we have considered. First, there is a very widespread feeling, an assumption, that public enterprises should be subject to a degree of public accountability. They cannot be left with the same degree of independence and secrecy of decision making as companies in full private ownership − indeed, if they were, there would be little point in taking them away from such ownership. It follows that the commercial type of audit, undertaken by fee-earning professional accountants, cannot suffice (though it may have a role to play), since private firms are themselves subject to this necessary but uninformative discipline.

Political and public opinion demands more: but within limits. There is a second widely shared assumption, counter to the first; this is that managements appointed with a commercial objective, even by governments, need a degree of freedom to make decisions, to take risks and confound their competitors (if they have any). They should, it is felt, have a wider independence than that of traditional departments of state, which owe direct obedience to a minister who is himself responsible to his political chiefs and often to a parliament. It is not impossible to conduct commercial affairs through such ministerial machinery; some countries, including West Germany and India, run their railways in this way, and Britain for many years applied it to the Post Office — various countries still do.

But the method is going out of fashion, and the vast majority of SOEs in countries with mixed economies are now directed by corporate boards with varying degrees of autonomy and outside the direct ministerial and civil service hierarchies.

So the common feeling about public accountability calls for a compromise: more accountability than that of private companies but rather less than that of ministerial departments. It is a compromise which some countries, including Britain and to a lesser degree France, have found exceedingly difficult to attain.

Since commercial-type auditing is insufficient, if not irrelevant, something must be added to augment the accountability up to the nationally desired level of compromise. Britain exhibits a whole range of choices: parliamentary questions and debates, annual reports and accounts published by the corporations, consumers' councils and the Select Committee on Nationalised Industries.[14] Other countries, while not necessarily neglecting some of these expedients (or substitutes), have preferred to depend chiefly upon their existing state audit departments.

Unaided parliamentary committees on SOEs, and not least that in the United Kingdom, have on occasions carried out an impressive and useful job of fact finding about the problems of specific industries. But such committees have defects. Lacking investigatory staffs, they must rely upon questioning the heads of industries: a report on any one may be based upon thousands of questions and answers, posed over a period of many months, and this can be an exhausting and distracting experience for the top management. The crucial disadvantage, however, is that examination by such a committee must be a rare event, falling on a given industry only once in many years. Public accountability, however, requires a sustained and regular flow of information and a frequent monitoring of performance.

Thus, the countries which have relied principally upon their national audit departments have been wise to do so. None of these departments, except perhaps the GAO, faced with a limited public sector, has yet fully resolved the difficulties posed by such a (to them) unfamiliar type of audit. Very few have sufficient staffs, so they may have to work in co-operation with professional auditors undertaking the bulk of the financial audit. But financial audit is not all that is needed; parliaments and the public require information about management problems, and generally about things which go wrong and call for corrective action. This is the true field of the state's own auditors, because they — in contrast to the private professionals — are trained in, and accustomed to, a long tradition of auditing with detailed, critical and impartial public reporting as its specific and principal objective.

Notes

1. Labour Party pamphlet, *Labour and the New Social Order* (1918).
2. W. Thornhill, *The Nationalized Industries: An Introduction* (London: Nelson, 1968), pp. 19–20.
3. *Ibid.*, p. 20.
4. Sidney and Beatrice Webb, *A Constitution for the Socialist Commonwealth of Great Britain* (London: Longmans Green, 1920); W.A. Robson, *Nationalized Industry and Public Ownership*, 2nd edn (London: Allen and Unwin, 1962), p. 203.
5. R. Kelf-Cohen, *Twenty Years of Nationalization: The British Experience* (London: Macmillan, 1969), p. 157.
6. *Ibid.*, p. 266.
7. Select Committee on Nationalized Industries (SCNI), 1st Report (Session 1967–68) (HC 371-1), paras 6, 7, 292, 782–7.
8. Expenditure Committee, 'The Civil Service', 11th Report (Session 1976–77) (HC 535-1), pp. 45–8.
9. Select Committee on Procedure, 1st Report (Session 1977–78) (HC 588-I), Ch. 8.
10. Public Accounts Committee, 8th Report (Session 1977–78) (HC 621): 'Accountability of Statutory Boards to Parliament'.
11. Green Paper, 'The Role of the Comptroller and Auditor General', presented to Parliament by the Chancellor of the Exchequer, Cmnd 7845 (March 1980).
12. Maurice Bernard, Conseiller Maître à la Cour des Comptes, *Le Contrôle des Entreprises Publiques, 1976.*
13. Cour des Comptes, Rapport au Président de la République (1978), pp. 73–8.
14. This has now been superseded by a new system of committees set up to scrutinize the activities of the major departments and their associated public bodies; these committees may establish a joint sub-committee to consider the affairs of the nationalized industries.

12 STATE TRADING

M.M. Kostecki

The implications of state trading for the economic and political relations of the industrialized countries is the focus of this study. 'State trading', in this context, refers to exports and imports conducted by agencies, enterprises and boards that are either state managed, state controlled, or both.[1] The study deals with state-trading agencies of the OECD area (Organization for Economic Cooperation and Development) and South Africa, including such diverse bodies as the Canadian Wheat Board, France's petroleum companies, the Wine and Spirit Company Ltd of Sweden and the State Fishing Equipment Corporation of Norway.

Three characteristics of state trading can be identified. First, objective functions and constraints imposed upon state traders by governments differ from those imposed upon private traders. Private traders are essentially free to determine the basket of their imports and exports; they decide at what prices to buy and sell. They may also determine other terms of foreign trade transactions.

State-trading agencies are much more restricted and are often subject to governmental directives that determine their business behaviour. Government's periodic instructions and imposed foreign trade prices or trade levels will be referred to as foreign trade targets.

General targets fix foreign trade levels for all potential trading partners *en bloc;* specific targets fix foreign trade levels for particular groups of countries, a particular country, or even a particular transaction. Foreign trade targets can implement protection, introduce discrimination or effect sudden, unpredictable changes in the level and direction of trade.

Second, state-trading agencies may receive special forms of public subsidy. In fact, their initial capital is often provided partially or totally by the government. Many state-trading enterprises also rely on more permanent financial links with the state treasury. When a state-trading agency suffers a loss, budgetary transfers equivalent to subsidies are used to maintain the agency's accounting balance. When a state-trading agency shows profits, transfers equivalent to tax payments take place. State-trading agencies also enjoy important tariff or tax exemptions, preferential transportation rates and other privileges

170

that are equivalent to subsidies.

Third, many state-trading agencies benefit from a monopoly status in their country's foreign trade system. State-trading monopolies separate domestic from foreign markets: domestic and foreign prices for a given range of products assigned to a particular agency are not necessarily linked.

There are two types of state-trading monopolies: one uses a single trading firm; the other uses target contracting. In target contracting, a central agency fixes prices and traded quantities, but private traders execute the foreign trade operations. The Egg Marketing Authority in New Zealand, the Banana Board and Milk Board of South Africa and, to a limited extent, the Australian Wheat Board practise target contracting.

Under state trading, quantities, prices and other terms of foreign trade transactions may become instruments of commercial policy. These instruments may be more efficient than tariffs, subsidies, quotas or other traditional trade controls. Whereas trade controls may encourage or discourage state traders to act, targets force state traders to act.

In the industrialized countries, state-trading operations respond to domestic objectives including price stabilization, expansion of domestic output, revenue support for domestic producers, maximization of government income, the strengthening of national defences and the maintenance of national health. External objectives include the use of international price-making power, linking trade with international politics, reducing overhead costs of foreign trade operations and fulfilling international commitments on quantities and prices. How the objectives are ranked has an important impact on the type of state-trading technique used. This study focuses on the implications that a particular choice of objectives and the state-trading techniques involved may have on commercial relations among the industrialized countries.

Foreign Trade

Agricultural products account for a major part of state trading by the industrialized countries. The history of agricultural state trading dates back at least to a state corn monopoly in ancient Rome, recorded in Gibbon's *Decline and Fall of the Roman Empire*. State export boards and state agencies importing agricultural products have flourished in this century in response to the economic crises of the 1920s, 1930s and the post-war period. South Africa today has 22 export marketing boards in agricultural products, New Zealand has eight and Australia has seven. Canada, too, trades heavily in agricultural products. The most important exporter of agricultural products, the United States, has not engaged in state trading since the early 1970s. However, in the 1960s, state trading in grain placed the United States among the major state traders in international markets. Today, Japan, Austria, Finland, Switzerland, France and Norway rank among the major agricultural state traders.

Petroleum, coal, iron and other minerals also account for a significant share of state trading. In these products, state trading is closely related to public ownership of mining industries, the government's desire to control mineral exports and, in a few cases, the government's concern for securing adequate supplies for the population (e.g., petroleum). The 1973-74 oil crisis made the governments of oil-dependent countries more aware of the risks involved in securing external oil supplies. To protect their interests, state-trading arrangements were introduced by France, Italy, Japan, Spain, Sweden and West Germany.

To remain in business, several industries and their related foreign trade operations have come under state ownership. The foreign trade operations of the National Coal Board in the United Kingdom and comparable operations in the coal industry in West Germany, Belgium, France and Japan are examples of government rescue projects.

It is often claimed that advanced countries do little state trading in industrial goods. However, given the total or partial public ownership of shipbuilding enterprises in West Germany, Italy, Spain, Sweden and the United Kingdom, it may be said that state trading exists in the international trade of these goods. In Austria, Belgium, Finland, Italy and the United Kingdom, the government owns part of the motor industries. In most of the major developed countries, the state either owns or tightly supervises the steel industries. Industrial equipment is also exported to developing countries under government contracts and channelled through state agencies as economic aid programmes or arrangements in industrial co-operation. Thus, governments control outputs, look for export contracts and provide financial backing. It is difficult to distinguish between state trading and private trading when the private and public sectors are so totally enmeshed.

A number of developed countries hold monopolies on alcoholic beverages and tobacco. State trading of these goods has for years proved profitable to state treasuries. Governments have chosen not to switch to an explicit tax system to secure revenue from drinkers and smokers.

The General Agreement on Tariffs and Trade (GATT) reports that state-trading agencies account for approximately 8 per cent of the imports and 2 per cent of the exports of the industrialized countries. The GATT, however, underestimates the extent of state trading by the developed market economies. Including the industries discussed above, it can be estimated that state trading accounts for 10 to 15 per cent of the foreign trade generated by advanced economies.

Domestic Objectives

For many state-trading agencies, exports and imports are determined first by domestic issues. Price stabilization, output expansion, revenue support and treasury income take priority over possible gains from trade and international market conditions. Most state-trading agencies, as well as many nationalized industries, plan their programmes in consideration of the larger macroeconomic concerns of production, distribution and foreign trade monopoly. This is especially true for agricultural agencies such as the Australian Dairy Corporation, the Grain Equalization Board of Austria and the Swiss Butter Supply Board.

Governments often claim they maintain state trading to assure stabilization of domestic agricultural prices — producer prices, consumer prices, or both. Price stabilization, however, is often linked with other domestic policy goals. As a result, it is difficult to assess its specific implications. The foreign trade of rice by the Food Agency in Japan and grains by the State Granary of Finland are examples of state trading for domestic price stabilization.

State trading, though widely used, is not required to achieve domestic price stabilization. Many industrialized countries prefer to divest their surpluses through private trading firms subject to more or less traditional trade control measures.

The economics of domestic price stabilization assume that self-sufficiency in a product is the aim of the country. A product is sold at a fixed domestic price; accidental surpluses are exported. Thus, foreign trade serves as an adjustment lever permitting the equilibrium of domestic supply and demand at a desired price level in domestic markets.

A state-trading agency exporting domestic surpluses has little bargaining power on international markets: it is forced to sell its surpluses at almost any price. Its bargaining power for imports is also rather weak. Thus, state-trading agencies operating to support domestic target prices need to be closely linked to the state treasury through a system of budgetary transfers. If the domestic target price exceeds the world market price, the state-trading agency can show excess profits when importing and suffer losses when exporting. When the responsibility for domestic consumer prices and exports lies with the same state-trading agency, budgetary transfers equal to export subsidies are not always required to compensate for export losses. Indeed, the agency may maximize its revenue in the domestic market, minimize its losses in foreign markets, and still show profits. This happens, of course, at the expense of domestic consumers.

State trading to promote domestic price stabilization is likely to increase the danger of market disruption in markets to which surpluses are exported. While the undernourished populations of some developing countries may welcome low export prices, the countries' producers may not. Marginal producers may be put out of business through cheap imports and aid programmes. As a result, there may be greater hunger when surpluses from industrialized countries are no longer available. This constitutes one of the major problems of agricultural trade among the industrialized countries and creates a difficult issue for the trade policies of developing countries.

Domestic price stabilization through state trading may imply greater international price instability, particularly when shortages or surpluses appear simultaneously in the major producing and consuming countries. The favourable prices at which food products have been bought on international markets are partly attributable to the weak bargaining power of state-trading agencies selling surpluses. Countries able to tighten or expand their domestic demand in response to available surpluses, therefore, benefit on the international market.

Many stabilization programmes set domestic target prices higher than expected equilibrium prices. Target prices are usually determined through a domestic bargaining process. As is often the case, a small group of individuals with much to lose will be more outspoken than a large group of individuals with seemingly little to lose. Thus, consumers tend to be the losers in every price battle as long as prices remain within a certain range. The political debates of the 1930s reveal that many governments considered state-trading monopolies to be a relatively costless (in terms of treasury income) way of satisfying producers' demands.[2]

A state-trading agency confronted with a domestic demand less elastic than a foreign demand may equalize the marginal production cost with marginal revenue separately in foreign and domestic markets. This strategy is equivalent to taxing domestic consumption to the advantage of domestic producers. The use of a state-trading agency rather than tax and trade controls, however, is frequently preferred by governments, for three major reasons.

First, implicit taxation of consumers may be more desirable for both political and procedural reasons than explicit taxation: monopoly profit is less visible and consequently receives less opposition than an imposed sales tax.

Second, a state-trading agency does not cost the state treasury much in terms of actual income, though it may be costly in terms of opportunities for taxation. Government has only to establish the agency and lend state power to reinforce its monopoly on the domestic market and in the foreign trade system.

Finally, farm producers prefer a revenue support system based on target prices rather than explicit subsidies. Subsidies require governmental appropriations and expenditures whereas target prices do not.

These three factors explain the existence of a number of state-trading agencies in the industrialized countries where both domestic price policy and export monopolies are the responsibility of state-backed central agricultural boards. The discriminatory price policies used by some of these agencies are evident in the grain-pricing strategies of several state-trading agencies in the late 1960s and early 1970s.[3]

In addition to revenue support, governments of advanced countries tend to support domestic output expansion policies. Here, too, state trading is commonly preferred to explicit subsidies to monitor domestic production. For example, a high-cost industry such as steel may be nationalized to protect against a sudden decline in the market. In the industrialized countries, farm production is rarely nationalized; however, state trading is often introduced somewhere in the distribution chain. The state-trading agency that monitors domestic production will meet the marginal social cost rather than the higher individual cost with marginal revenue from foreign markets. Output and exports will thus expand.[4]

The output expansion policies of the developed countries' agricultural sectors often reflect a lack of concern for world agricultural trade. In the early 1970s, for example, government-to-government sales of European Economic Community (EEC) butter were conducted at about one-third of the domestic producer price. French wheat has recently been exported at 50 per cent of the internal EEC price. At the end of 1977, New Zealand's Dairy Board held 67,000 tons of unsold butter in Britain despite the fact that New Zealand dairymen produce at approximately one-third the cost of their European counterparts. In general, governments prefer to subsidize exports rather than domestic consumption. A move towards shared responsibility for the management of the interdependent economies of the industrialized countries may well benefit international agricultural trade.

Industrialized countries, as a general rule, prefer to use taxation rather than state trading to collect revenue for the treasury. Nevertheless, a number of state-trading arrangements are maintained for products that have a relatively inelastic demand, including alcoholic beverages, tobacco, salt and matches.

A fiscal monopoly will try to maximize its income using its power as a monopolist. It will sell at a higher price than would be generated by a competitive domestic market. To maintain that price, the monopoly will find itself obliged to reduce imports below the free trade level. However, most fiscal monopolies do not follow policies designed to maximize their incomes. When monopolized sales are in part imported and in part produced domestically, state-trading agencies tend to favour domestic producers and pay higher prices. Since domestic supplies tend to be less elastic than foreign supplies, favouring domestic producers is clearly inconsistent with maximizing treasury revenue.

Still, fiscal monopolies today present a serious problem to international trade. Many fiscal monopolies for tobacco and alcoholic beverages impose mark-ups on imported products considerably higher than those on domestic output. For example, the liquor monopolies of Ontario and Quebec, Canada, have imposed mark-ups on imported wines 40 per cent higher than those on competing domestic wines.

Public health and security control are other domestic issues that promote state trading. The state monopoly on opium traded for medical purposes by the Japanese Ministry of Health and Welfare and the Norwegian Medical Import Centre trading in pharmaceutical products and drugs are examples of trading for public health control. The industrialized countries, in general, agree on the necessity of state trading for these purposes.

International Monopoly Power

Many state-trading agencies in industrialized countries benefit from some degree of price-making power on international markets. It appears that certain types of state trading may be better than tariffs in exploiting a country's price-making power. (See Appendix.)

In theory, a government whose economy has a monopoly in a given product in world markets could limit the volume of its sales and levy a tax on its exports that coincides exactly with the sales and mark-up policies of a monopolist. In practice, however, a state-trading monopoly is expected to perform better than a series of such regulatory measures. There are several explanations for this expectation. State-trading agencies usually specialize in one product, whereas ministries are more likely to work with a larger range of issues affecting different products and markets. Moreover, export performance usually affects state-trading manager pay levels; normally, no such link exists between the salary of a ministry employee and tariff revenue. Finally, state-trading agency managers have much greater flexibility in responding to changing market conditions than have trade ministries. Tariff changes are usually subject to complex, time-consuming procedures. Government manoeuvres regarding tariffs are limited by international tariff commitments, fear of retaliation or a complicated interplay of domestic pressure groups. In many cases, centralizing the decisions concerning prices, quantities and export marketing helps to maintain market equilibrium.

Establishing a state monopoly, especially when many producers are involved, may be the only realistic way to ensure that a country will benefit fully from its monopoly power. Such a state-trading agency should be free of foreign trade targets. A profit tax rather than an export tariff should be used to transfer the major part of the monopoly gain from the state-trading agency to the state budget. If these two requirements are fulfilled, the use of a country's price-making power will depend exclusively on the performance of the state-trading agency. In many cases, state-trading agencies use the familiar tactic of discriminating between monopolists, setting different prices for different markets. The economics of market-splitting strategies rely on the principle that a state-trading agency may do better equalizing returns from different foreign price markets or outlets than exploiting its monopoly power against a single world market. The Australian State Egg Board, for example, clearly uses its power to implement discriminatory export pricing. The Sugar Board in Australia also discriminates in pricing among its sugar importers. Application of this strategy, however, is only possible when there are barriers to the movement of goods between the different markets.

In addition, state-trading agencies are found implementing the terms of various bilateral trade agreements or government-to-government contract sales. Some of the purchases under long-term contracts by Eastern Europe from India of iron ore are good examples of bilateral state-trading arrangements to secure stable supplies.

The arrangements by which the New Zealand Dairy Board sells butter on the United Kingdom market also have included market-splitting policies employing specific targets. As soon as the industrialized countries started squeezing the New Zealand board out of the United Kingdom market, New Zealand began scrambling for new markets. The New Zealand government concluded bilateral contracts and established offices in developing countries. Government action, in this case, was probably much more efficient than what would have resulted had the board been left to recover on its own.

In some cases, a state-trading agency is introduced to re-establish a balance of bargaining power with another country's monopoly. The Meat Marketing Board of New Zealand, for example, was created to protect their meat producers from the effects of the buying practices of London marketing enterprises. Several state-trading agencies in Japan were established in part to restore the balance of bargaining advantages with exporting monopolies in Australia, New Zealand and some of the developing countries.[5]

Several smaller regulatory boards in New Zealand and South Africa have established their export targets to benefit from the relatively inelastic international demand; however, they confine the execution of specific export operations to private trading firms. The provincial government of Alberta, Canada, recently introduced an arrangement for potassium essentially equivalent to minimum export pricing.

Thus, state-trading arrangements may be useful devices in exploiting a country's price-making power on international markets. However, the realities of international trade are usually more complex than the factors considered here. Foreign trade targets are used frequently in the company of price-making power, for they permit governments to make commitments on quantities and prices to achieve the desired stability of bilateral relations. This stability may be indispensable if the importing country is to engage important resources in developing an industry in the exporting country.

One of the results of implementing state-trading practices such as market-splitting strategies will be to bring more and more of the world's trade in minerals under long-term contracts. Here, the role of state trading parallels that of multinational enterprises; accessibility to supplies is desired even when additional costs are involved. As a consequence, the international open market for these commodities is relatively small.

Accordingly, stability in bilateral trading may mean greater instability for the free international market. If important bilateral arrangements suddenly fail, the market may show sudden excessive price fluctuations; when shortages or surpluses occur, they will first affect quantities and prices of free trade rather than those regulated by long-term contracts.

Trade and International Politics

State trading is commonly used as the means of linking politics with trade. Trade is used for political objectives, particularly when monopoly or monopsony power in international markets is involved; it can rarely be used effectively when a country is buying or selling in a competitive market. The recent history of international trade in oil and agricultural products includes many illustrations of the use of commercial pressure for political ends.

State trading is particularly useful to governments that are trying to enlist politicians in support of their programmes for economic development. Governments of some developing countries prefer to seek favourable terms of supply for foreign industrial equipment and firm government commitments directly through government channels and state trading rather than through private business contracts. This preference may be explained in part by the fact that government officials in the developing countries feel more at ease negotiating with their political counterparts in the industrialized countries than dealing with businessmen. It may also be explained in part by the fact that development programmes by the government require a commitment to prices and other conditions of supply. In any case, the preference of some developing countries for dealing on a government-to-government basis has created a dilemma for some of the industrialized countries. Should governments establish state-trading agencies to channel exports of industrial equipment to the developing countries or are less structured arrangements more desirable?

Some developed countries, such as Canada and France, maintain quasi-state-trading centralized agencies to handle industrial co-operation with the developing world. The Canadian Commercial Company, for example, exports certain products under government contracts or programmes of economic aid. New quasi-state-trading arrangements are also likely to develop in some EEC member countries in response to the government-guided approach to north–south trade co-operation.

Although developing countries seem to favour the flow of industrial equipment through government-to-government channels, such a strategy contains certain risks. Government-to-government contracts are strongly influenced by political considerations. Favourable export terms are often linked to assurances of reciprocal supplies of raw materials or political favours. State trading increases the possibility that trade will be an extension of the political bargaining process.

Foreign Trade and Economies of Scale

Economies of scale in foreign trade operations are possible when a country's exporters or importers are replaced by a single trading enterprise. Under certain conditions, establishing a central agency to commercialize a country's products abroad necessitates the use of compulsory government power. In many cases, state trading appears to be the only device that reduces the overhead cost of foreign trade operations.

Centralized marketing is particularly important in the agricultural sector where many producers, dispersed over a large territory, are unable to combine their efforts to engage in foreign trade. A central state-trading agency or a central export-marketing board allows producers of some given export to share both the costs and the benefits of overseas promotion; at the same time, it reduces the risks of duplication of effort that might occur if individual exporters independently promoted their products. Moreover, the handling of large export volumes by a single export firm has resulted in significant economies of scale in shipping, port handling, brokerage and insurance; this has been an important consideration for countries located far from their traditional export markets, where marketing costs comprise an important part of the export price.

Centralized marketing at times facilitates vertical integration between production activities and marketing abroad. Farmers deliver their products to a purchasing station. Exportable products are stored, graded, processed, packed and transported to a port gate. Exporters operate from the port gate to the foreign market. Co-ordinating these activities is particularly important if goods are perishable; establishing a state-trading agency often assures the proper co-ordination.

A single state agency pooling a large volume of exports may be more successful than private trading in establishing standard quality grades which, in turn, will affect commodity pricing. When huge export quantities are involved, shipments are better organized and scheduled. Moreover, a centralized market affords an agency sufficient funds to own facilities for shipping, storing or packing. This includes agreeing to terms on heavy investments that a private investor would be unable to assume. In countries such as Australia, Canada, New Zealand and South Africa, export income from agricultural products accounts for an important percentage of producers' revenue and constitutes a significant proportion of these countries' foreign exchange earnings.

Prospects and Recommendations for International Action

State trading allows the advanced industrialized countries to stabilize domestic prices, implement revenue support policies and expand domestic output. International arrangements designed to deal with state trading of agricultural products need to rely upon international co-ordination of both trading and domestic policies.

The efforts of government to use state trading to prevent industries from having to close their doors raise a difficult problem. Governments have a tendency to risk unfair commercial behaviour on international markets to reduce the ill effects of lower domestic production. To avoid unfair practices, it may be helpful to incorporate state-trading activities into the international codes on subsidies, dumping and market disruption.

Another problem of state trading lies in linking trade with international politics. State trading linked with politics has a tendency to result in bilateralism, discrimination and divisiveness in economic and political relations based on such issues as ideological sympathies and military interests. Such a trade system jeopardizes the chances for politically harmonious relations among the industrialized countries.

The considerations mentioned above, along with a general commitment to the philosophy of private enterprise, have been at the root of the strong resistance to state trading in most of the advanced democracies. In spite of their ideological preference, support for state trading in the industrialized countries has grown. That growth can be attributed to the following factors: growing pressure of farmers' lobbies in developed countries to redistribute wealth and employment in their favour; government desire to control extraction and exports of raw materials; the necessity to assure stable access to supplies of resource goods by bilateral, long-term contracts; and government desire to boost exports while managing troubled domestic industries or engaging in industrial co-operation with developing countries.

The importance of state trading and government management of domestic output seems to suggest that international agreements based on price and quantity commitments are better suited to the logic of international trade. The approach of international codes towards state trading should probably be eclectic, depending upon the objectives for which state trading is maintained and the techniques it uses.

Figure 12.1: The Case of Pure International Monopoly

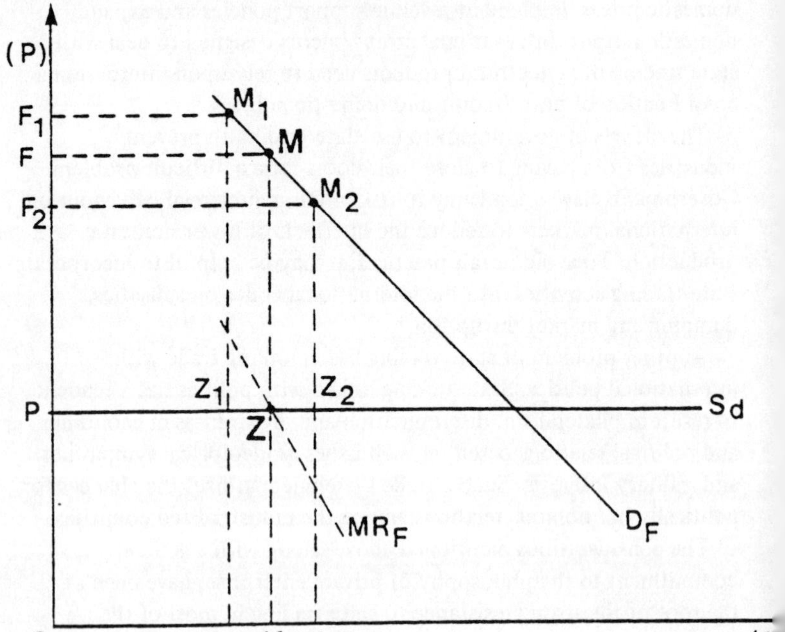

Appendix

The use of price-making power usually requires some restriction on the level of trade (a bilateral monopoly might be an exception to that rule). In Figure 12.1, the case of pure international monopoly is considered: the domestic supply curve (S_d) is assumed to be perfectly elastic; D_F is the foreign demand curve; MR_F is the marginal revenue curve derived from D_F. In order to exploit monopoly power, the country should equalize the marginal export revenue (MR_F) with marginal export cost (OP). This implies that the optimal export quantity OK will be sold on international markets at the price OF.

Notes

1. It is virtually impossible to give a clear-cut and economically meaningful definition of state trading acceptable to all concerned. The definition proposed in this study is inspired by the provisions of the General Agreement on Tariffs and Trade (GATT). See also M.M. Kostecki, *East-West Trade and the GATT System* (London: Macmillan Press, 1979), Ch. 3.

2. J.N. Lewis, 'Organized Marketing of Agricultural Products in Australia', *The Australian Journal of Agricultural Economics,* vol. 5, no. 1 (September 1961), p. 4.

3. Leslie A. Wheeler, 'The New Agricultural Protectionism', *Journal of Farm Economics,* vol. 42, no. 4 (November 1960), p. 801; and Keith Campbell, 'The State Marketing Board – Relic or Prototype?' *The Australian Journal of Agricultural Economics,* vol. 17, no. 3 (December 1973), p. 173.

4. See, for example, data on wheat prices for export and home consumption applied by the Australian Wheat Board; FAO, *National Grain Policies 1975* (Rome: FAO, 1976), p. 60.

5. D.F. Campbell, 'Control of Agricultural Marketing in New Zealand', in M.J. Moriarty (ed.), *New Zealand Farm Production and Marketing* (London: Oxford University Press, 1963), p. 81.

13 MANAGERIAL DISCRETION

Yair Aharoni

It is generally agreed that state ownership presents a different management situation from private ownership, that the behaviour of managers in state-owned enterprises differs from that of managers in private enterprises, and that these differences vary according to the national setting. This paper argues that differences in management behaviour are best analyzed in terms of managerial discretion. Managerial discretion, according to Williamson, is defined as the ability of managers to choose and pursue objectives and strategies that differ from those of the owners.[1]

We shall assume that the owners of private firms are largely motivated to maximize profits. According to Williamson, managers of private firms have discretion to the extent that they operate for reasons other than the maximization of profits, such as the expansion of staff or the increase of on-the-job leisure.

State-owned enterprises, on the other hand, do not exist solely to maximize profits; they have multiple objectives reflecting conflicting public needs and political pressures. Managerial discretion in state-owned enterprises cannot be stated simply in terms of divergence from profit maximization or from any other single objective. The absence of clearly defined goals for state-owned enterprises forms the basis for differences in managerial discretion between private and state-owned enterprises.

Managerial Discretion as an Agency Cost*

An agency relationship exists when one party, the agent, acts on behalf of another, the principal. The principal who uses an agent incurs certain costs. These costs arise from the fact that the interests of the agent and the principal are not identical, and that the agent will sometimes act to maximize his own interests. Therefore, the principal must include

---

* Editors' note: the principal–agent relationship explored here differs from that discussed in Raiffa where the manager's relationship to his subordinates is studied. Here it is the relationship of the owner to the manager that is being studied.

provisions in his agreement with the agent that will induce the agent to act as if he were maximizing the principal's interests. The costs incurred when the agent fails to maximize the principal's interests plus the cost of creating, monitoring and enforcing the contract between principal and agent are considered agency costs.

Relationships between owners and managers of business firms are examples of agency relationships. Managers of private firms contract to act on behalf of their shareholders. A perfect contract would structure the manager's incentives to correspond exactly to the shareholders' interests; however, given the uncertainties and complexities of actual situations, such perfect contracts are probably rare. Shareholders often choose to permit a degree of managerial discretion that entails some costs, especially if the only option of the shareholders is to replace the manager.

The existence of distinctive managerial interests, costs of monitoring and costs of replacement affect the relationships between managers and their principals in both state-owned and private enterprises. However, in state-owned enterprises, the principal cannot be identified. The owner of a state-owned enterprise is not a person, nor even a single organization. The state acts through a variety of people — ministers, legislators, civil servants — who are themselves agents of the general public. In many cases these agents lack the knowledge to determine and the power to enforce goals for state-owned enterprises. Moreover, different agents have different perceptions of their jobs. A government official concerned with foreign affairs may seek an increase in a public firm's research and development budget in order to reduce the state's dependence upon imported technology. The Minister of Labour may support an increase in labour-intensive procedures in order to maximize employment. The Minister of Finance, perceiving himself as a shareholder, may want the public firm to pay higher dividends. An entity that buys from the public firm may seek to reduce output prices. Who among these competing government representatives can be considered the principal of the firm? And which interests are to be paramount in the contract between principal and agent?

In the absence of clearly defined goals, state-owned enterprises often find themselves struggling with generalized, vague and conflicting interests. The statutes laying out the responsibilities of the British Steel Corporation and National Coal Board in the United Kingdom exemplify this struggle.

... to promote the efficient and economic supply of iron and steel products in such quantities and at such prices as may seem to them best calculated to meet the reasonable demands of customers and to further the public's interest.[2]

. . . making supplies of coal available of such qualities and sizes, and in such quantities and at such prices, as may seem to them best calculated to further the public interest in all respects, including the avoidance of any undue or unreasonable preference or advantage.[3]

A legislative proposal in a Canadian Privy Council report provides another example of the struggle state-owned enterprises face.

It is hereby declared that every Crown corporation is constituted an instrument for advancing the national interests of Canada and that in order to best advance those national interests it is the duty of the directors of every Crown corporation when managing the Crown corporation to take into consideration the national interests of Canada as well as the interests of the Crown corporation and, within the scope of their powers and the powers of the Crown corporations, to pursue those corporate policies that best advance such national interests.[4]

Defining and Measuring Managerial Discretion

Because governments have a tendency to state their goals in general, vague and conflicting terms, measuring the performance of a state-owned enterprise becomes difficult, if not impossible. In a private enterprise, the principal can measure performance, can use an incentive contract that ties rewards to measured performance, and can apply sanctions if measured performance differs significantly from expected performance. In state-owned enterprises, the existence of many goals and the vagueness in the definition of goals render measurement almost impossible. That situation increases the possibility of managerial discretion.

The managers of private enterprises may be able to respond to some secondary goals as they pursue their primary goal of profit maximization; the managers of state-owned enterprises, however, are usually free to choose much more widely, determining what goals are to be primary and what secondary.

Although managers of state-owned enterprises may be freer to choose their goals, they are, however, more constrained than private managers in their choice of strategies. Private managers are usually free to choose their strategies as long as they pursue profit maximization. Public managers may have to recognize employment policies, pricing policies, location policies and foreign investment policies as constraints on managerial discretion.

Managerial discretion may also vary depending upon the issue and the specific situation. For example, a union in a state-owned enterprise, confident of governmental support, may exert stronger pressure for higher wages or more job security than a labour union in a private firm. Such pressure, if supported by the government, may reduce managerial discretion. Indeed, managers of state-owned enterprises are subject to many different pressures from labour unions: unions demand generous wages, fringe benefits, labour conditions and job security; unions expect state-owned enterprises to commit themselves to policies beneficial to workers; unions use state-owned enterprises to set standards that later can be demanded of private enterprises; and unions use their political clout on government to receive concessions in collective bargaining.[5] When Labour governments are in power, these pressures become particularly strong. Indeed, in some cases, collective bargaining, which formally appears to be taking place between unions and management, is actually conducted between unions and ministers, who subsequently pressure managements to accept the resulting agreements.

The degree to which the managers of state-owned enterprises are obliged to respond to the pressures of outside groups, according to the record, seems quite overwhelming. The managers of state-owned enterprises are expected to choose domestic suppliers over foreign suppliers, even if foreign suppliers are able to fill orders more rapidly and less expensively. Managers of state-owned enterprises are also encouraged to choose other state-owned enterprises as suppliers rather than private enterprises. At the same time, constraints are placed on state-owned enterprises to prevent them from competing with private firms. Their ability to expand into new lines of business is constrained by treaty (as in the case of the Rome Treaty creating the European Economic Community), by the law of different countries and by government direction. For example, El Al, the Israeli state airline, is prevented from acquiring a major interest in a hotel, as a result of a government decree issued after pressure from private hotel owners. In many countries military industries are not allowed to produce goods for the civilian market, even if these industries have idle capacity and the machinery and expertise to produce these goods.

As other papers in this volume point out, state-owned enterprises are also expected to do many other things in support of the national interest: to refrain from raising prices in periods of inflation; to invest more during recessions; to borrow abroad in order to bring in needed foreign currency; not to borrow abroad in order to avoid balance-of-payments problems; and to act as trust busters by competing against strong private monopolies. The government also exerts pressure on state-owned enterprises to purchase ailing industries and to invest in laggard regions and weak sectors of the economy.*

To be sure, management does have some autonomy. Nevertheless, it would be premature to conclude that the managers of state-owned enterprises are hedged in any more than those of private enterprise. While the demands on the public managers may be greater and more diverse, their special privileges can restore some of the discretion that such demands have curbed. While governments may be reluctant to provide equity capital to their public enterprises, for instance, they are forthcoming in granting enterprises sizeable amounts of loans at subsidized rates of interest, in guaranteeing loans, in waiving requirements for the repayment of loans and in providing operating subsidies. State-owned enterprises at times are also offered special protection for their domestic markets, special waivers from government regulations, special exemptions from taxation.

What, then, are the net effects of these special duties and special privileges upon the discretion of public managers? Andrew Shonfield, a scholar of modern capitalism, believes that some state-owned enterprises successfully resist intervention:

> a fighting company like ENI [Ente Nazionale Idrocarburi], commanded by a dominant personality like Signor Mattei does not readily accept any form of outside supervision. Indeed it seems nowadays that the bosses of great public enterprises often operate with greater personal freedom of decision than the typical head of the big corporation in private industry. Few of them, however, have carried the method of personal rule to such lengths as Signor Mattei did in ENI. He worked on the *condottieri* principle: he had been handed fief to look after and he saw it as his task to enlarge its power and extent wherever possible — if at the expense of rivals, so much better.[6]

Nor is Signor Mattei altogether a unique case. Most managers of

* Editors' note: see the papers by Anastassopoulos and Grassini in this volume.

state-owned enterprises have much more discretion than would be supposed from scanning official documents. A French public committee on the state enterprises (the Nora Committee) reported that controllers who were set up to oversee state-owned enterprises became the advocates of the enterprise in the ministry, and that they neither had the expertise nor the inclination to control the enterprises. To be sure, these controllers did have very broad powers, including investigatory powers. However, most of them were superannuated civil servants unable to utilize the powers they enjoyed. The same high level of managerial discretion has been found in other countries.

Nevertheless, despite such cases, it is clear that some managers of state-owned enterprises are docile and passive receivers of governmental orders and parliamentary requests. In extreme cases, managers may develop what Phatak called the 'don't rock-the-boat syndrome'.[7] With this approach, managers avoid changes that may alienate any powerful groups: redundant workers are not dismissed, erring staff are not disciplined, obsolete plants remain open and faulty organizational structures remain unchanged. In short, managers simply develop apathy.

In the end, broad generalizations about the discretion of managers of state-owned enterprises prove elusive. In some cases, the formal discretion of the manager can be defined in fairly precise terms. In other cases, the manager's perception of his discretion can be precisely stated. But the actuality is more difficult to capture. Yet, if one day that actuality could be recorded in some meaningful way, it would surely reveal a very wide range of outcomes.

Key Variables Affecting Discretion

What is possible, however, is to reflect on the factors that are likely to determine the degree of the manager's discretion from case to case. If we disregard the personal traits of the manager, and assume he is eager to increase discretion, his ability to do so depends on a number of identifiable factors.

First and foremost, a manager who does not need to go to the government to ask for funds is a manager that has more discretion. This, of course, is why officials in Ministries of Finance grant little equity capital to state-owned enterprises, forcing the management to come back to the ministry with requests for funds.

Another variable that affects the discretion of the manager is the legal organization of the firm. Usually managers of enterprises that operate as integral parts of government departments have minimal discretion: their budgets are subject to annual legislative appropriations, they are not permitted to accumulate reserves and their employees are civil servants whose salaries, fringe benefits and incentives are controlled by the state. State-owned enterprises organized as corporations generally have much more discretion. Their employees are not usually civil servants, they are allowed to accumulate funds and they are subject to fewer day-to-day government directives.

In addition, governments tend to allow managers of joint ventures — that is, state-owned enterprises which have private partners — more discretion than is allotted to enterprises fully owned by the state. When a government goes into a joint venture with private partners, the government implicitly assumes certain constraints on its ability to force the enterprise to undertake social tasks, or even to take risks unacceptable to the private owners. Managers of joint ventures have been known to use the existence of private shareholders as a reason for rejecting a governmental intervention and have recruited the private shareholders to aid them in the conflict. Indeed, the private partners may have legal ways to impose their will and to avoid social or political direction.

Still another factor affecting discretion is the number and complexity of the goals that are associated with the enterprise. For the manager, the responsibility of responding to many masters may prove to be the privilege of responding to no masters at all.

Managers may also acquire more discretion from the fact that controllers perceive the very act of control as necessitating resources: their time, energy and attention. If the enterprise is large or is considered important for the national interest, it is monitored more carefully than otherwise. Thus, the manager of a state-owned electricity utility is subject to much closer scrutiny and may therefore have considerably less discretion than the manager of a small state-owned hotel.

Control functions are largely executed by civil servants. This point has particular importance because the capacity for control is a scarce resource in most countries. The degree of expertise and knowledge of these civil servants is necessarily limited, especially in relation to the enterprises which they confront. One reason is that the enterprises often pay higher salaries than the civil service and can attract more talented personnel. Another is that it is usually more challenging professionally to work for an enterprise than to control it. Pilots or aeronautical engineers usually work for the airline or the aerospace industry, not for the government. Generally, therefore, the more technical the information needed to operate the enterprise, and the more expertise concentrated at the management and firm level, the higher the managerial discretion.

Managers who are scarce and hard to replace also gain discretion by that very fact. A good manager may be hard to find, and not all good managers may be willing to work in the uncertain and ambiguous environment of the state-owned enterprise. The higher the perceived costs of replacing a manager, the higher his discretion. Very successful and effective managers can get away with ignoring many government demands, since the government may perceive the costs of replacing the manager as higher than the benefits.

Managerial discretion also depends on market structure. For example, state-owned, monopolistic firms, particularly public utilities, have less discretion than comparable firms in a competitive market. In one sense, the firm in the competitive market is already constrained, being obliged to match the prices of its competitors. Accordingly, a public enterprise that is expected to compete with other firms has to be compensated for its discretionary social activities, since it cannot recoup them through higher prices. On the other hand, if a monopolist is required to perform social services, it can be authorized by the government to recoup the costs of these services through higher prices, without the need for budgetary expenditures. Monopolies, therefore, are often the preferred social instrumentalities of governments, thus reducing the manager's discretion.

Another variable that affects discretion is the internationalization of the firm's operations. International enterprises enjoy greater discretion than domestic enterprises because of their ability to avoid foreign exchange controls and to avoid revealing the details of their offshore operations.

And, finally, a strategy of diversification on the part of the state-owned enterprise often proves to provide an escape toward increased discretion. With a large number of product lines, a state-owned enterprise enjoys added freedom. Many of its transactions are internalized, beyond the gaze of outsiders. If one product line becomes enmeshed in a web of government-imposed restrictions, the others may still be beyond the reach of government.

Techniques for Increasing Discretion

The various techniques for increasing discretion generally involve exploiting one or another of the factors mentioned above. But the manager can employ these factors in several different ways.[8]

One strategy of managers is to try to prevent apparent controls from becoming actual constraints. For instance, by appearing to pursue the objectives demanded by one government agency, managers can reduce the control of another government agency. Thus, managers may refuse to introduce pollution abatement equipment on the grounds that low-cost electricity was being demanded; they may refuse to pay dividends by pointing to the demand to maintain low prices; they may refuse to add workers to the plant on the grounds that profits were being demanded.

Managers of state-owned enterprises can also prevent the government's controls from becoming actual constraints by limiting the extent to which ministries have access to pertinent information. For example, if the state demands that the use of nuclear energy be safe, managers of state-owned enterprises can provide assurances that appropriate safety measures have been taken. In industries requiring specialized knowledge, particularly high-technology industries, government may be forced to defer to the expertise of the managers in determining whether the desired goals have been achieved.

A second line of strategy for managers, implicit in many of the factors listed earlier, is to reduce the firm's dependence on the government. As noted earlier, profitable firms increase their discretion by developing an internal source of discretionary funds for investment purposes and by reducing the opportunities for the media and legislature to scrutinize their operations. The strategy of diversification also reduces the risk of dependence for the firm by buffering it against possible losses in any one product.

Finally, managers of state-owned enterprises can sometimes affect the context in which control of their operations takes place, and can thereby increase their discretion. If managers are in a position to determine the rules that apply to the use of foreign exchange, for example, they may be able to place themselves in a position of using foreign currency without seeking government approval. If managers represent their governments in international negotiations, as they commonly do in the case of state-owned airlines, they may be able to negotiate international rules, such as the rules governing air fares, that increase their discretion. In complex technological fields, decisions on the extent and direction of research and development may be based upon the recommendations of experts inside the organization; and these recommendations may be aimed at increasing discretion.

Managers of state-owned enterprises, therefore, are not to be thought of as passive agents, required to live with the degree of discretion that the conditions of the environment produce.

This paper has put forth a number of variables and factors that may affect managerial discretion in state-owned enterprises. The actual weight of these factors in the management of public firms is still unknown. It is clear, however, that in the absence of a principal to dictate specific goals and monitor enterprises' activities, managerial discretion becomes a critical factor in the successful performance of state-owned enterprises. A better understanding of the mechanism of managerial discretion, its uses and the ways it is increased or constrained may help in designing more effective systems for managing state-owned enterprises.

Notes

1. O.E. Williamson, *The Economics of Discretionary Behavior: Management Objectives in a Theory of the Firm* (Englewood Cliffs, NJ: Prentice-Hall, 1964).

2. *Steel Nationalization*, Cmnd 2651 (London: HMSO, April 1976), para. 30 (a).

3. United Kingdom, Coal Industry Nationalization Act 1946, section 1 (1).

4. Canadian Privy Council Officer, *Crown Corporations: Direction, Control, Accountability* (Ottawa: Supply and Services, 1977), cat. no. CP 32-29/1977.

5. See Walter Kendall, 'Labour Relations', in Stuart Holland (ed.), *The State as Entrepreneur* (London: Weidenfeld and Nicolson, 1972).

6. Andrew Shonfield, *Modern Capitalism* (London: Oxford University Press, 1965), p. 185.

7. A. Phatak, 'Governmental Interference and Management Problems of Public Sector Firms', *Annals of Public and Co-operative Economy*, vol. 40, no. 3 (July–September 1969).

8. For a comparable analysis, see J. Pfeffer and G.R. Sallancik, *The External Control of Organizations* (New York: Harper and Row, 1978).

NOTES ON CONTRIBUTORS

Yair Aharoni is Professor of Business Policy at Tel-Aviv University, Israel.

Jean-Pierre C. Anastassopoulos is at the Centre d'Enseignement Supérieur des Affaires, Jouy-en-Josas, France.

Kenneth J. Arrow is Professor of Economics at Stanford University, California.

Michael Beesley is Professor of Economics at the London Graduate School of Business Studies.

Sabino Cassese is a Professor at the University of Rome and the High School for Advanced Studies in Public Administration, Italy.

Thomas Evans is at the London Graduate School of Business Studies.

Franco A. Grassini is Director and Vice President of Fiat do Brasil, Rio de Janeiro.

M.M. Kostecki is at the Centre for International Business Studies, Ecole des Hautes Etudes Commerciales, Université de Montréal, Canada.

John Lintner is Professor of Economics and Business Administration at Harvard Business School.

Alberto Martinelli is Professor at the School of Political Science, University of Milan, Italy.

Øystein Noreng is Professor at the Oslo Institute of Business Administration, Norway.

E. Leslie Normanton is a member of the International Board of Auditors for NATO, Brussels, Belgium.

Howard Raiffa is Professor of Managerial Economics at Harvard Business School.

Raymond Vernon is Professor of International Affairs, Harvard University.

INDEX

Accountability *see* Auditing
Adaptation to change, problems of 128
Advantages, granted by state-owned enterprises 13, 18
Aéroport de Paris (AP) 102-3
Agency for Energy Saving (AES) (France) 106
Agent 61, 63, 68
  objectives of 61
  principal and 61-2, 184-6
Agip (Italy) 133, 134, 136-7
  production, overseas 135
  see also ENI
Agriculture, state trade in 171-2
Airbus 13, 300
Air France 13, 164
  Aéroport de Paris and 102-3
  Caravelle jet and 100-2
  Charles de Gaulle Airport and 102-3
  government conflicts with 101-3
  losses of 101
  subsidies to 103
Alcohol *see* Trade, monopolies
Allocative efficiency 117-19
Anglo-Iranian Oil Company (Anglo-Persian Oil Company) 8, 133
  see also British Petroleum
Asquith, Paul 48
Audit commissions, efficiency 30
Auditing 157-69
  British enterprises and 159-64, 168
  French enterprises and 164-7
  summary of 167-9
  US enterprises and 157-9
Australian State Egg Board 177
Australian Wheat Board 171
Aziende municipalizzate 86

B 737 jet 101-2
Banana Board (South Africa) 171
Banque de France 164
Baumol, William 30
Beta 46, *see also* Systematic risk
Bilateral trade agreements *see* Trade
Board of directors 54, 59, 61, 67
  principal, relations of with 62
  veto voting model in 67-8

Boiteux, Marcel 30, 41
Bonuses and efficiency 30
Bradley, Michael 48
Breeder nuclear reactor 65-6
British Broadcasting Corporation 159
British National Coal Board 13
British National Oil Corporation (BNOC) 134, 138-9, 141, 163
  government relationship to 138
  political parties and 141
British Petroleum, overseas production of 135
  see also Anglo-Iranian Oil Company
British Rail 120-32
  capital goods replacement in 125
  corporate planning in 124-6
  financial appraisal of 125
  government management of 126-7
  investment constraints on 125
  management of 130-1
  passenger miles in 131
  passenger study (PBSS) of 125-6
  planning in 128
  resource allocation in 127
  social needs and 130
Bureau de Recherches de Pétrole (BRP) 133-4

Canadian Privy Council 186
Capital
  allocation of 36
  cost of, weighted average 36-7
  equity 36
Capital budgets 24, 31, 37
  criteria, bias in, for 47
  interest rates as criteria for 43-5
  optimal 36
  size selection of 39
Capital-intensive industries 23-4
Capital markets
  defects in 48
  informationally efficient 35, 48
  perfect 32, 34-5, 39, 43, 45
  private, efficiency of 38
Capital subsidies 19
  cost of 30
Caravelle jet 100-2
CAPM (Capital Asset Pricing Model) 45

196

of (Italy)
Mitbestimmungsrecht 15
'Mixed economy' 89
   Italy as 93
Monopoly 28
   trade 176
Multiple attribute utility theory 54

National Board for Electric Power
   (ENEL) (Italy) 151
National Coal Board (UK) 172, 184-
   5
National Economic Development
   Office (NEDO) (UK)
   audits and 162-3
   controls and 153
   efficiency and 154
   government intentions and 118-19
   1976 inquiry by 117-19
   policy councils and 119
   TDR, appraisal of, by 119
National Enterprise Board (UK) 163
National Railroad Passenger Corporation (AMTRAK) (US) 158-9
Nationalization Acts (UK) 161
Net present value rule 36
Nora Report (France) 146
   bureaucratic control and 148-9,
      189
   marketing control and 153
Norsk Hydro (Norway) 137, 138
Nuclear reactors
   in France 104-5
   see also Breeder nuclear reactor

Objectives 54, 57, 62
   conflicting, multiple 60, 90-2,
      93-4, 99, 122-3, 142, 145,
      150-1, 184, 185-8, 192
   profit-maximization as 70, 184
   quantification of 56
Office de Radiodiffusion Télévision
   Française (ORTF) 107
   government crackdown on 108
   reform of 107
Oil companies, state-owned, in
   Western Europe 133-44
   as private enterprises 135
   British *see* Anglo- Iranian;
      British National Oil;
      British Petroleum
   control of 143
   expansion by, desires for 141-2
   first generation 134-5
   French *see* CFP; Elf-ERAP

interests, multiple, of 142
   Italian *see* Agip
   Norwegian *see* Statoil
   objectives, multiple 142
   performance by 143
   reasons for 133-4
   second generation 134-5
Oil Directorate of the Ministry of
   Industry (France) 136, 139
   as oil industry representative
      139

Panama Canal Company (US) 158
Pareto optimality 26, 28, 31-2
   in capital markets 39, 44
Parliamentary committees, flaws in
   168
Passenger miles 131
Passenger study (PBSS) *see* British
   Rail
Perfectly competitive conditions 26,
   27-9, 67
   for capital markets 39, 43
   interest rates under 26
   marginal utility with 26
Performance, measuring 17, 111,
   119, 186
   oil companies, state-owned, and
      143
   see also Efficiency
Planning 129
   in Italy 96-7
   joint government and private 122
   reports 152
   situational 128-9
Political system, interactions with 12-
   13, 77-8, 83
Port of London Authority 159
Prices
   efficiency 63-4
   emphasis on 63
   list 27
   marginal cost 27, 41-2
   optimal 33, 64-5
   proper 30, 31
   shadow 27
   stabilization 173-4
   target 174
Principal-agent problem (manager-
   subordinate) 10-1, 60-1, 63,
      68
Principal-agent problem (owner-
   manager) 184-6
Private enterprises
   competition between state-owned